CONTENTS

ACKNOWLEDGEMENTS

We wish to acknowledge the valuable contributions of the following who have submitted information and provided photographs which have greatly enhanced this edition.

Kevin Clancy, *Royal Mint*
Paul Davies
David Fletcher
Andrew Jenkins, *Royal Mint*
Geoff Kitchen
Kerry Willecome, *Royal Mint*

FOREWORD

Welcome to the second edition of the new Coins of England Decimal Issues. It was necessary to create a second volume due to the quantity of new commemorative issues being released by the Royal Mint in recent years and the announcement that a new portrait of the Queen had been commissioned for the 2015 coinage so the compact nature of the single-volume format was being compromised.

There will obviously continue to be many new issues from the Royal Mint in the future so, in order to continue listing all of these new issues, we felt we had to migrate the Decimal Coinage to its own volume where it can benefit from the addition of new illustrations and new information as we work more closely with the Royal Mint to obtain as much accurate information as possible. The book retains the same format and numbering system as before but we intend to re-number and re-arrange the catalogue in future editions to create a more user friendly layout.

The prices in the catalogue represent the range of retail prices at which coins are being offered for sale at the time of going to press and NOT the price which a dealer will pay. These prices are based on our knowledge of the market and the current demand for particular coins. Where prices have not been given it is usually because they are very recent issues and a price has not yet been established for the secondary market. In addition to this, many coins are only issued as part of sets so prices for the individual coins are not relevant as they rarely appear in commerce.

In many cases the precious metal content of the coin is a major factor in deciding the value so the price of many coins will fluctuate with the value of the metal content.

Thank you to those of you who have contacted us with corrections and suggestions, we continue to welcome feedback from readers. Our aim is to make this catalogue more accurate and user-friendly so please feel free to write to us at Spink with your comments.

Happy collecting

Philip Skingley
Editor, Coins of England

INTRODUCTION

The decision to adopt decimal currency was announced in March 1966 following the recommendation of the Halsbury Committee of Enquiry which had been appointed in 1961. The date for the introduction of the new system was 15 February 1971 and it was evident that the Royal Mint facilities which had been located on Tower Hill for more than 150 years would be unable to strike the significant quantities of coins required on that site. The Government therefore decided to build a new mint at Llantrisant in South Wales.

The new system provided for three smaller bronze coins with the denominations of a half new penny, one new penny and two new pence, and very large numbers were struck and stock piled for D-Day. The cupro-nickel five and ten new pence denominations with the same specifications as the shilling and florin were introduced in 1968 and circulated along side the former denominations. A further change was the introduction in 1969 of a 50 new pence coin to replace the ten shilling banknote.

In 1982 and 1983 two more new coins were introduced; the 20 pence which helped to reduce demand for five and ten pence pieces, and the first circulating non-precious metal £1 coin which replaced the bank note of the same value.1982 also saw the removal of the word "NEW" from all denominations from half penny to fifty pence.

Increasing raw material costs, and inflation also play a part in the development of a modern coinage system and smaller 5 and 10 pence coins were introduced in 1990 and 1992 respectively. A further change in 1992 was the use of copper plated steel for the one and two pence bronze coins. The plated steel coins are magnetic unlike the solid bronze alloy. Further changes were made in 1997 when the fifty pence coin was reduced in size and a bimetallic circulating £2 was also introduced to reduce demand for the one pound value.

In 2008, 40 years after the introduction of the first of the decimal coin designs, a completely new series was issued. After an open competition that attracted more than 4,000 entries, designs by a young graphic designer, Matthew Dent, were selected, and represent a somewhat radical approach that uses elements of the shield of the Royal Arms for the denominations of 50 pence to 1 pence. The £1 shows the complete shield. Interestingly none of the coins show the value in numerical form.

The Mint offered sets of the new designs in various metals and qualities, and also gave collectors an opportunity to acquire the last issues of the original series. These, together with various commemorative issues, present collectors with a significant and varied range, and illustrate the importance of the sales of special issues to the Mint's business.

In the 40 years since Decimalisation there have been changes to the obverse portrait of Her Majesty The Queen with the exception of the Silver Maundy coins which retain the Mary Gillick design. The new effigy for the introduction of the decimal series was by Arnold Machin, followed then by Raphael Maklouf, Ian Rank-Broadley and now with a new portrait by Jody Clark.

Previous editions of the catalogue listed coins according to the portrait rather than by denomination. After discussion with dealers and contributors, it was decided that a radical change should be made so that users of the catalogue can see all issues of a particular denomination in sequence, starting with the lowest value and progressing to the highest. This will help collectors of, for example, £1, £2 and crown size coins. Catalogue numbers have been retained from the previous edition.

BRONZE

HALF PENCE COINS
Obverse portrait by Arnold Machin

4239 4240

4239 Half new penny. R. The Royal Crown and the inscription '1/2 NEW PENNY'
(Reverse design: Christopher Ironside)

1971...................... £0.50	1975 ....£0.50	1979..........................£0.50
— Proof *FDC** £1	— Proof *FDC** £1	— Proof *FDC** £1
1972 Proof *FDC** £2	1976 ....£0.50	1980..........................£0.50
1973...................... £0.50	— Proof *FDC** £1	— Proof *FDC**...........£1
— Proof *FDC**...... £1	1977 ....£0.50	1981..........................£0.50
1974...................... £0.50	— Proof *FDC** £1	— Proof *FDC** £1
— Proof *FDC**...... £1	1978 ....£0.50	
	— Proof *FDC** £1	

4240 Half penny. 'New' omitted. As illustration

1982...................... £0.50	1983 ....£0.50	1984*...........................£2
— Proof *FDC**...... £1	— Proof *FDC** £1	— Proof *FDC**..........£2

ONE PENCE COINS
Obverse portrait by Arnold Machin

4237 4238 4381

4237 One new penny. R. A portcullis with chains royally crossed, being the badge of Henry
VII and his successors, and the inscription 'NEW PENNY' above and the figure '1' below.
(Design: Christopher Ironside)

1971...................... £0.50	1975 ....£0.50	1979..........................£0.50
— Proof *FDC**...... £1	— Proof *FDC** £1	— Proof *FDC**...........£1
1972 Proof *FDC** £2	1976 ....£0.50	1980..........................£0.50
1973...................... £0.50	— Proof *FDC** £1	— Proof *FDC**...........£1
— Proof *FDC** £1	1977 ....£0.50	1981..........................£0.50
1974...................... £0.50	— Proof *FDC** £1	— Proof *FDC** £1
— Proof *FDC** £1	1978 ....£0.50	
	— Proof *FDC** £1	

4238 One penny. 'New' omitted, As illustration

1982...................... £0.50	1983 ....£0.50	1984..........................£1
— Proof *FDC**.......£1	— *FDC** £1	— Proof *FDC**...........£1

Obverse portrait by Raphael Maklouf

4381 One penny. R. Crowned portcullis with chains

1985...................... £0.50	1988 ....£0.50	1991..........................£0.50
— Proof *FDC** £1	— Proof *FDC** £1	— Proof *FDC**...........£1
1986...................... £0.50	1989 ....£0.50	1992..........................£0.50
— Proof *FDC** £1	— Proof *FDC** £1	— Proof *FDC** £1
1987..............................	1990	
— Proof *FDC** £1	— Proof *FDC** £1	

* Coins marked thus were originally issued in Royal Mint sets.

COPPER PLATED STEEL

4391 One penny R. Crowned portcullis with chains

1992 .... £0.50	1995 ....£0.50	1997 ....£0.50
1993 .... £0.50	— Proof *FDC** £1	— Proof *FDC** £1
— Proof *FDC** £1	1996 ....£0.50	
1994 .... £0.50	— Proof *FDC** £1	
— Proof *FDC** £1	— Proof in silver *FDC**£15	

Obverse portrait by Ian Rank-Broadley

4710

4710 One penny. R. Crowned portcullis with chains. (Illus. as 4381)

1998.................................£1	2004 .... £1
— Proof *FDC* * £3	— Proof *FDC*................. £3
1999.................................£1	2005 .... £1
— Proof *FDC* * £3	— Proof *FDC*................. £3
2000.................................£1	2006................................ £1
— Proof *FDC* * £3	— Proof *FDC*................. £3
— Proof in silver FDC (see PSS08)*£8	— Proof in silver *FDC* (see PSS22)* ... £8
2001 ....£1	2007................................ £1
— Proof *FDC* * £3	— Proof *FDC* *................ £3
2002.................................£1	2008................................ £1
— Proof *FDC* * £3	— Proof *FDC* *................ £3
— Proof in gold *FDC* (see PGJS1)*£200	— Proof in silver *FDC* (see PSS27)* ... £8
2003.................................£1	— Proof in gold *FDC* (see PGEBCS)*£225
— Proof *FDC* * £3	— Proof in platinum *FDC* (see PPEBCS)* £300

4711

4711 One penny. R. A section of Our Royal Arms showing elements of the first and third quartering accompanied by the words 'ONE PENNY'(Reverse design: Matthew Dent)

2008 ....£3
— Proof *FDC* (in 2008 set, see PS96)* £3
— Proof in silver *FDC* (in 2008 set, see PSS28)* £8
— Proof piedfort in silver *FDC* (in 2008 set, see PSS29)* £15
— Proof in gold *FDC* (in 2008 set, see PGRSAS)* £225
— Proof in platinum *FDC* (in 2008 set, see PPRSAS)* £300
2009
— Proof *FDC* (in 2009 set, see PS97)*
— BU in silver £15
— Proof in silver *FDC* (in 2009 set, see PSS 37)* £15

* Coins marked thus were originally issued in Royal Mint sets.

2010
— Proof *FDC* (in 2010 set, see PS101)* £3
— BU in silver £15
— Proof in silver *FDC* (in 2010 set, Edition: 3,500, see PSS41)* £15
2011 ....£3
— Proof *FDC* (in 2011 set, see PS104) * £3
— BU in silver..£15
— Proof in silver *FDC* (in 2011 set, Edition: 2,500, see PSS44)*............................£15
2012 ....£3
— Proof *FDC* (in 2012 set, see PS107) * £3
— BU in silver..£23
— Proof in silver *FDC* (Edition: 995, see PSS47)* £30
— Proof in silver with selected gold plating *FDC* (Edition: 2,012, see PSS48) * £30
— Proof in gold *FDC* (Edition: 150 see PGDJS)*...£225
2013 ....£3
— Proof *FDC* (in 2013 set, see PS109)* £5
— BU in silver £23
— Proof in silver *FDC* (Edition: 2,013, see PSS50)*....................................£30
— Proof in gold *FDC* (Issued: 59 see PGCAS)*...£225
2014 ....£5
— Proof *FDC* (in 2014 set, see PS112)*
— Proof in silver *FDC* (Edition: 2014 see PSS56)*
2015
— Proof *FDC* (in 2015 set, see PS115) * £5
— Proof in silver *FDC* (Edition: 7,500 see PSS61)*....................................£30
— Proof in gold *FDC* (Edition: 500 see PGC4P) * £225

Obverse portrait by Jody Clark
4712 One penny.
2015
— Proof *FDC* (in 2015 set, see PS116) * £5
— Proof in silver *FDC* (Edition: 7,500 see PSS62)*
— Proof in gold *FDC* (Edition: 500 see PGC5P) *

* Coins marked thus were originally issued in Royal Mint sets.

BRONZE

TWO PENCE COINS
Obverse portrait by Arnold Machin

    4235   4236

4235 Two new pence. R. The badge of the Prince of Wales, being three ostrich feathers enfiling a coronet of cross pattee and fleur de lys, with the motto 'ICH DIEN', and the inscription '2 NEW PENCE' (Reverse design: Christopher Ironside)

1971 .... £0.50	1976 ....£0.50	1979...........................£0.50
— Proof *FDC*...... £1	— Proof *FDC* £1	— Proof *FDC*...........£1
1972 Proof *FDC*...... £2	1977 ....£0.50	1980...........................£0.50
1973 Proof *FDC*...... £2	— Proof *FDC* £1	— Proof *FDC*...........£1
1974 Proof *FDC*...... £2	1978 ....£0.50	1981...........................£0.50
1975..................... £0.50	— Proof *FDC* £1	— Proof *FDC*...........£1
— Proof *FDC*....... £1		

4236 Two pence. 'New' omitted. As illustration

1982*........................ £1	1983*...............................£1	1984*...............................£1
— Proof *FDC*....... £2	— Proof *FDC* £2	— Proof *FDC*...........£2

4236A— Error reverse. The word 'new' was dropped from the reverse of the currency issues in 1982 but a number of 2 pence coins were struck in 1983 with the incorrect reverse die, similar to coins listed as 4235. Reports suggest that the error coins, or 'Mules' were contained in some sets packed by the Royal Mint for Martini issued in 1983 ....£750

Obverse portrait by Raphael Maklouf

          4376

4376 Two pence. R. Prince of Wales feathers

1985..................... £0.50	1988 ....£0.50	1991...........................£0.50
— Proof *FDC*........ £1	— Proof *FDC* £1	— Proof *FDC*...........£1
1986..................... £0.50	1989 ....£0.50	1992...........................£0.50
— Proof *FDC*........ £1	— Proof *FDC* £1	— Proof *FDC*...........£1
1987..................... £0.50	1990 ....£0.50	
— Proof *FDC*........ £1	— Proof *FDC* £1	

* Coins marked thus were originally issued in Royal Mint sets.

COPPER PLATED STEEL

4386 Two pence R. Plumes

1992.............................£1	1995 ....£1	1997...........................£0.50
1993.............................£1	— Proof *FDC** £1	— Proof *FDC** £1
— Proof *FDC** £1	1996 ....£1	
1994.............................£1	— Proof *FDC** £1	
— Proof *FDC**........£1	— Proof in silver *FDC**£15	

Obverse portrait by Ian Rank-Broadley

4690

4691

4690 Two pence. R. Prince of Wales feathers.

1998...£1	2004 ....£1
— Proof *FDC** £3	— Proof *FDC** £3
1999...£1	2005 ....£1
— Proof *FDC** £3	— Proof *FDC** £3
2000...£1	2006 ....£1
— Proof *FDC** £3	— Proof *FDC** £3
— Proof in silver FDC (see PSS08)* £8	— Proof in silver *FDC* (see PSS22)* £8
2001...£1	2007 ....£1
— Proof *FDC** £3	— Proof *FDC** £3
2002...£1	2008 ....£1
— Proof *FDC** £3	— Proof *FDC** £3
— Proof in gold *FDC* (see PGJS1)*£400	— Proof in silver *FDC* (see PSS27)* £10
2003	— Proof in gold *FDC* (see PGEBCS)* ...£450
— Proof *FDC** £3	— Proof in platinum *FDC* (see PPEBCS)* £550

4691 Two pence. R. A section of Our Royal Arms showing elements of the second quartering accompanied by the words 'TWO PENCE'(Reverse design: Matthew Dent)

2008...£3	
— Proof *FDC* (in 2008 set, see PS96)* £3	
— Proof in silver *FDC* (in 2008 set, see PSS28)* £10	
— Proof piedfort in silver *FDC* (in 2008 set, see PSS29)* £20	
— Proof in gold *FDC* (in 2008 set, see PGRSAS)* £450	
— Proof in platinum *FDC* (in 2008 set, see PPRSAS)* £550	
2009...£3	
— Proof *FDC* (in 2009 set, see PS97)* £3	
— Proof in silver *FDC* (in 2009 set, see PSS 37)* £10	
2010...£3	
— Proof *FDC* (in 2010 set, see PS101)* £3	
— Proof in silver *FDC* (in 2010 set, Edition: 3,500 see PSS41)* £10	
2011...£3	
— Proof *FDC* (in 2011 set, see PS104) * £3	
— Proof in silver *FDC* (in 2011 set, Edition: 2,500, see PSS44) * £15	

* Coins marked thus were originally issued in Royal Mint sets.

2012 .... £3
— Proof *FDC* (in 2012 set, see PS107) * £3
— Proof in silver *FDC* (Edition: 995, see PSS47)*.. £30
— Proof in silver with selected gold plating *FDC* (Edition: 2,012, see PSS48) * £30
— Proof in gold *FDC* (Edition: 150 see PGDJS)* £450
2013 .... £3
— Proof *FDC* (in 2013 set, see PS110) * £5
— Proof in silver *FDC* (Edition: 2,013, see PSS50)*.. £30
— Proof in gold *FDC* (Issued: 59 see PGCAS)*... £450
2014 .... £3
— Proof *FDC* (in 2014 set, see PS112) * £5
— Proof in silver *FDC* (Edition : 2,014 see PSS56)*
2015
— Proof *FDC* (in 2015 set, see PS115) * £5
— Proof in silver *FDC* (Edition: 7,500 see PSS61)*.. £30
— Proof in gold *FDC* (Edition: 500 see PGC4P) * £450

Obverse portrait by Jody Clark
4692 Two pence.
2015
— Proof *FDC* (in 2015 set, see PS116) * £5
— Proof in silver *FDC* (Edition: 7,500 see PSS62)*
— Proof in gold *FDC* (Edition: 500 see PGC5P) *

CUPRO-NICKEL
FIVE PENCE COINS
Obverse portrait by Arnold Machin

4233   4234

4233 Five new pence. R. A thistle royally crowned, being the badge of Scotland, and the inscription '5 NEW PENCE' (Reverse design: Christopher Ironside)

1968 .... £0.50	1974 Proof *FDC** £4	1979 .... £0.50
1969 .... £0.50	1975 ....£0.50	— Proof *FDC** £2
1970 .... £0.50	— Proof *FDC** £2	1980 .... £0.50
1971 .... £0.50	1976 Proof *FDC** £4	— Proof *FDC** £2
— Proof *FDC** £2	1977 .... £0.50	1981 Proof *FDC** £4
1972 Proof *FDC** £4	— Proof *FDC** £2	
1973 Proof *FDC** £4	1978 .... £0.50	
	— Proof *FDC** £2	

4234 Five pence. 'New' omitted. As illustration

1982* £2	1983* £2	1984* £2
— Proof *FDC** £4	— Proof *FDC** £4	— Proof *FDC** £4

* *Coins marked thus were originally issued in Royal*

Obverse portrait by Raphael Maklouf

4371   4372

4371 **Five pence.** R. Crowned thistle

1985*....................£2	1988 ....£1	1990*.............................£2
— Proof *FDC** £4	— Proof *FDC** £2	— Proof *FDC**............£2
1986*............................£2	1989 ....£1	— Proof in silver *FDC** £12
— Proof *FDC** £4	— Proof *FDC** £2	
1987............................£1		
— Proof *FDC** £2		

4372 **Five pence.** R. Crowned thistle: reduced diameter of 18mm

1990...............................£1	1992 ....£1	— Proof *FDC**...........£2
— Proof *FDC**..........£2	— Proof *FDC** £2	1996...............................£1
— Proof in silver *FDC** £10	1993*...............................£2	— Proof *FDC**...............£2
— Proof piedfort in silver	— Proof *FDC**...............£4	— Proof in silver *FDC** £15
FDC (Issued:20,000)£20	1994 ....£1	1997...............................£1
1991...............................£1	— Proof *FDC** £2	— Proof *FDC**...........£2
— Proof *FDC**..........£2	1995 ....£1	

Obverse portrait by Ian Rank-Broadley

4670

4670 **Five pence.** R. Crowned thistle

1998....................................£1	2004 ....£1	
— Proof *FDC* * £3	— Proof *FDC** £3	
1999 ....£1	2005 ....£1	
— Proof *FDC* * £3	— Proof *FDC** £3	
2000....................................£1	2006 ....£1	
— Proof *FDC* * £3	— Proof *FDC** £3	
— Proof in silver FDC (see PSS08)*£12	— Proof in silver *FDC* (see PSS22)* £12	
2001....................................£1	2007 ....£1	
— Proof *FDC* * £3	— Proof *FDC** £3	
2002....................................£1	2008 ....£1	
— Proof *FDC* * £3	— Proof *FDC*.* £3	
— Proof in gold *FDC* (see PGJS1) £225	— Proof in silver *FDC* (see PSS27)* £12	
2003....................................£1	— Proof in gold *FDC* (see PGEBCS)* £225	
— Proof *FDC* * £3	— Proof in platinum *FDC*	
	(see PPEBCS)* £325	

* Coins marked thus were originally issued in Royal

4671

4671 Five pence. R. A section of Our Royal Arms showing elements of all four quarterings
accompanied by the words 'FIVE PENCE'(Reverse design: Matthew Dent)
2008...£3
—   Proof *FDC* (in 2008 set, see PS96)*...£3
—   Proof in silver *FDC* (in 2008 set, see PSS28)*......................................£12
—   Proof piedfort in silver *FDC* (in 2008 set, see PSS29)*.........................£25
—   Proof in gold *FDC* (in 2008 set, see PGRSAS)*...................................£225
—   Proof in platinum *FDC* (in 2008 set, see PPRSAS)*.............................£325
2009...£1
—   Proof *FDC* (in 2009 set, see PS97)*...£3
—   Proof in silver *FDC* (in 2009 set, see PSS 37...£12
2010...£1
—   Proof *FDC* (in 2010 set, see PS101)*..£3
—   Proof in silver *FDC* (in 2010 set, Edition: 3,500 see PSS41)*................£12
2011...£3
—   Proof *FDC* (in 2011 set, see PS104) *..£3
—   Proof in silver *FDC* (in 2011 set, Edition: 2,500, see PSS44) *............£12

NICKEL PLATED STEEL

4672 Five pence.
2012...£3
—   Proof *FDC* (in 2012 set, see PS107) *..£5
—   Proof in silver *FDC* (Edition: 995, see PSS47) *....................................£30
—   Proof in silver with selected gold plating *FDC* (Edition: 2,012, see PSS48) *......£30
—   Proof in gold *FDC* (Edition: 150 see PGDJS)*.....................................£225
2013... £3
—   Proof *FDC* (in 2013 set, see PS109) *.. £5
—   Proof in silver *FDC* (Edition: 2,013, see PSS50)*..................................£30
—   Proof in gold *FDC* (Issued: 59 see PGCAS)*..£225
2014
—   Proof *FDC* (in 2014 set, see PS112) *.. £5
—   Proof in silver *FDC* (Edition: 2,014 see PSS56)*
2015
—   Proof *FDC* (in 2015 set, see PS115) *.. £5
—   Proof in silver *FDC* (Edition: 7,500 see PSS61)*..................................£30
—   Proof in gold *FDC* (Edition: 500 see PGC4P) *.....................................£225

* Coins marked thus were originally issued in Royal Mint sets.

Obverse portrait by Jody Clark

4673

4673 Five pence.
2015
— Proof *FDC* (in 2015 set, see PS116) * £5
— Proof in silver *FDC* (Edition: 7,500 see PSS62)*
— Proof in gold *FDC* (Edition: 500 see PGC5P) *

TEN PENCE COINS
Obverse portrait by Arnold Machin

4231

4231 Ten new pence. R. Lion passant guardant being royally crowned, being part of the crest of England, and the inscription 'Ten New Pence' (Reverse design: Christopher Ironside)

1968 .... £0.50	1974 .... £0.50	1978 Proof *FDC*..........£4
1969 .... £0.50	— Proof *FDC* £3	1979............................£0.50
1970 .... £0.50	1975 .... £0.50	— Proof *FDC* £3
1971 .... £0.50	— Proof *FDC* £3	1980..............................£1
— Proof *FDC* £3	1976 .... £0.50	— Proof *FDC*..........£3
1972 Proof *FDC*...... £4	— Proof *FDC* £3	1981..............................£1
1973 .... 0.40	1977 .... 0.50	— Proof *FDC*..........£3
— Proof *FDC* £3	— Proof *FDC* £3	

4232

4232 Ten pence. 'New' omitted. As illustration

1982* £3	1983* £3	1984*.............................£3
— Proof *FDC* £4	— Proof *FDC* £4	— Proof *FDC*..........£4

* Coins marked thus were originally issued in Royal Mint sets.

Obverse portrait by Raphael Maklouf

4366

4366 Ten pence. R. Lion passant guardant

1985*...........................£3	1988*..............................£3	1991*.................................£4
— Proof *FDC* *.......£4	— Proof *FDC**..............£4	— Proof *FDC*...........£4
1986*...........................£3	1989*...............................£4	1992*.................................£3
— Proof *FDC*........£4	— Proof *FDC**..............£4	— Proof *FDC*...........£4
1987*...........................£3	1990*...............................£4	— Proof in silver *FDC** £14
— Proof *FDC*........£4	— Proof *FDC**..............£4	

4367

4650

4367 Ten pence R Lion passant guardant: reduced diameter of 24.5mm

1992...£1	1995......................................£1
— Proof *FDC*...£3	— Proof *FDC*...................£3
— Proof in silver *FDC** £10.....................................	1996......................................£1
— Proof piedfort in silver *FDC** (Issued: 14,167)£30	— Proof *FDC*.....................£3
1993*...£3	— Proof in silver *FDC** ...£15
— Proof *FDC*...£4	1997......................................£1
1994*...£3	— Proof *FDC*...................£3
— Proof *FDC*...£4	

Obverse portrait by Ian Rank-Broadley

4650 Ten pence. R. Lion passant guardant. (Illus. as 4232)

1998*...................................£3	2004 ....£1
— Proof *FDC*..............................£4	— Proof *FDC* £3
1999*...................................£3	2005 ....£1
— Proof *FDC*..............................£4	— Proof *FDC* £3
2000.....................................£1	2006 ....£1
— Proof *FDC*..............................£3	— Proof *FDC* £3
— Proof in silver FDC (see PSS08)* £15	— Proof in silver *FDC* (see PSS22)*..........£15
2001.....................................£1	2007 ....£1
— Proof *FDC*..............................£3	— Proof *FDC* £3
2002.....................................£1	2008 ....£1
— Proof *FDC*..............................£3	— Proof *FDC* £3
— Proof in gold *FDC* (see PGJS1)*£500	— Proof in silver *FDC* (see PSS27)* ... £15
2003.....................................£1	— Proof in gold *FDC* (see PGEBCS)* £400
— Proof *FDC*..............................£3	— Proof in platinum *FDC* (see PPEBCS)*................................ £650

* Coins marked thus were originally issued in Royal Mint sets.

4651

4651 **Ten pence.** ℞. A section of Our Royal Arms showing elements of the first quartering accompanied by the words 'TEN PENCE'(Reverse design: Matthew Dent)

2008..£3
— Proof *FDC* (in 2008 set, see PS96)*...£6
— Proof in silver *FDC* (in 2008 set, see PSS28)*..£15
— Proof piedfort in silver *FDC* (in 2008 set, see PSS29)* £25
— Proof in gold *FDC* (in 2008 set, see PGRSAS)* £400
— Proof in platinum *FDC* (in 2008 set, see PPRSAS)*...............................£650
2009..£3
— Proof *FDC* (in 2009 set, see PS97)*...£6
— Proof in silver *FDC* (in 2009 set, see PSS 37)*..£15
2010..£3
— Proof *FDC* (in 2010 set, see PS101)*...£6
— Proof in silver *FDC* (in 2010 set, Edition: 3,500 see PSS 41)*..............£15
2011..£3
— Proof *FDC* (in 2011 set, see PS104) *..£3
— Proof in silver *FDC* (in 2011 set, Edition: 2,500, see PSS44) *............£15

NICKEL PLATED STEEL

4652 **Ten pence.**

2012..£3
— Proof *FDC* (in 2012 set, see PS107)*...£3
— Proof in silver *FDC* (Edition: 995, see PSS47)*.......................................£30
— Proof in silver with selected gold plating *FDC* (Edition: 2,012, see PSS48)*.......£30
— Proof in gold *FDC* (Edition: 150 see PGDJS)* £450
2013.. £3
— Proof FDC (in 2013 set, see PS109)*.. £5
— Proof in silver FDC (Edition: 2,013, see PSS50)*.......................................£30
— Proof in gold FDC (Issued: 59 see PGCAS)*..£450
2014
— Proof *FDC* (in 2014 set, see PS112)*... £5
— Proof in silver *FDC* (Edition: 2,014 see PSS56)*
2015
— Proof *FDC* (in 2015 set, see PS115) *... £5
— Proof in silver *FDC* (Edition: 7,500 see PSS61)*.....................................£30
— Proof in gold *FDC* (Edition: 500 see PGC4P) *.......................................£450

* Coins marked thus were originally issued in Royal Mint sets.

Obverse portrait by Jody Clark

4653

4653 Ten pence.
2015
— Proof FDC (in 2015 set, see PS116) * £5
— Proof in silver FDC (Edition: 7,500 see PSS62) £30
— Proof in gold FDC (Edition: 500 see PGC5P) *£30..£450

CUPRO-NICKEL

TWENTY PENCE COINS
Obverse portrait by Arnold Machin

4230

4230 Twenty pence. R. The Royal Badge of the Rose of England represented as a double rose
barbed and seeded, slipped and leaved and ensigned by a Royal Crown and the date of the
year with the inscription 'TWENTY PENCE' and the figure '20' superimposed on the stem
of the rose.(Reverse design: William Gardner)
1982...£0.50
— Proof FDC*...£3
— Proof piedfort in silver FDC (Issued: 10,000) £30
1983...£0.50
1984...£0.50
— Proof FDC*...£3

Obverse portrait by Raphael Maklouf

4361

4361 Twenty pence. R. Crowned double rose
1985...........................£1   1990 ....£1   1995...............................£1
— Proof FDC*........£3   — Proof FDC* ....£3   — Proof FDC*...........£3

* Coins marked thus were originally issued in Royal Mint sets.

1986*..........................£3	1991 ....£1	1996...............................£1
— Proof *FDC*........£4	— Proof *FDC* £3	— Proof *FDC*...........£3
1987...........................£1	1992...............................£1	— Proof in silver *FDC** £18
— Proof *FDC* £3	— Proof *FDC* £3	1997...............................£1
1988.........................£1	1993 ....£1	— Proof *FDC*...........£3
— Proof *FDC*........£3	— Proof *FDC* £3	
1989.........................£1	1994 ....£1	
— Proof *FDC*........£3	— Proof *FDC* £3	

Obverse portrait by Ian Rank-Broadley

4635

4635 Twenty pence. R. Crowned double rose.

1998...£1	2004 ....£1
— Proof *FDC*...............................£3	— Proof *FDC* £3
1999...£1	2005 ....£1
— Proof *FDC*...............................£3	— Proof *FDC* £3
2000...£1	2006 ....£1
— Proof *FDC*...............................£3	— Proof *FDC* £3
— Proof in silver *FDC* (see PSS08) *£20	— Proof in silver *FDC* (see PSS22)* £20
2001...£1	2007 ....£1
— Proof *FDC*...............................£3	— Proof *FDC* £3
2002...£1	2008 ....£1
— Proof *FDC*...............................£3	— Proof *FDC* £3
— Proof in gold *FDC* (see PGJS1)*£450	— Proof in silver *FDC* (see PSS27)* £20
2003...£1	— Proof in gold *FDC* (see PGEBCS)* £350
— Proof *FDC*...............................£3	— Proof in platinum *FDC*
	(see PPEBCS)* £550

4636

4636 Twenty pence. R. A section of Our Royal Arms showing elements of the second and forth quartering accompanied by the words 'TWENTY PENCE'(Reverse design: Matthew Dent)

2008...£3
— Proof *FDC* (in 2008 set, see PS96)* £3
— Proof in silver *FDC* (in 2008 set, see PSS28)*..£20
— Proof piedfort in silver *FDC* (in 2008 set, see PSS29)* £40
— Proof in gold *FDC* (in 2008 set, see PGRSAS)*...£350
— Proof in platinum *FDC* (in 2008 set, see PPRSAS)*..£550

* Coins marked thus were originally issued in Royal Mint sets.

2009...£3
— Proof *FDC* (in 2009 set, see PS97)* £6
— Proof in silver *FDC* (in 2009 set, see PSS 37)* £20
2010..£3
— Proof *FDC* (in 2010 set, see PS101)* £6
— Proof in silver *FDC* (in 2010 set, Edition: 3,500 see PSS 41)* £20
2011..£3
— Proof *FDC* (in 2011 set, see PS104) * £3
— Proof in silver *FDC* (in 2011 set, Edition: 2,500, see PSS44) * £15
2012..£3
— Proof *FDC* (in 2012 set, see PS107)* £3
— Proof in silver *FDC* (Edition: 995, see PSS47)* £30
— Proof in silver with selected gold plating *FDC* (Edition: 2,012, see PSS48)*.......£30
— Proof in gold *FDC* (Edition: 150 see PGDJS)* £350
2013..£3
— Proof *FDC* (in 2013 set, see PS109)* £5
— Proof in silver *FDC* (Edition: 2,013, see PSS50)* £30
— Proof in gold *FDC* (Issued: 59 see PGCAS)*.......................................£350
2014
— Proof *FDC* (in 2014 set, see PS112)* £5
— Proof in silver *FDC* (Edition: 2,014 see PSS56)*
2015
— Proof *FDC* (in 2015 set, see PS115) * £5
— Proof in silver *FDC* (Edition: 7,500 see PSS61)* £30
— Proof in gold *FDC* (Edition: 500 see PGC4P) * £350

4636A — **Error obverse – known as a Mule.** The new reverse design by Matthew Dent does
not include the year date and this should have appeared on the obverse. A number of coins
were struck using the undated obverse die that had previously been used with the dated
reverse of the crowned double rose. (See Illus. 4635) £100

Obverse portrait by Jody Clark

4637

4637 Twenty pence.
2015
— Proof *FDC* (in 2015 set, see PS116) * £5
— Proof in silver *FDC* (Edition: 7,500 see PSS62)*
— Proof in gold *FDC* (Edition: 500 see PGC5P) *

* Coins marked thus were originally issued in Royal Mint sets.

Obverse portrait by Arnold Machin

4223

4223 **Fifty new pence** (seven-sided). ℞. A figure of Britannia seated beside a lion, with a shield resting against her right side, holding a trident in her right hand and an olive branch in her left hand; and the inscription '50 NEW PENCE'. (Reverse design: Christopher Ironside)

1969	£3	1976	£2	1979	£2
1970	£4	— Proof *FDC**	£3	— Proof *FDC**	£3
1971 Proof *FDC**	£5	1977	£2	1980	£2
1972 Proof *FDC**	£5	— Proof *FDC**	£3	— Proof *FDC**	£3
1974 Proof *FDC**	£5	1978	£2	1981	£2
1975 Proof *FDC**	£5	— Proof *FDC**	£3	— Proof *FDC**	£3

4224   4225

4224 Accession to European Economic Community. ℞. The inscription 'FIFTY PENCE' and the date of the year, surrounded by nine hands, symbolizing the nine members of the community, clasping one another in a mutual gesture of trust, assistance and friendship. (Reverse design: David Wynne)

1973 ....£3

— Proof *FDC* ** £6

4224A—Design as 4224 above, but struck in very small numbers in silver on thicker blank. Sometimes referred to as a piedfort but not twice the weight of the regular cupro-nickel currency issue. The pieces were presented to EEC Finance Ministers and possibly senior officials on the occasion of the United Kingdom joining the European Economic Community..£2500

4225 **Fifty pence.** 'New' omitted. As illustration

1982	£3	1983	£2	1984*	£3
— Proof *FDC**	£3	— Proof *FDC**	£3	— Proof *FDC**	£3

* Coins marked thus were originally issued in Royal Mint sets
** Issued as an individual proof coin and in the year set

Obverse portrait by Raphael Maklouf

4351

4351 Fifty pence. R. Britannia

1985.............................£3	1990* £4	1996*...............................£3
— Proof *FDC*.........£3	— Proof *FDC* £5	— Proof *FDC*............£4
1986*...............................£3	1991*...................................£4	— Proof in silver *FDC** £20
— Proof *FDC*.........£3	— Proof *FDC* £5	1997.................................£2
1987*...............................£3	1992* £4	— Proof *FDC* £4
— Proof *FDC* £3	— Proof *FDC*..................£5	— Proof in silver *FDC**£20
1988*...............................£3	1993* £4	
— Proof *FDC*.........£4	— Proof *FDC* £4	
1989*...............................£4	1995* £3	
— Proof *FDC*.........£3	— Proof *FDC* £4	

4352

4352 Fifty pence Presidency of the Council of European Community Ministers and completion of the Single Market. R A representation of a table on which are placed twelve stars, linked by a network of lines to each other and also to twelve chairs, around the table, on one of which appear the letters 'UK', and with the dates '1992' and '1993' above and the value '50 PENCE' below. (Reverse design: Mary Milner Dickens)

1992-1993	£12
— Proof *FDC*...	£12
— Proof in silver *FDC** (Issued: 26,890	£28
— Proof piedfort in silver *FDC* (Issued: 10,993)	£60
— Proof in gold *FDC* (Issued: 1,864)..	£800

* Coins marked thus were originally issued in Royal Mint sets

4353

4353 **Fifty pence** 50th Anniversary of the Normandy Landings on D-Day. R: A design representing the Allied invasion force of the D-Day landings heading for Normandy and filling the sea and sky, Together with the value '50 PENCE' (Reverse design: John Mills)

1994...£3
— Specimen in presentation folder..£5
— Proof *FDC**...£5
— Proof in silver *FDC* (Issued: 40,000)...£35
— Proof piedfort in silver *FDC* (Issued: 10,000) £60
— Proof in gold *FDC* (Issued: 1,877)..£800

4354 **Fifty penc**e R. Britannia: reduced diameter of 27.3mm

1997...£2
— Proof *FDC**...£4
— Proof in silver *FDC* (Issued: 1,632)...£25
— Proof piedfort in silver *FDC* (Issued: 7,192) £40

Obverse portrait by Ian Rank-Broadley

4610

4610 **Fifty pence.** R. Britannia. (Illus. as 4351)

1998.........................£3	2006 ....£3
— Proof *FDC**...............£3	— Proof *FDC** £3
1999.........................£3	— Proof in silver *FDC* (see PSS22)*.....£25
— Proof *FDC**...............£3	2007 ....£3
2000.........................£3	— Proof *FDC** £3
— Proof *FDC**...............£3	2008 ....£3
— Proof in silver *FDC* (see PSS08)*£25	— Proof *FDC** £3
2001.........................£3	— Proof in silver *FDC* (see PSS27)*.....£30
— Proof *FDC**...............£3	— Proof in gold *FDC* (see PGEBCS)* £475
2002.........................£3	— Proof in platinum *FDC* (see PPEBCS)* £550
— Proof *FDC**...............£3	2009
— Proof in gold *FDC* (see PGJS1)* £450	— Proof *FDC* (in 2009 set, see PS100)*£15
2003 ....£3	— Proof in silver *FDC* (in 2009 set,
— Proof *FDC**...............£3	see PSS40)*.........................£30
2004 ....£3	— Proof in gold *FDC* (in 2009 set,
— Proof *FDC** £3	see PG50PCS)*........................ £475
2005 £3	— Proof piedfort in gold *FDC*
— Proof *FDC** £3	(see PG50PPCS)* £1200

* *Coins marked thus were originally issued in Royal Mint sets*

| 4611 | 4612 | 4613 |

4611 **Fifty pence.** R. Celebratory pattern of twelve stars reflecting the European flag with the dates 1973 and 1998 commemorating the 25th Anniversary of the United Kingdom's membership of the European Union and Presidency of the Council of Ministers. (Reverse design: John Mills)

1998 ....£2
— Proof *FDC** £5
— Proof in silver *FDC* (Issued: 8,859) £30
— Proof piedfort in silver *FDC* (Issued: 8,440) £60
— Proof in gold *FDC* (Issued: 1,177) £450

2009
— Proof *FDC* (in 2009 set, see PS100)* £15
— Proof in silver *FDC* (in 2009 set, see PSS40)* £30
— Proof in gold *FDC* (in 2009 set, see PG50PCS)* £450
— Proof piedfort in gold *FDC* (see PG50PPCS) * £1200

4612 **Fifty pence.** R. A pair of hands set against a pattern of radiating lines with the words 'FIFTIETH ANNIVERSARY' and the value '50 PENCE' accompanied by the initials 'NHS' which appear five times on the outer border. (Reverse design: David Cornell)

1998 ....£2
— Specimen in presentation folder £3
— Proof in silver *FDC* (Issued: 9,032) £30
— Proof piedfort in silver *FDC* (Issued: 5,117) £60
— Proof in gold *FDC* (Issued: 651) £450

2009
— Proof *FDC* (in 2009 set, see PS100)* £15
— Proof in silver *FDC* (in 2009 set, see PSS40)* £30
— Proof in gold *FDC* (in 2009 set, see PG50PCS)* £450
— Proof piedfort in gold *FDC* (see PG50PPCS) * £1200

4613 **Fifty pence.** Library commemorative. R. The turning pages of a book above the dates '1850 – 2000' and the value '50 PENCE', all above a classical library building on which the words 'PUBLIC LIBRARY' and, within the pediment , representations of compact discs. (Reverse design: Mary Milner Dickens)

2000 ....£2
— Specimen in presentation folder £5
— Proof *FDC** £5
— Proof in silver *FDC* (Issued: 7,634) £28
— Proof piedfort in silver *FDC* (Issued: 5,721) £60
— Proof in gold *FDC* (Issued: 710) £450

2009
— Proof *FDC* (in 2009 set, see PS100)* £15
— Proof in silver *FDC* (in 2009 set, see PSS40)* £30
— Proof in gold *FDC* (in 2009 set, see PG50PCS)* £450
— Proof piedfort in gold *FDC* (see PG50PPCS) * £1200

* *Coins marked thus were originally issued in Royal Mint sets.*

4614   4615   4616

4614 **Fifty pence**. Anniversary of the Suffragette Movement commemorative. R. The figure of a suffragette chained to railings and holding a banner on which appear the letters 'WSPU', to the right a ballot paper marked with a cross and the words 'GIVE WOMEN THE VOTE', to the left the value '50 PENCE' and below and to the far right the dates '1903' and '2003'. (Reverse design: Mary Milner Dickens)

2003 ....£2
  — Specimen in presentation folder (Issued: 9,582) £5
  — Proof *FDC* (in 2003 set, see PS78)* £5
  — Proof in silver *FDC* (Issued: 6,267) £28
  — Proof piedfort in silver *FDC* (Issued 6,795) £60
  — Proof in gold *FDC* (Issued: 942)..£450

2009
  — Proof *FDC* (in 2009 set, see PS100)* £15
  — Proof in silver *FDC* (in 2009 set, see PSS40)*..£30
  — Proof in gold *FDC* (in 2009 set, see PG50PCS)* £450
  — Proof piedfort in gold *FDC* (see PG50PPCS) * £1200

4615 **Fifty pence**. 50th anniversary of the first sub four-minute mile. R. The legs of a running athlete with a stylised stopwatch in the background and, below, the value '50 PENCE'. (Reverse design: James Butler)

2004 ....£2
  — Specimen in presentation folder (Issued: 10,371) £5
  — Proof *FDC* (in 2004 set, see PS81)* £5
  — Proof in silver *FDC* (Issued: 4,924)..£28
  — Proof piedfort in silver *FDC* (Issued: 4,054) £60
  — Proof in gold *FDC* (Issued: 644)...£450

2009
  — Proof *FDC* (in 2009 set, see PS100)* £15
  — Proof in silver *FDC* (in 2009 set, seePSS40)*...£30
  — Proof in gold *FDC* (in 2009 set, see PG50PCS)* £450
  — Proof piedfort in gold *FDC* (see PG50PPCS)*.. £1200

4616 **Fifty pence**. 250th anniversary of the publication of Samuel Johnson's Dictionary of the English Language. R. Entries from Samuel Johnson's Dictionary of the English Language for the words 'FIFTY' and 'PENCE', with the figure '50' above, and the inscription 'JOHNSON'S DICTIONARY 1755' below. (Reverse design: Tom Phillips)

2005 ....£2
  — Proof *FDC* (in 2005 set, see PS84)* £5
  — Proof in silver *FDC* (Issued: 4,029)..£28
  — Proof piedfort in silver *FDC* (Issued: 3,808) £60
  — Proof in gold *FDC* (Issued: 584)...£450

2009
  — Proof *FDC* (in 2009 set, see PS100)* £15
  — Proof in silver *FDC* (in 2009 set, see PSS40)*..£30
  — Proof in gold *FDC* (in 2009 set, see PG50PCS)* £450
  — Proof piedfort in gold *FDC* (see PG50PPCS)*..£1200

* Coins marked thus were originally issued in Royal Mint sets.

4617   4618   4619

4617 **Fifty pence.** 150th anniversary of the institution of the Victoria Cross. R. A depiction of the
obverse and reverse of a Victoria Cross with the date '29. JAN 1856' in the centre of the
reverse of the Cross, the letters 'VC' to the right and the value 'FIFTY PENCE'. (Reverse
design: Claire Aldridge)
2006..£2
—   Specimen in presentation folder with 4618...£7
—   Proof *FDC* (in 2006 set, see PS87)*...£5
—   Proof in silver *FDC* (Issued: 6,310)..£30
—   Proof piedfort in silver *FDC* (Issued: 3,532) (see PSS27)...£60
—   Proof in gold *FDC* (Issued: 866)...£450
2009
—   Proof *FDC* (in 2009 set, see PS100)*...£15
—   Proof in silver *FDC* (in 2009 set, see PSS40)*...£30
—   Proof in gold *FDC* (in 2009 set, see PG50PCS)*..£450
—   Proof piedfort in gold *FDC* (see PG50PPCS)*...£1200

4618 **Fifty pence.** 150th anniversary of the institution of the Victoria Cross. R. A Depiction of
a soldier carrying a wounded comrade with an outline of the Victoria Cross surrounded
by a sunburst effect in the background and the value 'FIFTY PENCE'. (Reverse design:
Clive Duncan)
2006..£2
—   Specimen in presentation folder with 4617...£7
—   Proof *FDC* (in 2006 set, see PS87)*...£5
—   Proof in silver *FDC* (Issued: 6,872)..£30
—   Proof piedfort in silver *FDC* (Issued: 3,415) (see PSS27)...£60
—   Proof in gold *FDC* (Issued: 804)...£450
2009
—   Proof *FDC* (in 2009 set, see PS100)*...£15
—   Proof in silver *FDC* (in 2009 set, see PSS40)*...£30
—   Proof in gold *FDC* (in 2009 set, see PG50PCS)*..£450
—   Proof piedfort in gold *FDC* (see PG50PPCS)*...£1200

4619 **Fifty pence.** Centenary of the Founding of the Scouting Movement. R. A Fleur-de-lis
superimposed over a globe and surrounded by the inscription 'BE PREPARED', and the
dates '1907' and '2007' and the denomination 'FIFTY PENCE' (Reverse design:
Kerry Jones)
2007..£2
—   Specimen in presentation folder..£7
—   Proof *FDC** (in 2007 set, see PS90) £5
—   Proof in silver *FDC* (Issued: 10,895)..£30
—   Proof piedfort in silver *FDC** (Issued; 1,555) £60
—   Proof in gold *FDC* (Issued: 1,250) £450
2009
—   Proof *FDC* (in 2009 set, see PS100)*...£15
—   Proof in silver *FDC* (in 2009 set, see PSS40)*...£30
—   Proof in gold *FDC* (in 2009 set, see PG50PCS)*..£450
—   Proof piedfort in gold *FDC* (see PG50PPCS)*...£1200

* *Coins marked thus were originally issued in Royal Mint sets.*

4620
4620 Fifty pence. R. A section of Our Royal Arms showing elements of the third and fourth
quarterings accompanied by the words 'FIFTY PENCE' (Reverse design: Matthew Dent)
2008 ....£3
— Proof *FDC* (in 2008 set, see PS96)* £5
— Proof in silver *FDC* (in 2008 set, see PSS28)* £30
— Proof piedfort in silver *FDC* (in 2008 set, see PSS29)* £60
— Proof in gold *FDC* (in 2008 set, see PGRSAS)* £450
— Proof in platinum *FDC* (in 2008 set, see PPRSAS)* £650
2009 ....£3
— Proof *FDC* (in 2009 set, see PS97)* £5
— Proof in silver *FDC* (in 2009 set, see PSS37)* £30
— Proof in gold *FDC* (in 2009 set, see PG50PCS)* £450
— Proof piedfort in gold *FDC* (see PG50PPCS)* £1200
2010 ....£3
— Proof *FDC* (in 2010 set, see PS101)* £5
— Proof in silver *FDC* (in 2010 set, Edition: 3,500, see PSS41)* £30
2011 ....£3
— Proof *FDC* (in 2010 set, see PS104)* £3
— Proof in silver *FDC* (in 2011 set, Edition: 2,500, see PSS44) * £15
2012 ....£3
— Proof *FDC* (in 2012 set, see PS107)* £3
— Proof in silver *FDC* (Edition: 995, see PSS47)* £30
— Proof in silver with selected gold plating *FDC* (Edition: 2,012, see PSS48) £30
— Proof in gold *FDC* (Edition: 150 see PGDJS)* £450
2013 .... £3
— Proof *FDC* (in 2013 set, see PS109) * £5
— Proof in silver *FDC* (Edition: 2,013, see PSS50)* £30
— Proof in gold *FDC* (Issued: 59 see PGCAS)* £475
2014
— Proof *FDC* (in 2014 set, see PS112)* £5
— Proof in silver *FDC* (Edition: 2,014 see PSS56)*
2015
— Proof *FDC* (in 2015 set, see PS115) * £5
— Proof in silver *FDC* (Edition: 7,500 see PSS61)* £30
— Proof in gold *FDC* (Edition: 500 see PGC4P) * £450

Coins marked thus were originally issued in Royal Mint sets.

4621

4621 Fifty pence. 250th Anniversary of the foundation of the Royal Botanical Gardens, Kew.
R. A design showing the pagoda, a building associated with the Royal Botanical Gardens
at Kew, encircled by a vine and accompanied by the dates '1759' and '2009', with the
word 'KEW' at the base of the pagoda.(Reverse design: Christopher Le Brun)
2009 ....£3
— Specimen in presentation pack (Issued: 128,364) £7
— Proof *FDC* (in 2009 set, see PS97)* £7
— Proof in silver *FDC* (Issued: 7,575) £30
— Proof piedfort in silver *FDC* (Issued: 2,967)) £55
— Proof in gold *FDC* (Issued: 629)...£450
— Proof piedfort in gold *FDC* (see PG50PPCS)* £1200

4622 Fifty new pence. R. Britannia (See 4223).
2009
— Proof *FDC* (in 2009 set, see PS100)* £15
— Proof in silver *FDC* (in 2009 set, see PSS40)* £30
— Proof in gold *FDC* (in 2009 set, see PG50PCS)* £450
— Proof piedfort in gold *FDC* (in 2009 set, see PG50PPCS)* £1200

4623 Fifty new pence. Accession to European Economic Community R. Clasped hands.
(See 4224)
2009
— Proof *FDC* (in 2009 set, see PS100)* £15
— Proof in silver *FDC* (in 2009 set, see PSS40)* £30
— Proof in gold *FDC* (in 2009 set, see PG50PCS)* £450
— Proof piedfort in gold *FDC* (in 2009 set, see PG50PPCS)* £1200

4624 Fifty pence. R. Presidency of the Council of European Community Ministers and
completion of the Single Market. R. Conference table top and twelve stars. (See 4352)
2009
— Proof *FDC* (in 2009 set, see PS100)* £15
— Proof in silver *FDC* (in 2009 set, see PSS40)* £30
— Proof in gold *FDC* (in 2009 set, see PG50PCS)* £450
— Proof piedfort in gold *FDC* (in 2009 set, see PG50PPCS)* £1200

4625 Fifty pence. 50th Anniversary of the Normandy Landings on D-Day. R. Allied Invasion
Force (See 4353)
2009
— Proof *FDC* (in 2009 set, see PS100)* £15
— Proof in silver *FDC* (in 2009 set, see PSS40)* £30
— Proof in gold *FDC* (in 2009 set, see PG50PCS)* £450
— Proof piedfort in gold *FDC* (in 2009 set, see PG50PPCS)* £1200

Coins marked thus were originally issued in Royal Mint sets.

4626   4627

4626 **Fifty pence.** 100th Anniversary of Girl Guides. R. A design which depicts a repeating pattern of the current identity of Girl Guiding, UK, accompanied by the inscription 'CELEBRATING ONE HUNDRED YEARS OF GIRLGUIDING UK' and the denomination 'FIFTY PENCE' (Reverse design: Jonathan Evans and Donna Hainan)
2010 ....£1
   — Specimen on presentation card (Issued: 99,075)) £5
   — Specimen in presentation folder (Edition: 50,000) £7
   — Proof *FDC* (in 2010 set, see PS101)* £7
   — Proof in silver *FDC* (Issued: 5,271))...£30
   — Proof piedfort in silver *FDC* (Issued: 2,879) £55
   — Proof in gold *FDC* (Issued: 355)..£525

4627 **Fifty pence.** Fifth Anniversary of the World Wildlife Fund. R. A design which features 50 different icons symbolising projects and programmes that the World Wildlife Fund has supported over the course of the last 50 years, with the Panda logo of the organisation in the centre and the date '2011' below. (Reverse design: Matthew Dent)
2011 ....£1
   — Specimen in presentation folder (Issued: 67,299) £7
   — Proof *FDC* (in 2011 set, see PS104)...£7
   — Proof in silver *FDC* (Issued: 24,870) £42
   — Proof piedfort in silver *FDC* (Issued: 2,244)..£73
   — Proof in gold *FDC* (Issued: 243) £725

4628

4628 **Fifty pence.** R. A version of the Royal Arms with the inscription 'FIFTY PENCE' above and the denomination '50' below. (Reverse design: Christopher Ironside).
2013
   — Specimen in presentation folder £8
   — Proof *FDC* (in 2013 set, see PS109)*..£5
   — Proof silver *FDC* (Issued: 1,823) £45
   — Proof piedfort in silver *FDC* (Issued: 816)...£90
   — Proof in gold *FDC* (Issued: 198) £800

Coins marked thus were originally issued in Royal Mint sets.

4629   4630

4629 Fifty pence. Centenary of the birth of Benjamin Britten. R. In the centre the name
'BENJAMIN BRITTEN' superimposed over musical staves with the inscription 'BLOW
BUGLE BLOW' above and 'SET THE WILD ECHOES FLYING' below. (Reverse
design: Tom Phillips).
2013
— Specimen in presentation folder £8
— Proof silver *FDC* (Issued: 717) £45
— Proof piedfort in silver *FDC* (Issued: 515)..£90
— Proof in gold *FDC*(Issued: 70) £800

4630 Fifty pence. Commonwealth Games R. A design of a cyclist and a sprinter with the
Scottish Saltire bisecting the coin and the inscription 'XX COMMONWEALTH GAMES
GLASGOW' and the date'2014' (Reverse design: Alex Loudon with Dan Flashman).
2014
— Specimen in presentation folde..£10
— Proof *FDC* (in 2014 set, see PS112)*..£5
— Proof silver *FDC* (Edition: 4,500 including coins in sets) £45
— Proof piedfort in silver *FDC* (Edition: 3,513 including coins in sets) £90
— Proof in gold *FDC* (Edition: 450)...£800

4631

4631 Fifty pence. Battle of Britain commemorative. R. A design showing airmen running
to their planes with enemy aircraft overhead with the inscription 'THE BATTLE OF
BRITAIN 1940' (Reverse design: Gary Breeze).
2015
— BU in presentation folder £8
— Proof *FDC* (in 2015 set, see PS116) * £5
— Proof in silver *FDC* (Edition: 3,000 see PSS63 and PSS64)..................................£50
— Proof piedfort in silver *FDC* (Edition: 1,500 see PSS65) £100
— Proof in gold *FDC* (Edition: 500 see PGC4P)) £675

* Coins marked thus were originally issued in Royal Mint sets.

Obverse portrait by Jody Clark

4632 4633

4632 Fifty pence.
2015
— Proof *FDC* (in 2015 set, see PS116) * ....
— Proof in silver *FDC* (Edition: 7,500 see PSS62)*
— Proof in gold *FDC* (Edition: 500 see PGC5P) *

4633 Fifty pence. Battle of Britain commemorative. R.A design showing airmen running to their planes with enemy aircraft overhead with the inscription 'THE BATTLE OF BRITAIN 1940' (Reverse design: Gary Breeze).
2015
— Proof in silver *FDC* (Edition: 4,200)...£50
— Proof piedfort in silver *FDC* (Edition: 1,940) £100
— Proof in gold *FDC* (Edition: 520)..£675

NICKEL-BRASS

ONE POUND COINS
Obverse portrait by Arnold Machin

4221 4222

4221 One pound. R. The Ensigns Armorial of Our United Kingdom of Great Britain and Northern Ireland with the value 'ONE POUND' below and the edge inscription 'DECUS ET TUTAMEN' (Reverse design: Eric Sewell)
1983 ....£5
— Specimen in presentation folder (Issued: 484,900) £5
— Proof *FDC* (in 1983 set, seePS33)* £5
— Proof in silver *FDC* (Issued: 50,000) £35
— Proof piedfort in silver *FDC* (Issued: 10,000) £125

4222 One pound. (Scottish design). R. A thistle eradicated enfiling a representation of Our Royal Diadem with the value 'ONE POUND' below and the edge inscription 'NEMO ME IMPUNE LACESSIT' (Reverse design: Leslie Durbin)
1984 ....£5
— Specimen in presentation folder (Issued: 27,960) £5
— Proof *FDC* (in 1984 set, see PS34)* £5
— Proof in silver *FDC* (Issued: 44,855) £30
— Proof piedfort in silver *FDC* (Issued: 15,000) £60

* Coins marked thus were originally issued in Royal Mint sets.

Obverse portrait by Raphael Maklouf

4331   4332   4333

4331 **One pound** (Welsh design). R. A leek eradicated enfiling a representation of Our Royal
Diadem with the value 'ONE POUND' below and the edge inscription 'PLEIDIOL
WYF I'M GWLAD". (Reverse design: Leslie Durbin)

1985 ....£4
— Specimen in presentation folder (Issued: 24,850) £4
— Proof *FDC* (in 1985 set, see PS35)* £5
— Proof in silver *FDC* (Issued: 50,000) £30
— Proof piedfort in silver *FDC* (Issued: 15,000) £60
1990 ....£5
— Proof *FDC* (in 1990 set, see PS45)* £6
— Proof in silver *FDC* (Issued: 23,277) £28

4332 **One pound** (Northern Irish design). R. A flax plant eradicated enfiling a representation
of Our Royal Diadem with value 'ONE POUND' below and the edge inscription
'DECUS ET TUTAMEN'. (Reverse design: Leslie Durbin)

1986 ....£5
— Specimen in presentation folder (Issued: 19,908) £5
— Proof *FDC* (in 1986 set, see PS37)* £4
— Proof in silver *FDC* (Issued: 37,958) £30
— Proof piedfort in silver *FDC* (Issued: 15,000) £60
1991 ....£5
— Proof *FDC* (in 1991 set, see PS47)* £6
— Proof in silver *FDC* (Issued: 22,922) £28

4333 **One pound** (English design). R. An oak tree enfiling a representation of Our Royal
Diadem with the value 'ONE POUND' below and the edge inscription 'DECUS ET
TUTAMEN'. (Reverse design: Leslie Durbin)

1987 ....£4
— Specimen in presentation folder (Issued: 72,607) £4
— Proof *FDC* (in 1987 set, see PS39)* £6
— Proof in silver *FDC* (Issued: 50,000) £30
— Proof piedfort in silver *FDC* (Issued: 15,000) £60
1992 ....£5
— Proof *FDC* (in 1992 set, see PS49)* £6
— Proof in silver *FDC* (Issued: 13,065) £30

4334 **One pound** (Royal Shield). R. A Shield of Our Royal Arms ensigned by a representation
of Our Royal Crown with the value 'ONE POUND' below and the Edge inscription
'DECUS ET TUTAMEN'. (Reverse design: Derek Gorringe)

1988 ....£5
— Specimen in presentation folder (Issued: 29,550) £6
— Proof *FDC* (in 1988 set, see PS41)* £6
— Proof in silver *FDC* (Issued: 50,000) £35
— Proof piedfort in silver *FDC* (Issued: 10,000) £60

* Coins marked thus were originally issued in Royal Mint sets.

4335 **One pound** (Scottish design). Edge 'NEMO ME IMPUNE LACESSIT' (Illus. as 4222)
1989 ....£5
— Proof *FDC* (in 1989 set, see PS43)* £6
— Proof in silver *FDC* (Issued: 22,275) £30
— Proof piedfort in silver *FDC* (Issued: 10,000) £60
4336 **One pound** (Royal Arms design). Edge 'DECUS ET TUTAMEN' (Illus. as 4221)
1993 ....£5
— Proof *FDC* (in 1993 set, see PS51)* £6
— Proof in silver *FDC* (Issued: 16,526) £30
— Proof piedfort in silver *FDC* (Issued: 12,500) £60
4337 **One pound** (Scottish design). R: A Lion rampant within a double tressure flory counter-flory, being that quartering of Our Royal Arms known heraldically as Scotland with the value 'ONE POUND' below and the edge inscription 'NEMO ME IMPUNE LACESSIT'. (Reverse design: Norman Sillman)
1994 ....£4
— Specimen in presentation folder £5
— Proof *FDC* (in 1994 set, see PS53)* £6
— Proof in silver *FDC* (Issued: 25,000) £30
— Proof piedfort in silver *FDC* (Issued: 11,722) £60
4338 **One pound** (Welsh design). R. A dragon passant, being Our badge for Wales with the value 'ONE POUND' below and the edge inscription 'PLEIDIOL WYF I'M GWLAD'. (Reverse design: Norman Sillman)
1995 ....£4
— Specimen in presentation folder, English version £5
— Specimen in presentation folder, Welsh version £10
— Proof *FDC* (in 1995 set, see PS55)* £5
— Proof in silver *FDC* (Issued: 27,445) £30
— Proof piedfort in silver *FDC* (Issued: 8,458) £70
4339 **One pound** (Northern Irish design). R. A Celtic cross charged at the centre with an Annulet therein a Pimpernel flower and overall an ancient Torque, symbolizing that part of Our Kingdom known as Northern Ireland with the value 'ONE POUND' below and the edge inscription 'DECUS ET TUTAMEN'. (Reverse design: Norman Sillman)
1996 ....£4
— Specimen in presentation folder £6
— Proof *FDC* (in 1996 set, see PS57)* £6
— Proof in silver *FDC* (Issued: 25,000) £30
— Proof piedfort in silver *FDC* (Issued: 10,000 ....£60

4340

4340 **One pound** (English design) R. Three lions passant guardant, being that quartering of Our Royal Arms known heraldically as *England*, with the value 'ONE POUND' below and the edge inscription 'DECUS ET TUTAMEN.(Reverse design: Norman Sillman)
1997 ....£4
— Specimen in presentation folder (Issued 56,996) £5
— Proof *FDC* (in 1997 set, see PS59)* £5
— Proof in silver *FDC* (Issued: 20,137) £30
— Proof piedfort in silver *FDC* (Issued: 10,000) £60

* Coins marked thus were originally issued in Royal Mint sets.

Obverse portrait by Ian Rank-Broadley

4590

4590 One pound (Royal Arms design). Edge: 'DECUS ET TUTAMEN' (rev. as 4221)

1998 .... £5
— Proof *FDC* (in 1998 set, see PS61)* £6
— Proof in silver *FDC* (Issued: 13,863) £30
— Proof piedfort in silver *FDC* (Issued: 7,894) £60
2003 .... £3
— Specimen in presentation folder (Issued: 23,760) £5
— Proof *FDC* (in 2003 set, see PS78)* £6
— Proof in silver *FDC* (Issued: 15,830) £30
— Proof piedfort in silver *FDC* (Issued: 9,871) £60
2008
— Specimen in presentation folder (Issued: 18,336) £7
— Proof *FDC* (in 2008 set, see PS93)* £6
— Proof in silver *FDC* (Issued: 8,441) £30
— Proof in gold *FDC* (Issued: 674) £600
— Proof in platinum *FDC* (in 2008 set, see PPEBCS)* £800
2013. 30th Anniversary of the introduction of the £1 coin
— Proof silver *FDC* (Issued: 1,311 in 3 coin sets, see PSS55) £60
— Proof in gold *FDC* (Issued: 17 in 3 coin sets, see PG31S) £1000
4590A 2008
— Proof in silver with selected gold plating on reverse *FDC* (in 2008 set,
see PSS30)* £40
4591 One pound. (Scottish lion design). Edge: 'NEMO ME IMPUNE LACESSIT' (rev as 4337)
1999 .... £3
— Specimen in presentation folder £5
— Proof *FDC* (in 1999 set, see PS63)* £6
— Proof in silver *FDC* (Issued: 16,328) £30
— Proof piedfort in silver *FDC* (Issued: 9,975) £60
2008
— Proof in gold *FDC* (in 2008 set, see PG1PCS)* £600
4591A 1999
— Proof in silver *FDC*, with reverse frosting, (Issued: 1,994)* £50
4591B 2008
— Proof in silver with selected gold plating on reverse *FDC* (in 2008 set, see PSS30)* £40
4592 One pound. (Welsh design). Edge: 'PLEIDIOL WYF I'M GWLAD' (rev. as 4338)
2000 .... £3
— Proof *FDC* (in 2000 set, see PS65)* £6
— Proof in silver *FDC* (Issued: 15,913) £30
— Proof piedfort in silver *FDC* (Issued: 9,994) £60
2008
— Proof in gold *FDC* (in 2008 set, see PG1PCS)* £600
4592A 2000
— Proof in silver *FDC*, with reverse frosting, (Issued: 1,994)* £50

* Coins marked thus were originally issued in Royal Mint sets.

4592B 2008
— Proof in silver with selected gold plating on reverse *FDC* (in 2008 set, see PSS30)* £40

4593 **One pound.** (Northern Irish design). Edge: 'DECUS ET TUTAMEN' (rev. as 4339)
2001 .... £3
— Proof *FDC* (in 2001 set, see PS68)* £6
— Proof in silver *FDC* (Issued: 11,697) £30
— Proof piedfort in silver *FDC* (Issued: 8,464) £60
2008
— Proof in gold *FDC* (in 2008 set, see PG1PCS)* £600

4593A 2001
— Proof in silver *FDC*, with reverse frosting, (Issued: 1,540)* £60

4593B 2008
— Proof in silver with selected gold plating on reverse *FDC* (in 2008 set, see PSS30)* £40

4594 **One pound.** (English design) Edge: 'DECUS ET TUTAMEN' (rev. as 4340)
2002 .... £3
— Proof *FDC* (in 2002 set, see PS72)* £6
— Proof in silver *FDC* (Issued: 17,693) £30
— Proof piedfort in silver *FDC* (Issued: 6,599) £60
— Proof in gold *FDC* (in 2002 set, see PGJS1)* £600
2008
— Proof in gold *FDC* (in 2008 set, see PG1PCS)* £600

4594A 2002
— Proof in silver *FDC*, with reverse frosting, (Issued: 1,540)* £60

4594B 2008
— Proof in silver with selected gold plating on reverse *FDC* (in 2008 set, see PSS30)* £40

4595

4595 **One pound.** Scotland R. A representation of the Forth Railway Bridge with a border of railway tracks and beneath, the value 'ONE POUND' and an incuse decorative feature on the edge symbolising bridges and pathways. (Reverse design: Edwina Ellis)
2004 .... £3
— Specimen in presentation folder (Issued: 24,014) £5
— Proof *FDC* (in 2004 set, see PS81)* £6
— Proof in silver *FDC* (Issued: 11,470) £30
— Proof piedfort in silver *FDC* (Issued: 7,013) £60
— Proof in gold *FDC* (Issued: 2,618) £600
2008
— Proof in gold *FDC* (in 2008 set, see PG1PCS)* £600

4595A **One pound pattern.** Scotland. R. Forth Railway Bridge but dated 2003 with plain edge and hallmark, reading "PATTERN" instead of "ONE POUND"
— Proof in silver *FDC** £25
— Proof in gold *FDC** £550

* Coins marked thus were originally issued in Royal Mint sets.

4595B   4596   4596B   4597

4595B **One pound pattern.** Scotland. ℞. Unicorn with the word "Pattern" below with plain
edge and hallmark and dated 2004. (Reverse design: Timothy Noad)
- — Proof in silver *FDC** £25
- — Proof in gold *FDC** £550

4595C 2008
- — Proof in silver as 4595 with selected gold plating on reverse *FDC* (in 2008 set, see
    PSS30)*...£40

4596 **One pound.** Wales. ℞. A representation of the Menai Straits Bridge with a border of
railings and stanchions, the value 'ONE POUND' and an incuse decorative feature on the
edge symbolising bridges and pathways. (Reverse design: Edwina Ellis)
2005 ....£3
- — Specimen in presentation folder (Issued: 24,802)..£6
- — Proof *FDC* (in 2005 set, see PS84)*..£6
- — Proof in silver *FDC* (Issued: 8,371) £35
- — Proof piedfort in silver *FDC* (Issued: 6,007) £60
- — Proof in gold *FDC* (Issued: 1,195)..£600

2008
- — Proof in gold *FDC* (in 2008 set, see PG1PCS)* £600

4596A **One pound pattern.** Wales. ℞. Menai Straits Bridge but dated 2003 with plain edge and
hallmark
- — Proof in silver *FDC* (in 2003 set, see PPS1)*..£25
- — Proof in gold *FDC* (in 2003 set, see PPS2)*...£550

4596B **One pound pattern.** Wales. ℞ Dragon and the word "Pattern" below with plain edge and
hallmark and dated 2004. (Reverse design: Timothy Noad)
- — Proof in silver *FDC* (in 2004 set, see PPS3)*..£25
- — Proof in gold *FDC* (in 2004 set, see PPS4)*...£550

4596C 2008
- — Proof in silver as 4596 with selected gold plating on reverse *FDC* (in 2008 set,
    see PSS30)*..£40

4597 **One pound.** Northern Ireland. ℞. A representation of the Egyptian Arch Railway Bridge
in County Down with a border of railway station canopy dags, the value 'ONE POUND'
and an incuse decorative feature on the edge symbolising bridges and pathways. (Reverse
design: Edwina Ellis)
2006..£4
- — Specimen in presentation folder £6
- — Proof *FDC* (in 2006 set, see PS87)*..£8
- — Proof in silver *FDC* (Edition: 20,000) £30
- — Proof piedfort in silver *FDC* (Edition: 7,500)..£60
- — Proof in gold *FDC* (Edition: 1,500) £600

2008
- — Proof in gold *FDC* (in 2008 set, see PG1PCS)* £600

4597A **One pound pattern.** Northern Ireland. ℞. MacNeill's Egyptian Arch Railway Bridge but
dated 2003 with plain edge and hallmark
- — Proof in silver *FDC* (in 2003 set, see PPS1)*..£25
- — Proof in gold *FDC* (in 2003 set, see PPS2)*...£550

* Coins marked thus were originally issued in Royal Mint sets.

| 4597B | 4598 | 4598A | 4598B |

4597B **One pound pattern.** Northern Ireland. ℞ Stag and the word 'Pattern' below with plain edge and hallmark and dated 2004. (Reverse design: Timothy Noad)
— Proof in silver *FDC* (in 2004 set, see PPS3)*...£25
— Proof in gold *FDC* (in 2004 set, see PPS4)*..£550

4597C 2008
— Proof in silver as 4597 with selected gold plating on reverse *FDC* (in 2008 set,
see PSS30)*...£40

4598 **One pound. England.** ℞. A representation of the Gateshead Millennium Bridge with a border of struts, the value 'ONE POUND' and an incuse decorative feature on the edge symbolising bridges and pathways. (Reverse design: Edwina Ellis)
2007...£4
— Specimen in presentation folder..£7
— Proof *FDC** (in 2007 set, see PS90) £8
— Proof in silver *FDC* (Issued: 10,110) £30
— Proof piedfort in silver *FDC* (Issued: 5,739) £60
— Proof in gold *FDC* (Issued: 1,112) £600
2008
— Proof in gold *FDC* (in 2008 set, see PG1PCS)*..£600

4598A **One pound pattern.** England. ℞. Millennium Bridge but dated 2003 with plain edge and hallmark
— Proof in silver *FDC* (in 2003 set, see PSS1)*...£25
— Proof in gold *FDC* (in 2003 set, see PPS2)*..£550

4598B **One pound pattern.** England. ℞. Lion with the word 'Pattern' below with plain edge and hallmark and dated 2004. (Reverse design: Timothy Noad)
— Proof in silver *FDC* (in 2004 set, see PPS3)*...£25
— Proof in gold *FDC* (in 2004 set, see PPS4)*..£550

4598C 2008
— Proof in silver as 4598 with selected gold plating on reverse *FDC* (in 2008 set,
see PSS30)*...£40

4599 **One pound.** (Scottish design). Edge 'NEMO ME IMPUNE LACESSIT' (rev. as 4222)
2008
— Proof in gold *FDC* (in 2008 set, see PG1PCS)*..£600

4599A 2008
— Proof in silver with selected gold plating on reverse *FDC* (in 2008 set,
see PSS30)*...£40

4600 **One pound.** (Welsh design). Edge 'PLEIDOL WYF I'M GWLAD' (rev. see 4331)
2008
— Proof in gold *FDC* (in 2008 set, see PG1PCS)*..£600

4600A 2008
— Proof in silver with selected gold plating on reverse *FDC* (in 2008 set,
see PSS30)*...£40

4601 **One pound.** (Northern Irish design). Edge 'DECUS ET TUTAMEN' (rev. see 4332)
2008
— Proof in gold *FDC* (in 2008 set, see PG1PCS)*..£600

* Coins marked thus were originally issued in Royal Mint sets.

4601A2008
—   Proof in silver with selected gold plating on reverse *FDC* (in 2008 set,
       see PSS30)* £40
4602 One pound. (English design). Edge 'DECUS ET TUTAMEN' (rev. see 4333)
       2008
—   Proof in gold *FDC* (in 2008 set, see PG1PCS)* £600
4602A2008
—   Proof in silver with selected gold plating on reverse *FDC* (in 2008 set,
       see PSS30)* £40

4603 One pound. (Royal Shield). Edge 'DECUS ET TUTAMEN' (rev.as 4334).
       2008
—   Proof in gold *FDC* (in 2008 set, see PG1PCS)* £600
       2013. 30th Anniversary of the introduction of the £1 coin.
—   Proof silver *FDC* (Issued: 1,311 in 3 coin sets, see PSS55)* £60
—   Proof in gold *FDC* (Issued: 17 in 3 coin sets, see PG31S)* £1000
4603A 2008
—   Proof in silver with selected gold plating on reverse FDC (in 2008 set,
       see PSS30)*..£40

4604
4604 One pound. R. A shield of Our Royal Arms with the words 'ONE' to the left and
       'POUND' to the right and the edge inscription 'DECUS ET TUTAMEN' (Reverse
       design: Matthew Dent)
       2008 ....£3
—   Proof *FDC* (in 2008 set, see PS96)* £5
—   Proof in silver *FDC* (Issued: 5,000) £30
—   Proof piedfort in silver *FDC* (Edition: 8,000)......................................£50
—   Proof in gold *FDC* (Issued: 860)*...£600
—   Proof in platinum *FDC* (in 2008 set, see PPRSAS)*............................£800
       2009 ....£3
—   Specimen in presentation folder (Edition: 15,000) £7
—   Proof *FDC* (in 2009 set, see PS97)*..£5
—   BU in silver (Edition: 50,000)..£30
—   Proof in silver *FDC* (Edition: 20,000 including coins in sets)..............£35
—   Proof in gold *FDC* (Edition: 1,000) £600
       2010 ....£3
—   Proof *FDC* (in 2010 set, see PS101)*..£5
—   BU in silver (Edition: 50,000)..£30
—   Proof in silver *FDC* (Edition: 20,000 including coins in sets)..............£35
       2011 ....£3
—   Proof *FDC* (in 2011 set, see PS104) *...£5
—   BU in silver...£30
—   Proof in silver *FDC* (in 2011 set, Edition: 2,500, see PSS44) *...........£35

* Coins marked thus were originally issued in Royal Mint sets.

2012 ....£3
— Proof *FDC* (in 2012 set, see PS107)* £3
— BU in silver £25
— Proof in silver with selected gold plating *FDC* (Edition: 2,012, see PSS48) £40
— Proof in gold *FDC* (Edition: 150 see PGDJS)* £600
2013 ....£3
— Proof *FDC* (in 2013 set, see PS109) * £7
— BU in silver £25
— Proof in silver *FDC* (Edition: 10,000 including coins in sets) £40
— Proof in gold *FDC* (Edition: 310 see PGCAS)* £1000
2014 ....£3
— Proof *FDC* (in 2014 set, see PS112) * £3
— BU in silver £25
— Proof in silver *FDC* (Edition: 2,014 see PSS56) * £35
2015
— Proof *FDC* (in 2015 set, see PS115) * £5
— Proof in silver *FDC* (Edition: 7,500 see PSS61)* £35
— Proof in gold *FDC* (Edition: 500 see PGC4P) * £600

4605   4606

4605 – One pound. London. R. A design which depicts the official badges of the capital
cities of the United Kingdom, with the badge of London being the principal focus,
accompanied by the name 'LONDON' and the denomination 'ONE POUND' with the
edge inscription 'DOMINE DIRIGE NOS'. (Reverse design: Stuart Devlin)
2010 ....£3
— Specimen on presentation card (Issued: 66,313) £5
— Specimen in presentation folder with **4606** (Edition: 10,000) £14
— Proof *FDC* (in 2010 set, see PS101)* £5
— Proof in silver *FDC* (Issued: 7,693) £35
— Proof piedfort in silver *FDC* (Issued: 3,682) £55
— Proof in gold *FDC* (Issued: 950) £600
4606 – One pound. Belfast. R. A design which depicts the official badges of the capital cities
of the United Kingdom, with the badge of Belfast being the principal focus, accompanied
by the name 'BELFAST' and the denomination 'ONE POUND' with the edge inscription
'PRO TANTO QUID RETRIBUAMUS' (Reverse design: Stuart Devlin)
2010 ....£3
— Specimen on presentation card (Issued: 64,461) £5
— Specimen in presentation folder with **4605** (Edition: 10,000) £14
— Proof *FDC* (in 2010 set, see PS101)* £5
— Proof in silver *FDC* (Issued: 5,805) £35
— Proof piedfort in silver *FDC* (Issued: 3,503) £55
— Proof in gold *FDC* (Issued: 585) £600

* Coins marked thus were originally issued in Royal Mint sets.

4607   4608

4607 **One pound. Edinburgh.** R. A design which depicts the official badges of the capital cities of the United Kingdom, with the badge of Edinburgh being the principal focus, accompanied by the name 'EDINBURGH' and the denomination 'ONE POUND' with the edge inscription 'NISI DOMINUS'. (Reverse design: Stuart Devlin)

2011 ....£3
— Specimen in presentation folder with **4608** (Edition: 10,000) £14
— Proof *FDC* (in 2011 set, see PS104)*..£8
— Proof in silver *FDC* (Issued: 4,973) £45
— Proof piedfort in silver *FDC* (Issued: 2,696)..£78
— Proof in gold *FDC* (Issued: 499) £950

4608 **One pound. Cardiff.** R. A design which depicts the official badges of the capital cities of the United Kingdom, with the badge of Cardiff being the principal focus, accompanied by the name 'CARDIFF' and the denomination 'ONE POUND' with the edge inscription 'Y DDRAIG GOCH DDYRY CYCHWYN ' (Reverse design: Stuart Devlin)

2011 ....£3
— Specimen in presentation folder with **4607** (Edition: 10,000)...................£14
— Proof *FDC* (in 2011 set, see PS104) *..£8
— Proof in silver *FDC* (Issued: 5,553) £45
— Proof piedfort in silver *FDC* (Issued: 1,615)..£78
— Proof in gold *FDC* (Issued: 524) £950

4720   4721

4720 **One pound. England.** R. Depicts an oak branch paired with a Tudor-inspired rose with the denomination 'ONE POUND' below and the edge inscription 'DECUS ET TUTAMEN'. (Reverse design: Timothy Noad)

2013 ....£3
— Specimen in presentation folder with **4721** £18
— Proof *FDC* (in 2013 set, see PS109) *..£7
— Proof in silver *FDC* (Issued: 1,858) £50
— Proof piedfort in silver *FDC* ((Issued: 1,071) £100
— Proof in gold *FDC* ((Issued: 185)..£1000

4721 **One pound. Wales.** R. Depicts a leek and a daffodil with their leaves entwined and the denomination 'ONE POUND' below and the edge inscription 'PLEIDIOL WYF I'M GWLAD'. (Reverse design: Timothy Noad)

2013 ....£3
— Specimen in presentation folder with **4720** £18
— Proof *FDC* (in 2013 set, see PS109) *..£7
— Proof in silver *FDC* ((Issued: 1,618) £50
— Proof piedfort in silver *FDC* ((Issued: 860) £100
— Proof in gold *FDC* ((Issued: 175)..£1000

4722   4723

4722 One pound. Northern Ireland. R. Depicts a flax and shamrock being the principle
focus for Northern Ireland accompanied by the denomination 'ONE POUND' and
the edge inscription 'DECUS ET TUTANEM. (Reverse design: Timothy Noad)
2014 ....£3
— Specimen in presentation folder with **4723** £18
— Proof *FDC* (in 2014 set, see PS112)*..£7
— Proof in silver *FDC* (Edition: 6,028 including coins in sets) £50
— Proof piedfort in silver *FDC* (Edition: 3,014 including coins in sets) £100
— Proof in gold *FDC* (Edition: 560 including coins in sets)................................£1000

4723 One pound. Scotland. R. Depicts the thistle and bluebell being the principle focus for
Scotland accompanied by the denomination 'ONE POUND' and the edge inscription
'NEMO ME IMPUNE LACESSIT'. (Reverse design: Timothy Noad)
2014 ....£3
— Specimen in presentation folder with **4722** £18
— Proof *FDC* (in 2014 set, see PS112)*..£7
— Proof in silver *FDC* (Edition: 6,028 including coins in sets) £50
— Proof piedfort in silver *FDC* (Edition: 3,014 including coins in sets) £100
— Proof in gold *FDC* (Edition: 560 including coins in sets)................................£1000

Obverse portrait by Jody Clark

4625

4624 One pound. R. A shield of Our Royal Arms with the words 'ONE' to the left and
'POUND' to the right and the edge inscription 'DECUS ET TUTAMEN'
(Reverse design: Matthew Dent) 2015
— Proof *FDC* (in 2015 set, see PS116) *..£5
— Proof in silver *FDC* (Edition: 7,500 see PSS62)*
— Proof in gold *FDC* (Edition: 500 see PGC5P) *

4625 One Pound R. A depiction of Our Royal Arms accompanied by the inscription 'ONE
POUND' below with the edge inscription 'DECUS ET TUTAMEN' (Reverse design:
Timothy Noad)
2015
— BU in presentation pack £10
— Proof in silver *FDC* (Edition: 3,500)..£50
— Proof piedfort in silver *FDC* (Edition: 2,000) £100
— Proof in gold *FDC* (Edition: 500)..£850

* Coins marked thus were originally issued in Royal Mint sets.

NICKEL-BRASS

TWO POUND COINS
Obverse portrait by Raphael Maklouf

4311

4311 **Two pounds.** R. St. Andrew's cross with a crown of laurel leaves and surmounted by a
thistle of Scotland with date '1986' above. Edge 'XIII COMMONWEALTH GAMES
SCOTLAND' (Reverse design: Norman Sillman)

1986 ....£5
— Specimen in presentation folder £8
— Proof *FDC** £10
— 500 silver (Issued: 58,881) £18
— Proof in silver *FDC* (Issued: 59,779) £35
— Proof in gold *FDC* (Issued: 3,277)..£525

4312   4313

4312 **Two pounds** 300th Anniversary of Bill of Rights. R Cypher of W&M (King William
and Queen Mary) interlaced surmounting a horizontal Parliamentary mace and a
representation of the Royal Crown above and the dates '1689'and '1989' below, all
within the inscription 'TERCENTENARY OF THE BILL OF RIGHTS'. (Reverse
design: John Lobban)

1989 ....£5
— Specimen in presentation folder £8
— Proof *FDC* (in 1989 set, see PS43)* £10
— Proof in silver *FDC* (Issued: 25,000) £35
— Proof piedfort in silver *FDC* (in 1989 set, seePSS01)* £60

4313 **Two pounds** 300th Anniversary of Claim of Right (Scotland). R. As 4312, but with
Crown of Scotland and the inscription 'TERCENTENARY OF THE CLAIM OF
RIGHT'. (Reverse design: John Lobban)

1989 ....£15
— Specimen in presentation folder £20
— Proof *FDC* (in 1989 set, see PS43)* £15
— Proof in silver *FDC* (Issued: 24,852) £35
— Proof piedfort in silver *FDC* (in 1989 set, seePSS01)* £60

* *Coins marked thus were originally issued in Royal Mint sets.*

4314 4315 4316

4314 Two pounds 300th Anniversary of the Bank of England. R: Bank's original Corporate Seal, with Crown & Cyphers of William III & Mary II and the dates '1694' and '1994'. Edge 'SIC VOS NON VOBIS'on the silver and base metal versions. (Reverse design: Leslie Durbin)

1994 ....£5
— Specimen in presentation folder £8
— Proof *FDC* (in 1994 set, see PS53)* £10
— Proof in silver *FDC* (Issued: 27, 957) £35
— Proof piedfort in silver *FDC* (Issued: 9,569) £60
— Proof in gold *FDC* (Issued: 1,000) £550

4314A— Gold Error – known as a Mule coin. £2500
The obverse of the 1994 Bank of England issue should have included the denomination 'TWO POUNDS' as this was not included in the design of the commemorative reverse. An unknown number of coins were struck and issued in gold using the die that was reserved for the Double Sovereign or Two Pound coins in the sovereign series. The Royal Mint wrote to its retail customers inviting them to return the error coin for replacement with the correct design. No details are known as to how many were returned, nor how many exist in the market. The incorrect obverse can be seen at **4251** in the section listing Gold Sovereigns; the correct obverse is at **4311**.

4315 Two pounds 50th Anniversary of the End of World War II. R: A stylised representation of a dove as the symbol of Peace. Edge '1945 IN PEACE GOODWILL 1995'. (Reverse design: John Mills)

1995 ....£5
— Specimen in presentation folder £8
— Proof *FDC* (in 1995 set, see PS55)* £10
— Proof in silver *FDC* (Issued: 35,751) £35
— Proof piedfort in silver *FDC* (Edition: 10,000) £60
— Proof in gold *FDC* (Issued: 2,500) £525

4316 Two pounds 50th Anniversary of the Establishment of the United Nations. R: 50th Anniversary symbol and a fanning pattern of flags with the inscription 'NATIONS UNITED FOR PEACE' above and the dates '1945-1995'below. (Reverse design: Michael Rizzello)

1995 ....£5
— Specimen in presentation folder £7
— Specimen in card (issued as part of multi country United Nations Collection)..........£7
— Proof in silver *FDC* (Edition: 175,000) £35
— Proof piedfort in silver *FDC* (Edition: 10,000) £60
— Proof in gold *FDC* (Edition: 17,500) £525

* Coins marked thus were originally issued in Royal Mint sets.

4317

4317 Two pounds European Football Championships. R: A stylised representation of a football with the date '1996' centrally placed and surrounded by sixteen small rings. Edge: 'TENTH EUROPEAN CHAMPIONSHIP'. (Reverse design: John Mills)

1996	£6
— Specimen in presentation folder	£8
— Proof *FDC* (in 1996 set, see PS57)*	£10
— Proof in silver *FDC* (Issued: 25,163)	£35
— Proof piedfort in silver *FDC* (Issued: 7,634)	£60
— Proof in gold *FDC* (Issued: 2,098)	£525

4317A Incorrect blank. When struck the coins have a dished appearance on both the obverse and reverse but several pieces in gold have been reported where the surface of the coins is flat. Enquiries at the Mint are continuing with a view to understanding how this could have occurred £1500

Bimetallic issues

4318

4318 Two pounds Bimetallic currency issue. R. Four concentric circles representing the Iron Age, 18th Century industrial development, silicon chip, and Internet. Edge: 'STANDING ON THE SHOULDERS OF GIANTS'. (Reverse design: Bruce Rushin)

1997	£5
— Specimen in presentation folder	£8
— Proof *FDC* (in 1997 set, see PS59)*	£10
— Proof in silver FDC (Issued: 29,910)	£32
— Proof piedfort in silver *FDC* (Issued: 10,000)	£60
— Proof in gold *FDC* (Issued: 2,482)	£525

* Coins marked thus were originally issued in Royal Mint sets.

Obverse portrait by Ian Rank-Broadley

4570

4570 Two pounds. Bimetallic currency issue. R. Four concentric circles, representing the Iron Age, 18th Century industrial development, silicon chip and Internet. Edge: 'STANDING ON THE SHOULDERS OF GIANTS'. (Rev. as 4318)

1998	£5
— Proof *FDC* (in 1998 set, see PS61)*	£10
— Proof in silver *FDC* (Issued: 19,978)	£32
— Proof piedfort in silver *FDC* (Issued: 7,646)	£60
1999	£4
2000	£4
— Proof *FDC* (in 2000 set, see PS65)*	£10
— Proof in silver *FDC* (in 2000 set, see PSS10)*	£35
2001	£4
— Proof *FDC* (see PS68)*	£10
2002	£4
— Proof *FDC* (in 2002 set, see PS72)*	£10
— Proof in gold *FDC* (in 2002 set, see PGJS1)*	£525
2003	£4
— Proof *FDC* (see PS78)*	£10
2004	£4
— Proof *FDC* (in 2004 set, see PS81)*	£10
2005	£4
— Proof *FDC* (see PS84)*	£10
2006	£4
— Proof *FDC* (in 2006 set, see PS87)*	£10
— Proof in silver *FDC* (in 2006 set, see PSS22)*	£35
2007	£4
2008	£4
— Proof *FDC* (in 2008 set, see PS93)*	£10
2009	£4
— Proof *FDC* (in 2009 set, see PS97)	£10
— Proof in silver *FDC* (in 2009 set, see PSS37)*	£35
2010	£4
— Proof *FDC* (in 2010 set, see PS101)*	£10
— Proof in silver *FDC* (in 2010 set, see PSS41)*	£35
2011	£4
— Proof *FDC* (in 2010 set, see PS104)*	£10
— Proof in silver *FDC* (in 2010 set, see PSS44)*	£35
2012	£4
— Proof *FDC* (in 2012 set, see PS107)*	£3
— Proof in silver *FDC* (Edition: 2,012, see PSS47)*	£30
— Proof in gold *FDC* (Edition: 150 see PGDJS)*	£800

* Coins marked thus were originally issued in Royal Mint sets.

2013 ....£4
— Proof *FDC* (in 2013 set, see PS109)* £5
— Proof in silver *FDC* (Edition: 2,013, see PSS50)* £30
— Proof in gold FDC (Edition: 50 see PGCAS)* £1000
2014 ....£4
— Proof *FDC* (in 2014 set, see PS112)* £5
— Proof in silver *FDC* (Edition: 2,014 see PSS56)*
2015 ....£4
— Proof *FDC* (in 2015 set, see PS115) * £5
— Proof in silver *FDC* (Edition: 9,000 see PSS61 and PSS63)*
— Proof in gold *FDC* (Edition: 500 see PGC4P) *

4571 Two pounds. Rugby World Cup. R. In the centre a rugby ball and goal posts surrounded by a stylised stadium with the denomination 'TWO POUNDS' and the date '1999'. Edge: 'RUGBY WORLD CUP 1999'. (Reverse design: Ron Dutton)
1999 ....£5
— Specimen in presentation folder £8
— Proof *FDC* (in 1999 set, see PS63)* £10
— Proof in silver *FDC* (Issued: 9,665) £40
— Proof in gold *FDC* (Issued: 311) £550

4571A　　　　　　　　4572

4571A— Proof piedfort in silver with coloured hologram on reverse *FDC* (Issued: 10,000) ..£150

4572 Two pounds. Marconi commemorative. R. Decorative radio waves emanating from a spark of electricity linking the zeros of the date to represent the generation of the signal that crossed the Atlantic with the date '2001' and the denomination 'TWO POUNDS'. Edge: 'WIRELESS BRIDGES THE ATLANTIC MARCONI 1901'. (Reverse design: Robert Evans)
2001 ....£5
— Specimen in presentation folder £7
— Proof *FDC* (in 2001 set, see PS68)* £10
— Proof in silver *FDC* (Issued: 11,488) £35
— Proof piedfort in silver *FDC* (Issued: 6,759) £60
— Proof in gold *FDC* (Issued: 1,658) £525

4572A— Proof in silver *FDC*, with reverse frosting. (Issued: 4,803 in a 2-coin set with a Canadian $5 Marconi silver proof) £60

* Coins marked thus were originally issued in Royal Mint sets.

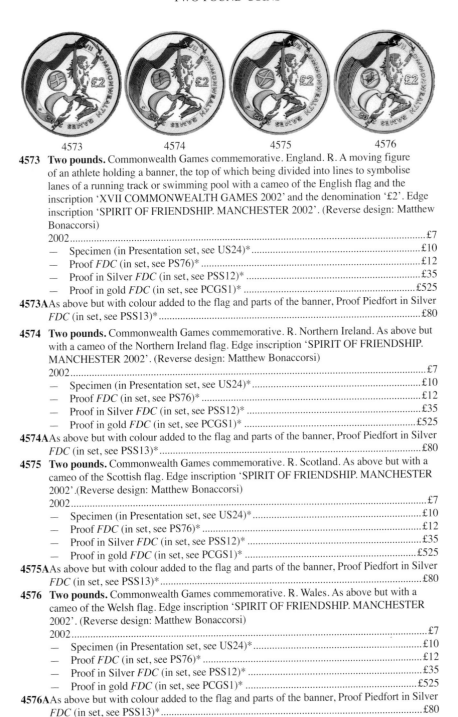

| 4573 | 4574 | 4575 | 4576 |

4573 **Two pounds.** Commonwealth Games commemorative. England. R. A moving figure of an athlete holding a banner, the top of which being divided into lines to symbolise lanes of a running track or swimming pool with a cameo of the English flag and the inscription 'XVII COMMONWEALTH GAMES 2002' and the denomination '£2'. Edge inscription 'SPIRIT OF FRIENDSHIP. MANCHESTER 2002'. (Reverse design: Matthew Bonaccorsi)

2002...£7
— Specimen (in Presentation set, see US24)*..£10
— Proof *FDC* (in set, see PS76)*...£12
— Proof in Silver *FDC* (in set, see PSS12)*..£35
— Proof in gold *FDC* (in set, see PCGS1)*..£525

4573A As above but with colour added to the flag and parts of the banner, Proof Piedfort in Silver *FDC* (in set, see PSS13)*..£80

4574 **Two pounds.** Commonwealth Games commemorative. R. Northern Ireland. As above but with a cameo of the Northern Ireland flag. Edge inscription 'SPIRIT OF FRIENDSHIP. MANCHESTER 2002'. (Reverse design: Matthew Bonaccorsi)

2002...£7
— Specimen (in Presentation set, see US24)*..£10
— Proof *FDC* (in set, see PS76)*...£12
— Proof in Silver *FDC* (in set, see PSS12)*..£35
— Proof in gold *FDC* (in set, see PCGS1)*..£525

4574A As above but with colour added to the flag and parts of the banner, Proof Piedfort in Silver *FDC* (in set, see PSS13)*..£80

4575 **Two pounds.** Commonwealth Games commemorative. R. Scotland. As above but with a cameo of the Scottish flag. Edge inscription 'SPIRIT OF FRIENDSHIP. MANCHESTER 2002'.(Reverse design: Matthew Bonaccorsi)

2002...£7
— Specimen (in Presentation set, see US24)*..£10
— Proof *FDC* (in set, see PS76)*...£12
— Proof in Silver *FDC* (in set, see PSS12)*..£35
— Proof in gold *FDC* (in set, see PCGS1)*..£525

4575A As above but with colour added to the flag and parts of the banner, Proof Piedfort in Silver *FDC* (in set, see PSS13)*..£80

4576 **Two pounds.** Commonwealth Games commemorative. R. Wales. As above but with a cameo of the Welsh flag. Edge inscription 'SPIRIT OF FRIENDSHIP. MANCHESTER 2002'. (Reverse design: Matthew Bonaccorsi)

2002...£7
— Specimen (in Presentation set, see US24)*..£10
— Proof *FDC* (in set, see PS76)*...£12
— Proof in Silver *FDC* (in set, see PSS12)*..£35
— Proof in gold *FDC* (in set, see PCGS1)*..£525

4576A As above but with colour added to the flag and parts of the banner, Proof Piedfort in Silver *FDC* (in set, see PSS13)*..£80

* Coins marked thus were originally issued in Royal Mint sets.

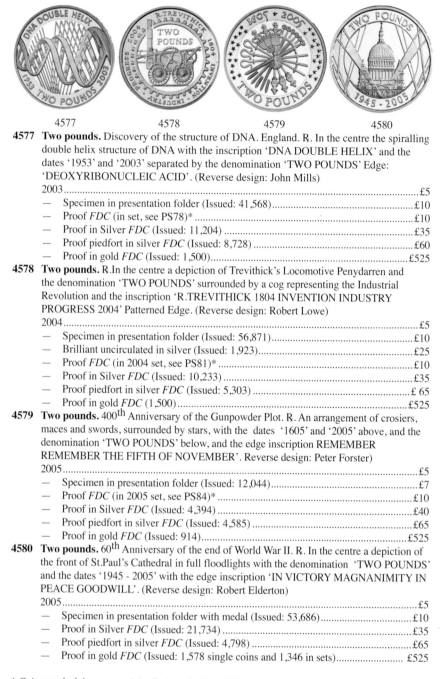

| 4577 | 4578 | 4579 | 4580 |

4577 Two pounds. Discovery of the structure of DNA. England. ℞. In the centre the spiralling double helix structure of DNA with the inscription 'DNA DOUBLE HELIX' and the dates '1953' and '2003' separated by the denomination 'TWO POUNDS' Edge: 'DEOXYRIBONUCLEIC ACID'. (Reverse design: John Mills)
2003 ....£5
— Specimen in presentation folder (Issued: 41,568) £10
— Proof *FDC* (in set, see PS78)* £10
— Proof in Silver *FDC* (Issued: 11,204) £35
— Proof piedfort in silver *FDC* (Issued: 8,728) £60
— Proof in gold *FDC* (Issued: 1,500) £525

4578 Two pounds. ℞.In the centre a depiction of Trevithick's Locomotive Penydarren and the denomination 'TWO POUNDS' surrounded by a cog representing the Industrial Revolution and the inscription 'R.TREVITHICK 1804 INVENTION INDUSTRY PROGRESS 2004' Patterned Edge. (Reverse design: Robert Lowe)
2004 ....£5
— Specimen in presentation folder (Issued: 56,871) £10
— Brilliant uncirculated in silver (Issued: 1,923) £25
— Proof *FDC* (in 2004 set, see PS81)* £10
— Proof in Silver *FDC* (Issued: 10,233) £35
— Proof piedfort in silver *FDC* (Issued: 5,303) ....£ 65
— Proof in gold *FDC* (1,500) £525

4579 Two pounds. 400th Anniversary of the Gunpowder Plot. ℞. An arrangement of crosiers, maces and swords, surrounded by stars, with the dates '1605' and '2005' above, and the denomination 'TWO POUNDS' below, and the edge inscription REMEMBER REMEMBER THE FIFTH OF NOVEMBER'. Reverse design: Peter Forster)
2005 ....£5
— Specimen in presentation folder (Issued: 12,044) £7
— Proof *FDC* (in 2005 set, see PS84)* £10
— Proof in Silver *FDC* (Issued: 4,394) £40
— Proof piedfort in silver *FDC* (Issued: 4,585) £65
— Proof in gold *FDC* (Issued: 914) £525

4580 Two pounds. 60th Anniversary of the end of World War II. ℞. In the centre a depiction of the front of St.Paul's Cathedral in full floodlights with the denomination 'TWO POUNDS' and the dates '1945 - 2005' with the edge inscription 'IN VICTORY MAGNANIMITY IN PEACE GOODWILL'. (Reverse design: Robert Elderton)
2005 ....£5
— Specimen in presentation folder with medal (Issued: 53,686) £10
— Proof in Silver *FDC* (Issued: 21,734) £35
— Proof piedfort in silver *FDC* (Issued: 4,798) £65
— Proof in gold *FDC* (Issued: 1,578 single coins and 1,346 in sets) £525

* Coins marked thus were originally issued in Royal Mint sets.

4581 4582 4583

4581 Two pounds. 200th Anniversary of the birth of Isambard Brunel. ℞. In the centre a portrait of the engineer with segments of a wheel and bridge in the background surrounded by links of a heavy chain and the date '2006' and the denomination 'TWO POUNDS', with the edge inscription '1806 - 1859 ISAMBARD KINGDOM BRUNEL ENGINEER'. (Reverse design: Rod Kelly)

2006..£5
— Specimen in presentation folder (with **4582**)..£10
— Proof *FDC* (in 2006 set, see PS87)*..£10
— Proof in silver *FDC* (Issued: 7,251)..£35
— Proof piedfort in silver *FDC* (Issued: 3,199) (see PSS25)* £65
— Proof in gold *FDC* (Issued: 1,071)..£525

4582 Two pounds. 200th Anniversary of the birth of Isambard Brunel. ℞. In the centre a section of the roof of Paddington Station with 'BRUNEL' below and the date '2006' and the denomination 'TWO POUNDS', with the edge inscription 'SO MANY IRONS IN THE FIRE'. (Reverse design: Robert Evans)

2006..£4
— Specimen in presentation folder (with **4581**)..£10
— Proof *FDC* (in 2006 set, see PS87)*..£10
— Proof in silver *FDC* (Issued: 5,375)..£35
— Proof piedfort in silver *FDC* (Issued: 3,018) (see PSS25)*................................£65
— Proof in gold *FDC* (Issued: 746)..£525

4583 Two pounds. Tercentenary of the Act of Union between England and Scotland. ℞. A design dividing the coin into four quarters, with a rose and a thistle occupying two of the quarters, and a portcullis in each of the other two quarters. The whole is overlaid with a linking jigsaw motif and surrounded by the dates '1707' and '2007' and the denomination 'TWO POUNDS', with an edge inscription 'UNITED INTO ONE KINGDOM' (Reverse design : Yvonne Holton)

2007..£5
— Specimen in presentation folder..£8
— Proof *FDC* (in 2007 set, see PS90)*..£10
— Proof in Silver *FDC* (Issued: 8,310) £35
— Proof piedfort in silver *FDC* (Issued: 4,000) £60
— Proof in gold *FDC* (Issued: 750)..£700

4583A — Error edge. The obverse and reverse designs of the Act of Union silver proof combined with the edge inscription of the Abolition of Slave Trade issue (4584 below). The edge inscription is impressed on the blanks prior to the striking of the obverse and reverse designs and whilst one example has been reported, and confirmed as genuine by the Royal Mint, it seems possible that a small batch may have been produced and other pieces have yet to be detected. £1000

* *Coins marked thus were originally issued in Royal Mint sets.*

| 4584 | 4585 | 4586 |

4584 **Two pounds.** Bicentenary of the Abolition of the Slave Trade in the British Empire. R. The date '1807' with the '0' depicted as a broken chain link , surrounded by the inscription 'AN ACT FOR THE ABOLITION OF THE SLAVE TRADE', and the date '2007', with an edge inscription 'AM I NOT A MAN, AND A BROTHER' (Reverse design : David Gentleman)

2007...£5
—   Specimen in presentation folder with..£8
—   Proof *FDC* (in 2007 set, see PS90)* £10
—   Proof in Silver *FDC* (Issued: 7,095) £35
—   Proof piedfort in silver *FDC* (Issued: 3,990)* £60
—   Proof in gold *FDC* (Issued: 1,000)..£550

4585 **Two pounds.** 250th Anniversary of the birth of Robert Burns. R. A design featuring a quote from the song *Auld Lang Syne* 'WE'LL TAK A CUP A' KINDNESS YET, FOR AULD LANG SYNE ', the calligraphy of which is based on the handwriting of Robert Burns with the inscription '1759 ROBERT BURNS 1796' and the denomination 'TWO POUNDS' with the edge inscription 'SHOULD AULD ACQUAINTANCE BE FORGOT' (Reverse design: Royal Mint Engraving Team)

2009 ....£5
—   Specimen in celebration card (Issued: 120,223) £6
—   Specimen in presentation folder (Edition: 50,000) £8
—   Proof *FDC* (in 2009 set, see PS97)* £10
—   Proof in Silver *FDC* (Issued: 9,188)) £35
—   Proof piedfort in silver *FDC* (Issued: 3,500) £60
—   Proof in gold *FDC* (Issued: 1,000)..£550

4586 **Two pounds.** 200th Anniversary of the birth of Charles Darwin. R A design showing a portrait of Charles Darwin facing an ape surrounded by the inscription '1809 DARWIN 2009' and the denomination 'TWO POUNDS' and the edge inscription 'ON THE ORIGIN OF SPECIES 1859' (Reverse design: Suzie Zamit)

2009 ....£5
—   Specimen in presentation folder (Edition: 25,000) £8
—   Proof *FDC* (in 2009 set, see PS97)* £10
—   Proof in Silver *FDC* (Issued: 9,357)) £35
—   Proof piedfort in silver *FDC* (Issued: 3,282) £60
—   Proof in gold *FDC* (Issued: 1,000)..£550

* *Coins marked thus were originally issued in Royal Mint sets.*

4587

4587 Two pounds. The Centenary of the death of Florence Nightingale and the One
hundred and fiftieth Anniversary of the publication of *NOTES ON NURSING*. R.
A design depicting the pulse of a patient being taken, surrounded by the inscription
'FLORENCE NIGHTINGALE – 1910' and the denomination 'TWO POUNDS'.
The design being set against a background texture of lines symbolising rays of light
from a lamp with the edge inscription '150 YEARS OF NURSING' on the precious
metal versions. (Reverse design: Gordon Summers)
2010..£3
— Specimen on presentation card £5
— Specimen in presentation folder (Edition: 25,000) £8
— Proof *FDC* (in 2010 set, see PS101)*..£10
— Proof in silver *FDC* (Issued: 5,117)..£35
— Proof piedfort in silver *FDC* (Issued: 2770) £60
— Proof in gold *FDC* (Issued: 472)..£550

4588

4588 Two pounds. 500th Anniversary of the launch of the Mary Rose. R. A depiction
of the ship based on a contemporary painting, surrounded by a cartouche bearing
the inscription 'THE MARY ROSE' above, the denomination 'TWO POUNDS'
below, and a rose to the left and right. The lettering on the reverse is rendered in the
Lombardic style employed on the coins of Henry VII, and with the edge inscription
'YOUR NOBLEST SHIPPE 1511' (Reverse design: John Bergdahl)
2011..£3
— Specimen in presentation folder (Edition: 20,000)...£8
— Proof *FDC* (in 2011 set, see PS104)*..£10
— Proof in silver *FDC* (Issued: 6,618)..£50
— Proof piedfort in silver *FDC* (Issued: 2,394)...£88
— Proof in gold *FDC* (Issued: 692) £800

* Coins marked thus were originally issued in Royal Mint sets.

4589 4730 4731

4589 **Two pounds.** The 400th Anniversary of the King James Bible. R. A design focusing on the opening verse of St John's Gospel, 'IN THE BEGINNING WAS THE WORD', showing the verse as printing blocks on the left and the printed page on the right, with the inscription 'KING JAMES BIBLE' above and the dates '1611-2011'below with the edge inscription 'THE AUTHORISED VERSION'. (Reverse design: Paul Stafford and Benjamin Wright)

2011 ....£3
— Specimen in presentation folder (Edition: 20,000) £8
— Proof *FDC* (in 2011 set, see PS104)* £10
— Proof in silver *FDC* (Issued: 4,494)..£50
— Proof piedfort in silver *FDC* (Issued: 2,394)...£88
— Proof in gold *FDC* (Issued: 355) £800

4730 **Two pounds.** The 200th Anniversary of the birth of Charles Dickens. R. A silhouette profile of the writer through the titles of his works, greater prominence being given to those that are more well known, with the inscription 'CHARLES DICKENS 1870' to the left with the edge inscription 'SOMETHING WILL TURN UP' (Reverse design:)

2012 ....£3
— Specimen in presentation folder (Issued: 15,035) £8
— Proof *FDC* (in 2012 set, see PS107)* £10
— Proof in silver *FDC* (Issued: 2,631) £50
— Proof piedfort in silver *FDC* (Issued: 1,279) £88
— Proof in gold *FDC* (Issued: 202)...£800

4731 **Two pounds.** 350th Anniversary of the Guinea, R. A depiction of the Royal Arms based on that on the reverse of the 'SPADE GUINEA' of George III with and surrounded by the inscription 'ANNIVERSARY OF THE GOLDEN GUINEA' and the date '2013' below with the edge inscription 'WHAT IS A GUINEA ? 'TIS A SPENDID THING'. (Reverse design: Anthony Smith).

2013 ....£4
— Specimen in presentation folder £10
— Proof *FDC* (in 2013 set, see PS109)* £10
— Proof in silver *FDC* (Issued: 1,640) £50
— Proof piedfort in silver *FDC* (Issued: 969) £100
— Proof in gold FDC (Issued: 284) £900

* *Coins marked thus were originally issued in Royal Mint sets.*

4732   4733

4732 Two pounds. 150th Anniversary of the London Underground. R.The Roundel logo of
the London underground system with the dates '1863' above and '2013' below and the
edge inscription 'MIND THE GAP'. (Reverse design: Edwina Ellis).
2013 ....£4
— Specimen in presentation folder with 4733 ....£20
— Proof *FDC* (in 2013 set, see PS109)* £10
— Proof in silver *FDC* (Issued: 1,185) £50
— Proof piedfort in silver *FDC* (Issued: 162) £100
— Proof in gold *FDC* (Issued: 132)..£900

4733 Two pounds. 150th Anniversary of the London Underground. R. Depicts a train
emerging from a tunnel with the date '1863' to the left and the inscription 'LONDON
UNDERGROUND' and the date '2013' to the right with a patterned edge inspired by the
map of the underground network. (Reverse design: Edward Barber and Jay Osgerby).
2013 ....£4
— Specimen in presentation folder with 4732 ....£20
— Proof *FDC* (in 2013 set, see PS109)* £10
— Proof in silver *FDC* (Edition: Issued: 2,042) £50
— Proof piedfort in silver *FDC* (Issued: 186) £100
— Proof in gold *FDC* (Issued: 140)..£900

4734

4734 Two pounds. Trinity House R. A depiction of a lighthouse lens, surrounded by the
inscription 'TRINITY HOUSE' and the dates '1514' and '2014' with the denomination
'TWO POUNDS' with the edge inscription 'SERVING THE MARINER' (Reverse
design: Joe Whitlock Blundell with David Eccles).
2014 ....£4
— Specimen in presentation folder £10
— Proof *FDC* (in 2014 set, see PS112)* £10
— Proof in silver *FDC* (Edition: 3,714 including coins in sets)..............................£50
— Proof piedfort in silver *FDC* (Edition: 3,514 including coins in sets) £100
— Proof in gold *FDC* (Edition: including coins in sets)...£900

* Coins marked thus were originally issued in Royal Mint sets.

4735

4735 Two pounds. World War I R. A depiction pf Lord Kitchener pointing, with the
inscription 'YOUR COUNTRY NEEDS YOU' below the effigy of Lord Kitchener,
and the inscription 'THE FIRST WORLD WAR 1914-1918' and the date '2014'
with the edge inscription 'THE LAMPS ARE GOING OUT ALL OVER EUROPE'
(Reverse design: John Bergdahl).

2014...£4
— Specimen in presentation folder...£10
— Proof *FDC* (in 2014 set, see PS112)*...£10
— Proof in silver *FDC* (Edition: 8,014 including coins in sets) £50
— Proof piedfort in silver *FDC* (Edition: 4,514 including coins in sets).................£100
— Proof in gold *FDC* (Edition: 825 including coins in sets) £750

4736

4736 Two pounds. World War 1 – The Royal Navy R. The designs shows a dreadnought
at sea with the inscription 'THE FIRST WORLD WAR 1914 – 1918' and the date
of the year below with the edged inscription 'THE SURE SHIELD OF BRITAIN'
(Reverse design : David Rowlands).

2015
— BU in presentation pack £10
— Proof *FDC* (in 2015 set, see PS117) * £5
— Proof in silver *FDC* (Edition: 8,500 including coins in sets)....................£50
— Proof piedfort in silver *FDC* (Edition: 4,000 including coins in sets).................£100
— Proof in gold *FDC* (Edition: 900) £750

* Coins marked thus were originally issued in Royal Mint sets.

4737

4737 Two pounds. 800th Anniversary of the signing of Magna Carta R. The design shows King John flanked by figures representing the clergy on one side and the barons on the other with the inscription 'MAGNA CARTA' and '1215 – 2015' and the edge inscription ' FOUNDATION OF LIBERTY'. (Reverse design: John Bergdahl).
2015
— BU in presentation pack £10
— Proof *FDC* (in 2015 set, see PS117) * £5
— Proof in silver *FDC* (Edition: 3,000 see PSS63 and PSS64)*
— Proof piedfort in silver *FDC* (Edition: 1,500)...£
— Proof in gold *FDC* (Edition: 100) ....£

Obverse portrait by Jody Clark

4737A

4737A Two pounds. 800th Anniversary of the signing of Magna Carta. R. As above.
2015
— Proof in silver *FDC* (Edition: 7,500)
— Proof piedfort in silver *FDC* (Edition: 2,000)...£100
— Proof in gold *FDC* (Edition: 500)

4738

4738 Two pounds. R. A depiction of Britannia holding a shield and trident with the inscription 'TWO POUNDS' and the edge inscription 'QUATUOR MARIA VINDICO' (Reverse design: Antony Dufort).
2015
— Proof *FDC* (in 2015 set, see PS116)*..£5
— Proof in silver *FDC* (Edition: 7,500 see PSS61)*
— Proof in gold *FDC* (Edition: 500 see PGC4P) *
— Proof piedfort in platinum *FDC* (Edition:)

For further £2 commemorative issues, see Olympic and Paralympic coins on page 143.
* Coins marked thus were originally issued in Royal Mint sets.

CUPRO-NICKEL

Note for Collectors

The collecting of crown size coins is one of the most popular pursuits among new and established coin collectors. Before decimalisation in 1971, crowns had a nominal denomination of five shillings and this was then changed to twenty five pence in 1972 when the Silver Wedding commemorative was issued. Over time with increasing metal, manufacturing and distribution costs, the production of coins with such a low face value was not economic and the decision was taken to change to a higher value that would last for many years. The first of the five pound crowns was issued in 1990 to mark the ninetieth birthday of The Queen Mother. It seems sensible to group all of the crown size coins together and therefore the earlier twenty five pence issues are not listed between the twenty pence and fifty pence denominations but appear below.

Obverse portrait by Arnold Machin

4226

4226 Twenty-five pence (crown). Silver Wedding Commemorative R. The initials E P on a background of foliage, figure of Eros above the Royal Crown with the inscription 'ELIZABETH AND PHILIP'above and the dates '20 NOVEMBER 1947 – 1972' below.(Reverse design: Arnold Machin)

1972...£2
— Proof *FDC* (in 1972 Set, See PS22)*...£6
— Silver proof *FDC* (Issued: 100,000) £45

4227

4227 Twenty-five pence (crown). Silver Jubilee Commemorative R. The Ampulla and Anointing Spoon encircled by a floral border and above a Royal Crown. (Obverse and reverse design: Arnold Machin)

1977...£2
— Specimen in presentation folder..£2
— Proof *FDC* (in 1977 Set, See PS27)*...£5
— Silver proof *FDC* (Issued: 377,000) £40

* Coins marked thus were originally issued in Royal Mint sets.

4228

4228 **Twenty-Five pence** (crown). Queen Mother 80th Birthday Commemorative Ꝛ. In the centre a portrait of The Queen Mother surrounded by bows and lions with the inscription 'QUEEN ELIZABETH THE QUEEN MOTHER 4 AUGUST 1980' (Reverse design: Richard Guyatt)

1980..£3
— Specimen in presentation folder..£5
— Silver proof *FDC* (Issued: 83,672) £45

* Coins marked thus were originally issued in Royal Mint sets.

4229

4229 **Twenty-five pence.**(crown). Royal Wedding Commemorative R.Portrait of the Prince of Wales and Lady Diana Spencer with the inscription 'HRH THE PRINCE OF WALES AND LADY DIANA SPENCER 1981' (Reverse design: Philip Nathan)

1981..£3
— Specimen in presentation folder...£5
— Silver proof *FDC* (Issued: 218,142) £45

Obverse portrait by Raphael Maklouf

4301

4301 **Five pounds** (crown). Queen Mother's 90th birthday commemorative. R. A Cypher in the letter E in duplicate above a Royal Crown flanked by a rose and a thistle all within the inscription 'QUEEN ELIZABETH THE QUEEN MOTHER' and the dates '1900 – 1990' (Reverse design: Leslie Durbin)

1990..£10
— Specimen in presentation folder (Issued: 45,250)......................................£12
— Proof in silver *FDC* (Issued: 56,102)...£45
— Proof in gold *FDC* (Issued: 2,500)...£1250

* Coins marked thus were originally issued in Royal Mint sets.

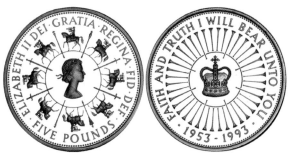

4302

4302 Five pounds (crown). 40th Anniversary of the Coronation. R. St Edward's Crown encircled by forty trumpets all within the inscription 'FAITH AND TRUTH I WILL BEAR UNTO YOU' and the dates '1953 – 1993'(Reverse design: Robert Elderton) 1993...£7

— Specimen in presentation folder...£9

— Proof *FDC* (in 1993 set, see PS51)* £12

— Proof in silver *FDC* (Issued: 58,877)...£45

— Proof in gold *FDC* (Issued: 2,500)..£1250

4303

4303 Five pounds (crown). 70th Birthday of Queen Elizabeth II. R. A representation of Windsor Castle with five flag poles, two holding forked pennants with anniversary dates '1926' and '1996', the other flags are Royal Arms, the Union flag and Our Personal flag. Edge inscription: 'VIVAT REGINA ELIZABETHA'. (Reverse design: Avril Vaughan) 1996..£10

— Specimen in presentation folder (issued: 73,311) £12

— Proof *FDC* (in 1996 set, See PS57)* £12

— Proof in silver *FDC* (Issued: 39,336)...£50

— Proof in gold *FDC* (Issued: 2,127)..£1250

* Coins marked thus were originally issued in Royal Mint sets.

4304

4304   **Five pounds** (crown). Golden Wedding of Queen Elizabeth II and Prince Philip.
Conjoint portraits of The Queen and Prince Philip. R. A pair of shields, chevronwise, on
the left, OurRoyal Arms, on the right, the shield of Prince Philip, above a Royal Crown
separating the dates '1947' and '1997' with the date '20 NOVEMBER', below an
anchor cabled with the denomination 'FIVE POUNDS'.
(Obverse design: Philip Nathan, reverse design: Leslie Durbin)
1997...£7
—   Specimen in presentation folder...£10
—   Proof *FDC* (in 1997 set, See PS59)*..£15
—   Proof in silver *FDC* (Issued: 33,689)...£50
—   Proof in gold *FDC* (Issued: 2,574)..£1250

Obverse portrait by Ian Rank-Broadley

4550

4550   **Five pounds** (crown). Prince Charles' 50th Birthday. R. A portrait of Prince
Charles and in the background words relating to the work of The Prince's Trust.
A circumscription of 'FIFIETH BIRTHDAY OF HRH PRINCE OF WALES' and
below 'FIVE POUNDS' flanked by the anniversary dates '1948' and '1998'.
(Reverse design: Michael Noakes / Robert Elderton)
1998...£7
—   Specimen in presentation folder...£10
—   Proof *FDC* (in 1998 set, see PS 61)*...£15
—   Proof in silver *FDC* (Issued: 13,379)...£60
—   Proof in gold *FDC* (Issued: 773)..£1250

* Coins marked thus were originally issued in Royal Mint sets.

4551

4551 Five pounds (crown). Diana, Princess of Wales Memorial. ℞. A portrait of Diana, Princess of Wales with the dates '1961' and '1997', and the circumscription 'IN MEMORY OF DIANA, PRINCESS OF WALES' with the value 'FIVE POUNDS' (Reverse design: David Cornell)

1999..£7
— Specimen in presentation folder..£12
— Proof *FDC* (in 1999 set, see PS63)*...£15
— Proof in silver *FDC* (Issued: 49,545)..£50
— Proof in gold *FDC* (Issued: 7,500)..£1250

4552   4552A

4552 Five pounds (crown). Millennium commemorative. ℞. A representation of the dial of a clock with hands set at 12 o'clock with a map of the British Isles and the dates '1999' and '2000' and the words 'ANNO DOMINI' and the value 'FIVE POUNDS'. Edge: 'WHAT'S PAST IS PROLOGUE' in serif or sans serif font. (Reverse design: Jeffrey Matthews)

1999..£7
— Specimen in presentation folder..£10
— Proof in silver *FDC* (Issued: 49,057)..£50
— Proof in gold *FDC* (Issued: 2,500)..£1250
2000
— Specimen in presentation folder..£20
— Proof *FDC* (in 2000 set, see PS65)*...£15
— Proof in gold *FDC* (Issued: 1,487)..£1250

4552A2000
— Specimen in presentation folder with Dome mint mark £20
(See illustration above - the mintmark is located within the shaded area at 3 o'clock).

4552B 2000
— Proof in silver *FDC* (Issued: 14,255)..£60

(The reverse design is the same as the 1999 issue but with the British Isles highlighted with 22 ct. gold)

* Coins marked thus were originally issued in Royal Mint sets.

4553   4554

4553 **Five pounds** (crown). Queen Mother commemorative. R. A portrait of the Queen
Mother flanked by groups of people with the circumscription 'QUEEN ELIZABETH
THE QUEEN MOTHER' the anniversary dates '1900' and '2000' below, and the
denomination 'FIVE POUNDS'. Below the portrait a representation of her signature.
(Reverse design: Ian Rank-Broadley)

2000 ....£7
   —   Specimen in presentation folder £10
   —   Proof in silver *FDC* (Issued: 31,316) £50
   —   Proof piedfort in silver *FDC* (Issued: 14,850) £80
   —   Proof in gold *FDC* (Issued: 3,000) £1250

4554 **Five pounds** (crown). Victorian anniversary. R. A classic portrait of the young Queen
Victoria based on the Penny Black postage stamp with a V representing Victoria, and
taking the form of railway lines and in the background the iron framework of the Crystal
Palace, and the denomination '5 POUNDS' and the dates '1901' and '2001'.
(Reverse design: Mary Milner-Dickens)

2001 ....£7
   —   Specimen in presentation folder £10
   —   Proof *FDC* (in 2001 set, see PS68)* £15
   —   Proof in silver *FDC* (Issued: 19,216) £55
   —   Proof in gold *FDC* (Issued: 2,098) £1250

4554A —   Proof in silver *FDC* with 'reverse frosting' giving matt appearance (Issued:596)
(Crown issued with sovereigns of 1901 and 2001)* £200

4554B —   Proof in gold *FDC* with 'reverse frosting' giving matt appearance.(Issued:733)
(Crown issued with four different type sovereigns of Queen Victoria, - Young
Head with shield, and Young Head with St.George reverse, Jubilee Head and
Old Head.)* £1350

* Coins marked thus were originally issued in Royal Mint sets.

4555

4555 Five pounds (crown). Golden Jubilee commemorative 2002. O. New portrait of The Queen with the denomination 'FIVE POUNDS'. R. Equestrian portrait of The Queen with the inscription 'ELIZABETH II DEI GRA REGINA FID DEF' around the circumference and 'AMOR POPULI PRAESIDIUM REG' within, and the date '2002' below separated by the central element of the Royal Arms.
(Obverse and reverse designs: Ian Rank-Broadley)

2002...£7
— Specimen in presentation folder...£10
— Proof *FDC* (in 2002 set, see PS 72)* £15
— Proof in silver *FDC* (Issued: 54,012)...£55
— Proof in gold *FDC* (Issued: 3,500)..£1250

4556

4556 Five pounds (crown). Queen Mother Memorial 2002. R. Three quarter portrait of the Queen Mother within a wreath with the inscription 'QUEEN ELIZABETH THE QUEEN MOTHER' and the dates '1900' and '2002', with an edge inscription 'STRENGTH, DIGNITY AND LAUGHTER'. (Reverse design: Avril Vaughan)

2002...£8
— Specimen in presentation folder...£15
— Proof in silver *FDC* (Issued: 16,117) £55
— Proof in gold *FDC* (Issued: 2,086)..£1250

* Coins marked thus were originally issued in Royal Mint sets.

4557

4557 Five pounds (crown). Coronation commemorative 2003. O. Profile portrait of
The Queen in linear form facing right with the inscription 'ELIZABETH II DEI
GRATIA REGINA F D'. R. In the centre the inscription 'GOD SAVE THE QUEEN'
surrounded by the inscription 'CORONATION JUBILEE' the denomination 'FIVE
POUNDS' and the date '2003'. (Obverse and reverse designs: Tom Phillips)

2003...£8
— Specimen in presentation folder (Issued: 100,481)..£10
— Proof *FDC* (in 2003 set, see PS 78)*..£15
— Proof in silver *FDC* (Issued: 28,758)...£55
— Proof in gold *FDC* (Issued: 1,896)...£1250

4558

4558 Five pounds (crown). Centenary of Entente Cordiale 2004. R. In the centre the head
and shoulders of Britannia and her French counterpart Marianne with the inscription
'ENTENTE CORDIALE' separated by the dates '1904' and '2004'. Obv. as 4556.
(Reverse design: David Gentleman)

2004...£8
— Specimen in presentation folder (Issued: 16,507)..£20
— Proof *FDC* with reverse frosting (Issued: 6,065)..£20
— Proof in silver *FDC* (Issued: 11,295)...£60
— Proof Piedfort in silver *FDC* (Issued: 2,500)...£150
— Proof in gold *FDC* (Issued: 926)..£1250
— Proof Piedfort in platinum *FDC* (Issued: 501)..£3600

* *Coins marked thus were originally issued in Royal Mint sets.*

4559   4560

4559 Five pounds (crown). Two hundredth anniversary of the Battle of Trafalgar 2005. R.
A depiction of the two British ships, HMS Victory and Temeraine, in the midst of the
battle, the central design surrounded by the inscription 'TRAFALGAR' and the dates
'1805' and '2005' with the edge inscription 'ENGLAND EXPECTS THAT EVERY
MAN WILL DO HIS DUTY'. Obv. as 4556. (Reverse design: Clive Duncan)
*Note: Only the precious metal versions have edge inscriptions, the CuNi coins have a
milled edge.*
2005...£9
— Specimen in presentation folder (Issued: 79,868)...£12
— Proof *FDC* (in 2005 set, see PS84)*...£12
— Proof in silver *FDC* (Issued: 21,448)...£55
— Proof piedfort in silver *FDC* (see PSS21)*..£90
— Proof in gold *FDC* (Issued: 1,805)...£1250

4560 Five pounds (crown). Two hundredth anniversary of the death of Nelson 2005. R. A
portrait of Lord Nelson in the uniform of a Vice Admiral accompanied by the inscription
'HORATIO NELSON' and the dates '1805' and '2005' with the edge inscription
'ENGLAND EXPECTS THAT EVERY MAN WILL DO HIS DUTY'. Obv. as 4556.
(Reverse design: James Butler)
*Note: Only the precious metal versions have edge inscriptions, the CuNi coins have a
milled edge.*
2005...£10
— Specimen in presentation folder (Issued: 72,498)...£12
— Proof *FDC* (in 2005 set, see PS84)*...£12
— Proof in silver *FDC* (Issued: 12,852)...£60
— Proof piedfort in silver *FDC* (see PSS21)*..£90
— Proof in gold *FDC* (Issued: 1,760) £1250
— Proof piedfort in platinum *FDC* (Edition: 200) £3600

* Coins marked thus were originally issued in Royal Mint sets.

4561

4561 Five pounds (crown). 80th Birthday of Her Majesty Queen Elizabeth II. R. A fanfare of
regal trumpets with the inscription 'VIVAT REGINA' and the dates '1926' and '2006',
and the edge inscription 'DUTY SERVICE FAITH'. Obv. as 4556.
(Reverse design: Danuta Solowiej-Wedderburn)
2006..£7
— Specimen in presentation folder..£10
— Proof *FDC* (in 2006 set, see PS87)*..£15
— Proof in silver *FDC* (Issued: 20,790)..£55
— Proof in gold *FDC* (Issued: 2,750)...£1250
— Proof piedfort in platinum *FDC* (Issued: 250)...£3600

4561A— Proof piedfort in silver with selected gold plating *FDC* (Issued: 5,000)...................£80

4562

4562 Five pounds (crown). Diamond Wedding Anniversary of Her Majesty Queen
Elizabeth II and The Duke of Edinburgh. O. Conjoint portrait of The Queen and
Prince Philip. R. The Rose window of Westminster Abbey with the inscription
'TVEATVR VNITA DEVS', the dates '1947' and '2007', the denomination 'FIVE
POUNDS', and the edge inscription 'MY STRENGTH AND STAY'
(Obverse design: Ian Rank-Broadley, reverse design: Emma Noble)
2007..£7
— Specimen in presentation folder..£10
— Proof *FDC* (in 2007 set, see PS90)*..£15
— Proof in silver *FDC* (Issued: 15,186)..£55
— Proof piedfort in silver *FDC* (Issued: 2,000) £80
— Proof in gold *FDC* (Issued: 2,380)...£1250
— Proof piedfort in platinum *FDC* (Issued: 250)...£3600

* Coins marked thus were originally issued in Royal Mint sets.

4563   4564

4563 Five pounds (crown). 450th Anniversary of the Accession of Queen Elizabeth I.
R A portrait of Queen Elizabeth I surrounded by four Tudor roses placed at the
centre points of connecting arches, with two side panels containing details taken
from carvings made by Robert Dudley, Earl of Leicester, found at the Tower of
London, the design being encircled by the inscription 'ELIZABETH REGINA' with
the dates 'MDLVIII' and 'MMVIII' with the edge inscription 'I HAVE REIGNED
WITH YOUR LOVES' on the precious metal versions. Obv. as 4556.
(Reverse design: Rod Kelly).

2008..£7
— Specimen in presentation folder (Issued: 26,700)....................................£10
— Proof *FDC* (in 2008 set, see PS93)* £15
— Proof in silver *FDC* (Issued: 10,398)..£60
— Proof piedfort in silver *FDC* (Edition: 5,000)...£90
— Proof in gold *FDC* (Issued: 1,500)...£1250
— Proof piedfort in platinum *FDC* (Issued: 150)..£3600

4564 Five pounds (crown). Prince of Wales 60th Birthday. R. A profile portrait of
His Royal Highness The Prince of Wales with the inscription 'THE PRINCE
OF WALES' above and '1948 ICH DIEN 2008' below with the edge inscription
'SIXTIETH BIRTHDAY' on the precious metal versions. Obv. as 4556. (Reverse
design : Ian Rank-Broadley)

2008..£7
— Specimen in presentation folder (Issued: 54,746)....................................£10
— Proof *FDC* (in 2008 set, see PS93)* £15
— Proof in silver *FDC* (Issued: 7,446)...£60
— Proof piedfort in silver *FDC* (Edition: 5,000)...£90
— Proof in gold *FDC* (Issued: 867)...£1250
— Proof in platinum *FDC* (Issued: 54) £3600

* Coins marked thus were originally issued in Royal Mint sets.

4565 4566

4565 Five pounds (crown). 500th Anniversary of the accession of Henry VIII. R. A
design inspired By a Holbein painting of King Henry VIII, set within a tressure and
surrounded by the inscription 'THE ACCESSION OF HENRY VIII 1509' and the
denomination 'FIVE POUNDS', with the edge inscription 'ROSA SINE SPINA' on
the precious metal versions. Obv. as 4551. (Reverse design: John Bergdahl)

2009 ....£7
— Specimen in presentation folder (Edition: 100,000) £10
— Proof *FDC* (in 2009 set, see PS97)* £15
— Proof in silver *FDC* (Issued: 10,419)) £60
— Proof piedfort in silver *FDC* (Issued: 3,580) £90
— Proof in gold *FDC* (Issued: 1,130) £1250
— Proof piedfort in platinum *FDC* (Edition: 100) £3600

4566 Five pounds (crown). Commemorating the three hundred-and fiftieth anniversary
of the restoration of the Monarchy. R. A design featuring a crown, a spray of oak
leaves, interlinked 'C's, the date '1660', the inscription 'RESTORATION OF THE
MONARCHY' and the denomination 'FIVE POUNDS' with the edge inscription 'A
QUIET AND PEACEFUL POSSESSION' on the precious metal versions. Obv. as
4551. (Reverse design: David Cornell)

2010 ....£7
— Specimen on presentation card (Edition: 150,000) £8
— Specimen in presentation folder (Edition: 50,000) £10
— Proof *FDC* (in 2010 set, see PS101)* £15
— Proof in silver *FDC* (Issued: 6,518) £50
— Proof piedfort in silver *FDC* (Issued: 4,435) £90
— Proof in gold *FDC* (Issued: 1,182) £1250
— Proof piedfort in platinum *FDC* (Edition: 100) £3600

* Coins marked thus were originally issued in Royal Mint sets.

4567

4567 Five pounds (crown). Royal Wedding Commemorative. R.A design featuring facing portraits of His Royal Highness Prince William and Miss Catherine Middleton with the inscription 'WILLIAM AND CATHERINE' above and the date '29 APRIL 2011 below. (Reverse design: Mark Richards)

2011
- — Specimen in presentation folder (Issued: 250,000) £18
- — Proof in silver *FDC* (Issued: 26,069)..£75
- — Proof in silver with gold plating *FDC* (Issued: 7,451) £90
- — Proof piedfort in silver *FDC* (Issued: 2,991)...£120
- — Proof in gold *FDC* (Issued: 2,066) £1250
- — Proof piedfort in platinum *FDC* (Edition: 200)...£4500

4568

4568 Five pounds (crown). 90th Birthday of Prince Philip. R. A profile portrait of His Royal Highness The Duke of Edinburgh with the inscription 'PRINCE PHILIP 90TH BIRTHDAY ' and the denomination 'FIVE POUNDS' and the date '2011' (Reverse design: Mark Richards)

2011
- — Specimen in presentation folder (Edition: 50,000)...£10
- — Proof *FDC* (in 2011 set, see PS104)*..£15
- — Proof in silver *FDC* (Issued: 4,599) £83
- — Proof piedfort in silver *FDC* (Issued: 2,659)...£145
- — Proof in gold *FDC* (Issued: 636) £1250
- — Proof piedfort in platinum *FDC* (Edition: 90)...£4500

* Coins marked thus were originally issued in Royal Mint sets.

4569

4569 Five pounds (crown). Diamond Jubilee commemorative 2012. O. For the obverse impression, Our Effigy, inspired by the sculpture mounted in the entrance to the Supreme Court building on Parliament Square, with the inscription 'ELIZABETH. II. D. G. REG. F. D. FIVE POUNDS', and for the reverse an adaptation of Our Effigy first used on United Kingdom coins from 1953, with an olive branch and ribbon below, the date '2012' to the left and the inscription 'DIRIGE DEVS GRESSVS MEOS' to the right. With the edge inscription 'A VOW MADE GOOD' on the precious metal coins. (Obverse and reverse designs: Ian Rank-Broadley) 2012

  — Specimen in presentation folder (Issued: 484,775 .... £13
  — Proof *FDC* (in 2012 set, see PS107)* £10
  — Proof in silver *FDC* (Issued: 16,370 including coins in sets) £83
  — Proof in silver with gold plating *FDC* (Issued: 12,112) £100
  — Proof piedfort in silver *FDC* (Issued: 3,187) £145
  — Proof in gold *FDC* (Issued: 1,085) £1250
  — Proof piedfort in platinum *FDC* (Issued: 20) £4500

4751

4751 Five pounds (crown). Coronation Anniversary commemorative 2013. R. In the centre The Imperial State Crown with the inscription 'TO REIGN AND SERVE' and 'A VOW MADE GOOD' (Reverse design: Emma Noble). 2013

  — Specimen in presentation folder £13
  — Proof *FDC* (in 2013 set, see PS109)* £10
  — Proof in silver *FDC* (Issued: 4,050 including coins in sets) £80
  — Proof in silver with gold plating *FDC* (Issued: 2,547) £100
  — Proof piedfort in silver *FDC* (Issued: 2,686 including coins in sets) £160
  — Proof in gold *FDC* (Issued: 418 including coins in sets) £2400
  — Proof piedfort in platinum *FDC* (Issued: 106) £6400

* Coins marked thus were originally issued in Royal Mint sets.

4752

4752 Five pounds (crown). Commemorative coin to mark the birth of a son to the Duke and Duchess of Cambridge. R. A depiction of St. George armed, sitting on horseback, attacking the dragon with a sword, and a broken spear upon the ground, and the date of the year.(Reverse design: Benedetto Pistrucci). 2013

— Proof in silver *FDC* (Issued: 7,460) £80

4753

4753 Five pounds (crown) Commemorative coin to mark the christening of Prince George of Cambridge. R. A deconstructed silver lily font incorporating cherubs and roses, with a Baroque-style cartouche with the inscription 'DIEU ET MON DROIT' and ' TO CELEBRATE THE CHRISTENING OF PRINCE GEORGE OF CAMBRIDGE 2013' in the centre of the coin. (Reverse design: John Bergdahl). 2013

— Specimen in presentation folder.. £13
— Proof in silver *FDC* (Issued: 7,264)... £80
— Proof piedfort in silver *FDC* (Issued: 2,251) £160
— Proof in gold *FDC* (Issued: 486).. £2000
— Proof piedfort in platinum *FDC* (Issued: 38).. £6400

* Coins marked thus were originally issued in Royal Mint sets.

4754

4754 **Five pounds** (crown). Obverse design depicts the Royal Arms with the date
'2013' below. R. The portrait of The Queen by Mary Gillick with the inscription
'ELIZABETH II DEI GRATIA REGINA F.D.' and the denomination 'FIVE
POUNDS' below. (Obverse design: James Butler).
2013
—   Proof in silver *FDC* (Issued: 1,465 in sets, see PSS53)* £100
—   Proof piedfort in silver *FDC* (Issued: 697 in sets, see PSS54)* £200
—   Proof in gold *FDC* (Issued: 148 in sets, see PGQPS)* £2400

4755

4755 **Five pounds** (crown). Obverse design depicts the Royal Arms with the date 2013' below.
R. The portrait of The Queen by Arnold Machin with the inscription 'ELIZABETH II D:
G REG: F: D: FIVE POUNDS'. (Obverse design: James Butler).
2013
—   Proof in silver *FDC* (Issued: 1,465 in sets, see PSS53)* £100
—   Proof piedfort in silver *FDC* (Issued: 697 in sets, see PSS54)* £200
—   Proof in gold *FDC* (Issued: 148 in sets, see PGQPS)* £2400

* Coins marked thus were originally issued in Royal Mint sets.

4756   4757

4756 **Five pounds** (crown). Obverse design depicts the Royal Arms with the date '2013' below. R. The portrait of The Queen by Raphael Maklouf with the inscription 'ELIZABETH II DEI. GRATIA. REGINA. F. D.' and the denomination 'FIVE POUNDS' below. (Obverse design: James Butler).
2013
—   Proof in silver *FDC* (Issued: 1,465 in sets, see PSS53)* £100
—   Proof piedfort in silver *FDC* (Issued: 697 in sets, see PSS54)* £200
—   Proof in gold *FDC* (Issued: 148 in sets, see PGQPS)* £2400

4757 **Five pound**s (crown). Obverse design depicts the Royal Arms with the date '2013' below. R. The portrait of The Queen by Ian Rank-Broadley with the inscription 'ELIZABETH II D. G. REG. F.D and the denomination 'FIVE POUNDS' below. (Obverse design: James Butler).
2013
—   Proof in silver *FDC* (Issued: 1,465 in sets, see PSS53)* £100
—   Proof piedfort in silver *FDC* (Issued: 697 in sets, see PSS54)* £200
—   Proof in gold *FDC* (Issued: 148 in sets, see PGQPS)* £2400

4758

4758 **Five pounds** (crown). Queen Anne commemorative. R. The effigy pf Queen Anne enclosed by baroque decoration including the Royal Arms from the reign of Queen Anne and surrounded by the inscription 'QUEEN ANNE DEI GRATIA 1665-1714' (Reverse design: Mark Edwards).
2014
—   Specimen in presentation folder.. £13
—   Proof *FDC* (in 2014 set, see PS112)* £10
—   Proof in silver *FDC* (Edition: 60,000 including coins in sets)............................ £80
—   Proof in silver with gold plating *FDC* (Edition: 5,114) £100
—   Proof piedfort in silver *FDC* (Edition: 4,028 including coins in sets)................ £160
—   Proof in gold *FDC* (Edition: 2,060 including coins in sets) £2400
—   Proof piedfort in platinum *FDC* (Edition: 150) £6400

* *Coins marked thus were originally issued in Royal Mint sets.*

4759

4759 **Five pounds** (crown). Commemorative coin to mark the first birthday of Prince
      George of Cambridge. R. The four Quarterings of Our Royal Arms each contained in
      a shield and arranged in saltire with, in the intervening spaces, a Rose, a Thistle, both
      slipped and leaved, a sprig of shamrock and a Leek, in the centre the Crown and in the
      base the date of the year. (Reverse design: Edgar Fuller)
      2014
      —   Proof in silver *FDC* (Edition: 7,500) £80

4760   4761

4760 **Five pounds** (crown). Celebrating British Landmarks. R. A design depicting the
      head of one of the lions in Trafalgar Square with Nelson's Column in the background
      and the inscription 'FIVE POUNDS' (Reverse design: Glyn Davies and Laura Clancy)
      2014
      —   Proof in silver *FDC* with colour printing (Edition: 5,000 see PSS59)*
4761 **Five pounds** (crown). Celebrating British Landmarks. R. A design depicting a view
      of the Elizabeth Tower with the inscription 'FIVE POUNDS' (Reverse design:
      Glyn Davies and Laura Clancy)
      2014
      —   Proof in silver *FDC* with colour printing (Edition: 5,000 see PSS59)*

      * *Coins marked thus were originally issued in Royal Mint sets.*

4762   4763

4762 **Five pounds** (crown). Celebrating British Landmarks. R. A design depicting Tower Bridge with the inscription 'FIVE POUNDS' (Reverse design: Glyn Davies and Laura Clancy)
2014
—   Proof in silver *FDC* with colour printing (Edition: 5,000 see PSS59)*

4763 **Five pounds** (crown). Celebrating British Landmarks. R. A design depicting the Victoria Memorial with Buckingham Palace in the background and the inscription 'FIVE POUNDS' (Reverse design: Glyn Davies and Laura Clancy)
2014
—   Proof in silver FDC with colour printing (Edition: 5,000 see PSS59)*

4764

4764 **Five pounds.** (Crown) Fifth Anniversary of the death of Winston Churchill, R. A portrait of Winston Churchill with the inscription 'CHURCHILL' with the edge inscription on the precious metal versions 'NEVER FLINCH, NEVER WEARY, NEVER DESPAIR' (Reverse design: Mark Richards).
2015
—   BU in presentation pack £13
—   Proof *FDC* (in 2015 set, see PS115) * £5
—   Proof in silver *FDC* (Edition: 10,875 including coins in sets) £80
—   Proof piedfort in silver *FDC* (Edition: 4,150 including coins in sets)...................£160
—   Proof in gold *FDC* (Edition: 770)..£1800
—   Proof piedfort in platinum *FDC* (Edition: 90) ....£

4765

4765   Five pounds. (Crown) Bicentenary pf the Battle of Waterloo, R. A depiction of the
       Duke of Wellington greeting the Prussian General Gebhard Leberecht von Blucher
       after the Battle of Waterloo with the inscription 'THE BATTLE OF WATERLOO
       1815'with the edge inscription on the precious metal versions 'THE NEAREST RUN
       THING YOU EVER SAW' (Reverse design: David Lawrence).
       2015
       —   BU in presentation pack £13
       —   Proof FDC (in 2015 set, see PS117) * £5
       —   Proof in silver FDC (Edition: 3,000 see PSS63 and PSS64) ....£
       —   Proof piedfort in silver FDC (Edition: 1,500)..£

Obverse portrait by Jody Clark

4765A

4765A **Five pounds.** (Crown) Bicentenary pf the Battle of Waterloo, R. A depiction of the
       Duke of Wellington greeting the Prussian General Gebhard Leberecht von Blucher
       after the Battle of Waterloo with the inscription 'THE BATTLE OF WATERLOO
       1815'with the edge Inscription on the precious metal versions 'THE NEAREST RUN
       THING YOU EVER SAW' (Reverse design David Lawrence)
       2015
       —   Proof in silver *FDC* (Edition: 3,000) £80
       —   Proof piedfort in silver *FDC* (Edition: 1,500) £160
       —   Proof in gold *FDC* (Edition: 500)...£1650

* *Coins marked thus were originally issued in Royal Mint sets.*

4766

4766 **Five pounds.** (Crown) The second child of The Duke and Duchess of Cambridge.
R. An ornamental cartouche in the centre featuring the inscription 'THE DUKE
AND DUCHESS OF CAMBRIDGE 2015' surrounded by the inscription 'TO
CELEBRATE THE BIRTH OF THE SECOND CHILD' (Reverse design: John
Bergdahl)
2015
— BU in presentation pack...£13
— Proof in silver *FDC* (Edition: 9,500)..£80
— Proof in gold *FDC* (Edition: 350)...£1800

4767   4768

4767 **Five pounds.** (Crown) Commemorating the Christening of Princess Charlotte of
Cambridge R. A design depicting a deconstructed silver lily font incorporating
cherubs,with a Baroque - Style cartouche and 'DIEU ET – MON DROIT' below
and in the centre the inscription 'TO CELEBRATE THE CHRISTENING OF
PRINCESS CHARLOTTE ELIZABETH DIANA OF CAMBRIDGE 2015'
(Reverse design: John Bergdahl)
2015
— BU in presentation pack...£13
— Proof in silver *FDC* (Edition: 5,000)..£80
— Proof in gold *FDC* (Edition: 350)...£1800

4768 **Five pounds.** (Crown) Prince George's second birthday. R. A design depicting
St George slaying the dragon and the date '2015' (Reverse design: Christopher
Le Brun)
2015
— Proof in silver *FDC* (Edition: 7,500)...£80

Obverse portrait by James Butler

4769

4769 Five pounds. (Crown) The Longest serving monarch.. R. St Edwards crown in the
centre and the date '1952'and '2015' above and 'ONE CROWN' below with the
edge inscription on the precious metal versions 'LONG TO REIGN OVER US'
(Reverse design: James Butler)
2015
— BU in presentation pack £13
— Proof in silver *FDC* (Edition:15,000) £80
— Proof piedfort in silver *FDC* (Edition: 4,200) £160
— Proof in gold *FDC* (Edition: 350)..£1800

Obverse portrait by Ian Rank Broadley

4640

4640 Ten pounds (five ounce). Diamond Jubilee commemorative 2012. O. For the obverse
impression, Our Effigy, inspired by the sculpture mounted in the entrance to the
Supreme Court building on Parliament Square, with the inscription 'ELIZABETH.
II. D. G. REG. F. D. TEN POUNDS', and for the reverse an enthroned representation
of Ourself surrounded by the inscription 'DILECTA REGNO MCMLII – MMXII'
(Obverse and reverse design: Ian Rank-Broadley)
2012
— Proof in silver *FDC* (Issued: 1,933)...£350
— Proof in gold *FDC* (Issued: 140)..£7500
Illustration shown at reduced size – actual coin diameter 65 mm.

4641

4641 **Ten pounds** (five ounce). Coronation Anniversary. R. In the foreground the Orb and Sceptre resting upon the Coronation Robe with the arches of Westminster Abbey in the background with the inscription 'HER MAJESTY QUEEN ELIZABETH II CORONATION ANNIVERSARY' (Reverse design: Jonathan Olliffe).
2013
— Proof in silver (0.999) *FDC* (Issued: 1,604) £450
— Proof in gold (0.9999) *FDC* (Issued: 74) £9500
Illustration shown at reduced size – actual coin diameter 63mm

4642

4642 **Ten pounds** (five ounce) Commemorative coin to mark the christening of Prince George of Cambridge. R. A deconstructed silver lily font incorporating cherubs and roses, with a Baroque-style cartouche with the inscription 'DIEU ET MON DROIT' and ' TO CELEBRATE THE CHRISTENING OF PRINCE GEORGE OF CAMBRIDGE 2013' in the centre of the coin. (Reverse design: John Bergdahl).
2013
— Proof in silver (0.999) *FDC* (Issued: 912) £450
— Proof in gold (0.9999) *FDC* (Issued: 48) £9500
Illustration shown at reduced size – actual coin diameter 63mm

4643

4643 Ten pounds (five ounce). 100th Anniversary of the outbreak of the First World War.
R. A depiction of a lion behind the figure of Britannia holding a shield and a trident,
watching over departing ships from a cliff top, with the inscription 'THE FIRST
WORLD WAR 1914 1918' and the date at the base of the coin. (0.999 fine silver.)
(Reverse design: John Bergdahl)
2014
—   Proof in silver (0.999) *FDC* (Edition: 1,300)...£395
—   Proof in gold (0.9999) *FDC* (Edition: 100)..£7500

4644

4644 Ten pounds. Churchill R. A depiction of Sir Winston Churchill with the inscription
'CHURCHILL' at the base of the coin. (Reverse design: Etienne Millner)
2015
—   Proof on silver *FDC* (5 oz. fine silver) (Edition: 900) £395
—   Proof in gold *FDC* (5 oz. fine gold) (Edition: 60) £7,500

Obverse portrait by Jody Clark

4645

4645 Ten pounds. World War One. R.A depiction of the landscape of the Western Front
with the inscription '1914 – 1918' Reverse design: James Butler)
2015
— Proof on silver *FDC* (5 oz. fine silver) (Edition: 500)
— Proof in gold *FDC* (5 oz. fine gold) (Edition: 50)

Obverse portrait by James Butler

4646

4646 Ten pounds. The Longest serving monarch R. A design depicting Our Royal
Cypher below Our five definitive coinage portraits and the inscription
'THE LONGEST REIGN'.(Reverse design: Stephen Taylor)
2015
— Proof on silver *FDC* (5 oz. fine silver) (Edition: 1,500) £395
— Proof in gold *FDC* (5 oz. fine gold) (Edition: 180) £6950

Obverse portrait by Ian Rank-Broadley

4770

4770 Twenty pounds. R. A depiction of St. George armed, sitting on horseback, attacking
the dragon with a sword, and a broken spear upon the ground and the date of the
year. (0.999 fine silver) (Reverse design: Benedetto Pistrucci).
2013
—   Bu in silver (Issued: 250,000) £20

4771

4771 Twenty pounds. R. A depiction of a lion behind the figure of Britannia holding
a shield and a trident, watching over departing ships from a cliff top, with the
inscription 'THE FIRST WORLD WAR 1914 1918' and the date at the base of the
coin. (0.999 fine silver) (Reverse design: John Bergdahl)
2014
—   Bu in silver (Edition: 250,000)..£20

4772   4773

4772 Twenty pounds. Churchill R. A depiction of Sir Winston Churchill with the
inscription 'CHURCHILL' at the base of the coin. (Reverse design: Etienne Millner)
2015
—   BU (Edition : 200,000)

4773 Twenty pounds. The Longest serving monarch. R. A design depicting Our Royal
Cypher below Our five definitive coinage portraits and the inscription 'THE
LONGEST REIGN' (Reverse design: Stephen Taylor)
2015
—   (Edition: 150,000)..£20

4775 **One hundred pounds.** World War I R. A depiction of Lord Kitchener pointing above the inscription 'YOUR COUNTRY NEEDS YOU' and the inscription 'THE FIRST WORLD WAR 1914-1918' and the date '2014' surrounding the design. (Reverse design: John Bergdahl).
2014
— Proof in Platinum *FDC*

4774

4774 **One hundred pounds.** Elizabeth Tower (Reverse design: Glyn Davies and Laura Clancy)
2015
— BU (Edition: 50,000)

Obverse portrait by Jody Clark

4777

4777 **One hundred pounds,** R. A design the Victoria Memorial with Buckingham Palace in the background Reverse design: Glyn Davies and Laura Clancy)
2015
— BU

Obverse portrait by Ian Rank-Broadley

4780

4780 Five hundred pounds (one kilo). Diamond Jubilee commemorative 2012. O. For the
obverse impression, Our Effigy, inspired by the sculpture mounted in the entrance to the
Supreme Court building on Parliament Square, with the inscription 'ELIZABETH. II. D.
G. REG. F. D. 500 POUNDS', and for the reverse a full achievement of the Royal Arms
based on those mounted on the front gates of Buckingham Palace with the date '2012'
below. (Obverse and reverse design: Ian Rank-Broadley)
2012

—   Proof in silver *FDC* (Issued: 206)..£2000
Illustration shown at reduced size – actual coin diameter 100 mm.

4781 Five hundred pounds (one kilo). R. Coronation commemorative 2013. R. In the
foreground the Orb and Sceptre with the St. Edward's Crown behind surrounding
by flowers representing the constituent parts of the United Kingdom and in the
background a ribbon showing the '2nd JUNE 1953' with the inscription 'QUEEN
ELIZABETH II' and 'THE 60TH ANNIVERSARY OF THE CORONATION'
(Reverse design: John Bergdahl)
2013

—   Proof in silver *FDC* (0.999) (Issued: 301))..£2600

4782

4782 Five hundred pounds (1 kilo of fine silver). Commemorative coin to mark the christening
of Prince George of Cambridge. R. A deconstructed silver lily font incorporating cherubs
and roses, with a Baroque-style cartouche with the inscription 'DIEU ET MON DROIT'
and 'TO CELEBRATE THE CHRISTENING OF PRINCE GEORGE OF CAMBRIDGE
2013' in the centre of the coin. (Reverse design: John Bergdahl).
2013

—   Proof in silver (0.999) *FDC* (Issued: 194)).. £2000
Illustration shown at reduced size – actual coin diameter 100mm

4783

4783 Five hundred pounds. (1 kilo of fine silver). World War 1. R. A design depicting
British soldiers marching through no man's land with the figure of a British soldier
with rifle and helmet in the foreground and the dates '1914-1918' at the base of the coin.
(Reverse design: Michael Sandle).
2014
   —   Proof in silver (0.999) *FDC* (Edition: 430)..£2000
Illustration shown at reduced size – actual coin diameter 100mm

Obverse portrait by James Butler

4784

4784 Five hundred pounds. (1 kilo of fine silver).The Longest serving monarch R. A
design depicting Our Royal Cypher below Our five definitive coinage portraits and
the inscription 'THE LONGEST REIGN'. (Reverse design: Stephen Taylor)
2015
   —   Proof on silver *FDC* (Edition: 320) £2000

4790

4790 One thousand pounds (one kilo). Diamond Jubilee commemorative 2012. O. For the obverse impression, Our Effigy, inspired by the sculpture mounted in the entrance to the Supreme Court building on Parliament Square, with the inscription 'ELIZABETH. II. D. G. REG. F. D. 1000 POUNDS', and for the reverse a full achievement of the Royal Arms based on those mounted on the front gates of Buckingham Palace with the date '2012' below. (Reverse design: 2012

—   Proof in gold *FDC* (Issued: 21)) £60000
Illustration shown at reduced size – actual coin diameter 100mm

4791 One thousand pounds (One kilo). Coronation commemorative 2013. R. In the foreground the Orb and Sceptre with the St. Edward's Crown behind surrounding by flowers representing the constituent parts of the United Kingdom and in the background a ribbon showing the '2nd JUNE 1953' with the inscription 'QUEEN ELIZABETH II' and 'THE 60TH ANNIVERSARY OF THE CORONATION' (Reverse design: John Bergdahl)
2013

—   Proof in gold *FDC* (0.9999) (Issued: 13)) £60000

4792

4792 One thousand pounds (1 kilo of fine gold). Commemorative coin to mark the christening of Prince George of Cambridge. R. A deconstructed silver lily font incorporating cherubs and roses, with a Baroque-style cartouche with the inscription 'DIEU ET MON DROIT' and 'TO CELEBRATE THE CHRISTENING OF PRINCE GEORGE OF CAMBRIDGE 2013'in the centre of the coin. (Reverse design: John Bergdahl).
2013

—   Proof in gold *FDC* (0.9999) (Issued: 19) £50000
Illustration shown at reduced size – actual coin diameter 100mm

4793

4793 One thousand pounds. (1 kilo of fine gold). World War 1. R. A design depicting British soldiers marching through no man's land with the figure of a British soldier with rifle and helmet in the foreground and the dates '1914-1918' at the base of the coin. (Reverse design: Michael Sandle).

2014

— Proof in gold *FDC* (0.9999) (Edition: 25)..£45000

Illustration shown at reduced size – actual coin diameter 100mm

GOLD SOVEREIGN ISSUES

Obverse portrait by Ian Rank-Broadley

4445   4446

4445 Quarter sovereign. R. The image of St George armed, sitting on horseback, attacking the dragon with a sword, and a broken spear upon the ground, and the date of the year. (Reverse design: Benedetto Pistrucci)

2009 Bullion type (Edition: 50,000)...£110

— Proof *FDC* (Issued: 13,495 including coins in sets) £130

2010 Bullion type (Edition: 250,000)...£110

— Proof *FDC* (Issued: 6,007 including coins in sets) £130

2011 Bullion type (Edition: 50,000)...£110

— Proof *FDC* (Issued: 7,764 including coins in sets) £130

2013 Bullion type

— Proof *FDC* (Issued: 1,729)*

2014 Bullion type

— Proof *FDC* (Issued: 1,696 including coins in sets)* £110

2015

— Proof (Edition: 4,600 including coins in sets)..£110

4446 Quarter sovereign. R. The image of St George on horseback, attacking the dragon with a lance, with date of the year to the left. (Reverse design: Paul Day)

2012 Bullion type (Edition: 250,000) £80

— Proof *FDC* (Issued: 7,579)..£110

* Coins marked thus were originally issued in Royal Mint sets.

Obverse portrait by Jody Clark

4447

4447   Quarter sovereign.
2015 Proof (Edition: 4,600 including coins in sets) £110

Obverse portrait by Arnold Machin

4205

4205   Half-sovereign. R. The image of St George armed, sitting on horseback, attacking the
dragon with a sword, and a broken spear upon the ground, and the date of the year.
(Reverse design: Benedetto Pistrucci)

1980 Proof *FDC* (Issued: 76.700). £125	1983 Proof *FDC* (Issued: 19,710)** £125
1982 Unc £100	1984 Proof *FDC* (Issued: 12,410) £125
— Proof *FDC* (Issued: 19,090).. £125	

Obverse portrait by Raphael Maklouf

4276   4277

4276   Half-sovereign. R. St. George (as 4205)

1985 Proof *FDC* (Issued: 9,951) ... £160	1992 Proof *FDC* (Issued: 3,783) £175
1986 Proof *FDC* (Issued: 4,575) ... £160	1993 Proof *FDC* (Issued: 2,910) £175
1987 Proof *FDC* (Issued: 8,187) ... £160	1994 Proof *FDC* (Issued: 5,000) £150
1988 Proof *FDC* (Issued: 7,074) ... £160	1995 Proof *FDC* (Issued: 4,900) £150
1990 Proof *FDC* (Issued: 4,231) ... £175	1996 Proof *FDC* (Issued: 5,730) £150
1991 Proof *FDC* (Issued: 3,588) ... £175	1997 Proof *FDC* (Issued: 7,500) £150

4277   Half-sovereign 500th Anniversary of Sovereign. For the obverse impression a
representation Of Ourself as at Our Coronation, seated in King Edward's Chair and
having received the Sceptre with the Cross and the Rod with the Dove, all within the
circumscription 'ELIZABETH. II.DEI.GRA.REG.FID.DEF' and for the reverse a
Shield of Our Royal Arms ensigned by an open Royal Crown, the whole superimposed
upon a double Rose, and with the circumscription 'ANNIVERSARY OF THE GOLD
SOVEREIGN 1489-1989' (Designs: Bernald Sindall)
1989 Proof *FDC (*Issued: 8,888)...£400

* Coins marked thus were originally issued in Royal Mint sets.
** Numbers include coins sold in sets

Obverse portrait by Ian Rank-Broadley

| 4440 | 4441 | 4442 |

4440 **Half sovereign.** R. St.George

1998 Proof *FDC* (Issued: 6,147)... £175	2004 Bullion type (Issued: 34,924) £140
1999 Proof *FDC* (Issued: 7,500)... £175	— Proof *FDC* (Issued: 4,446) £175
2000 Bullion type (Issued: 146,822). £140	2006 Bullion type £140
— Proof *FDC* (Issued: 7,458).... £175	— Proof *FDC* (Issued: 4,173) £175
2001 Bullion type (Issued: 94,763) .£140	2007 Bullion type (Edition: 75,000)........ £140
— Proof *FDC* (Issued: 4,596).... £175	— Proof *FDC* (Issued: 2,442) £175
2003 Bullion type (Issued: 47,818)£140	2008 Bullion type (Edition: 75,000)........ £140
— Proof *FDC* (Issued: 4,868).... £175	— Proof *FDC* (Issued: 2,465) £175

4441 **Half sovereign** R. The Shield of Arms of Our United Kingdom of Great Britain and Northern Ireland within an open wreath of laurel and ensigned by Our Royal Crown and beneath the date of the year. (Reverse design: Timothy Noad)

2002 Bullion type (Issued: 61,347)..£150
— Proof *FDC* (Issued: 10,000)..£250

4442 **Half sovereign.** R. A depiction of St George, carrying a shield and a sword, slaying the dragon, with the date '2005' beneath the wing of the dragon. (Reverse design: Timothy Noad)

2005 Bullion type (Issued: 30,299)...£150
— Proof *FDC* (Issued: 5,011)..£250

4443

4443 **Half sovereign.** R. St George. Based on the original design of 1893 with reduced ground below design and larger exergue with no BP initials

2009 Bullion type (Edition: 50,000)...£165
— Proof *FDC* (Issued: 5,412 including coins in sets) £225
2010 Bullion type (Edition: 250,000)...£165
— Proof *FDC* (Issued: 5,370 including coins in sets) £225
2011 Bullion type (Edition: 50,000)...£160
— Proof *FDC* (Issued 5,287 including coins in sets)..£250
2013 Bullion type (Issued: 1,051)
— BU (Issued: 124 in sets, see PGS70)
— Proof *FDC* (Issued: 1,863 including coins in sets)*
2014 Bullion type
— BU (Edition: 9,900)...£170
— Proof *FDC* (Edition: 4,075 including coins in sets)...£195
2015
— BU (Edition: 5,000)...£175
— Proof (Edition ; 4,600 including coins in sets)..£190

* Coins marked thus were originally issued in Royal Mint sets.

4444

4444 Half sovereign. R. The image of St George on horseback, attacking the dragon with
a lance, with date of the year to the left. (Reverse design: Paul Day)
2012 Bullion type (Edition: 250,000)..£175
— Proof *FDC* (Issued: 2,303

Obverse portrait by Jody Clark
4415 Half sovereign
— 2015 Proof (Edition ; 1,100)..£190

Obverse portrait by Arnold Machin

4204

4204 Sovereign. R. The image of St George armed, sitting on horseback, attacking the
dragon with a sword, and a broken spear upon the ground, and the date of the year.
(Reverse design: Benedetto Pistrucci)

1974 Unc £225	1981 Unc..£225
1976 Unc £225	— Proof *FDC* (Issued: 32,960) £250
1976 VIP Proof *FDC*......*Extremely rare*	1982 Unc..£225
1978 Unc £225	— Proof *FDC* (Issued: 20,000) £250
1979 Unc £225	1983 Proof *FDC* (Issued: 21,250)** £250
— Proof *FDC* (Issued: 50,000) £250	1984 Proof *FDC* (Issued: 12,880) £250
1980 Unc £225	
— Proof *FDC* (Issued: 81,200) £250	

* Coins marked thus were originally issued in Royal Mint sets.
** Numbers include coins sold in sets

Obverse portrait by Raphael Maklouf

4271   4272

4271 Sovereign. R. St. George (as 4204)

1985 Proof *FDC* (Issued: 11,393). £300
1986 Proof *FDC* (Issued: 5,079)... £300
1987 Proof *FDC* (Issued: 9,979)... £300
1988 Proof *FDC* (Issued: 7,670)... £300
1990 Proof *FDC* (Issued: 4,767)... £350
1991 Proof *FDC* (Issued: 4,713)... £350

1992 Proof *FDC* (Issued: 4,772) £350
1993 Proof *FDC* (Issued: 4,349) £400
1994 Proof *FDC* (Issued: 4,998) £350
1995 Proof *FDC* (Issued: 7,500) £325
1996 Proof *FDC* (Issued: 7,500) £325
1997 Proof *FDC* (Issued: 7,500) £325

4272 Sovereign. 500th Anniversary of Sovereign. For the obverse impression a representation Of Ourself as at Our Coronation, seated in King Edward's Chair and having received the Sceptre with the Cross and the Rod with the Dove, all within the circumscription 'ELIZABETH.II.DEI.GRA.REG.FID.DEF' and for the reverse a Shield of Our Royal Arms ensigned by an open Royal Crown, the whole superimposed upon a double Rose, and with the circumscription 'ANNIVERSARY OF THE GOLD SOVEREIGN 1489-1989' (Designs: Bernald Sindall)

1989 Proof *FDC* (Issued: 10,535) £1200

Obverse portrait by Ian Rank-Broadley

4430

4430 Sovereign. R. St.George

1998 Proof *FDC* (Issued: 10,000). £325
1999 Proof *FDC* (Issued: 10,000). £350
2000 Bullion type (Issued: 129,069).£225
— Proof *FDC* (Issued: 9,909).... £325
2001 Bullion type (Issued: 49,462)£225
— Proof *FDC* (Issued: 8,915).... £325
2003 Bullion type (Issued: 43,230)£225
— Proof *FDC* (Issued: 12,433).. £325

2004 Bullion type (Issued: 30,688) £225
— Proof *FDC* (Issued: 10,175) £325
2006 Bullion type £225
— Proof *FDC* (Issued: 9,195) £325
2007 Bullion type (Edition: 75,000)........£225
— Proof *FDC* (Issued: 8,199) £325
2008 Bullion type (Edition: 75,000)........£225
— Proof *FDC* (Edition: 12,500)...........£325

Where numbers of coins issued or the Edition limit is quoted, these refer to individual coins. Additional coins were included in sets which are listed in the appropriate section.

4431   4433

4431 Sovereign ℞. The Shield of Arms of Our United Kingdom of Great Britain and Northern Ireland within an open wreath of laurel and ensigned by Our Royal Crown and beneath the date of the year. (Reverse design: Timothy Noad)

2002 Bullion type (Issued: 75,264) £300

— Proof *FDC* (Issued: 12,500) £400

4432 Sovereign ℞. A depiction of St George, carrying a shield and a sword, slaying the dragon, with the date '2005' beneath the wing of the dragon.(Reverse design: Timothy Noad)

2005 Bullion type (Issued: 45,542) £300

— Proof *FDC* (Issued: 12,500) £400

4433   Sovereign. R. St George. Based on the original design of 1820 with the plumed helmet without its streamer.

2009 Bullion type (Edition: 75,000)...£325

— Proof *FDC* (Issued: 9,770 including coins in sets)..£400

2010 Bullion type (Edition: 250,000)..£325

— Proof *FDC* (Issued: 8,828 including coins in sets)..£400

2011 Bullion type (Edition: 250,000) £325

— Proof *FDC* (Edition: 15,000 including coins in sets) £450

2013 Bullion type (Issued: 2,695)

— BU (Issued: 124 in sets, see PGS70)

— Proof *FDC* (Issued: 8,243 including coins in sets)

2014 Bullion type

— BU (Edition: 15,000) £325

— Proof *FDC* (Edition: 9,725 including coins in sets) £390

2015

— BU (Edition: 10,000)

— Proof (Edition : 9,800 including coins in sets) £360

4433A Sovereign. R. St George as 4433 above but with 'I' mint mark on reverse for coins struck in India.

2013 BU

4434

4434 Sovereign. ℞. The image of St George on horseback, attacking the dragon with a lance, with date of the year to the left. (Reverse design: Paul Day)

2012 Bullion type (Edition: 250,000)...£275

— Proof *FDC* (Issued: 5,501)) £400

Obverse portrait by Jody Clark

4435

4435 Sovereign.
2015
— BU (Edition ; 10,000)
— Proof (Edition :8,800 including coins in sets) £360

Obverse portrait by Arnold Machin

4203

4203 Two pounds R. The image of St George armed, sitting on horseback, attacking the dragon
with a sword, and a broken spear upon the ground, and the date of the year.(Reverse design:
Benedetto Pistrucci)
1980 Proof *FDC* (see PGS01)* ....£525   1983 Proof *FDC* (Issued: 12,500) ** £525
1982 Proof *FDC* (see PGS03)* £525

Obverse portrait by Raphael Maklouf

4261

4261 Two pounds. R. St. George (as 4203)
1985 Proof *FDC* (see PGS06)* ....£525   1991 Proof *FDC* (Issued: 620) £525
1987 Proof *FDC* (Issued: 1,801) ....£525   1992 Proof *FDC* (Issued: 476) £525
1988 Proof *FDC* (Issued: 1,551) ....£525   1993 Proof *FDC* (Issued: 414) £525
1990 Proof *FDC* (Issued: 716) ....£525   1996 Proof *FDC* (see PGS24)* £525

* Coins marked thus were originally issued in Royal Mint sets.
** Numbers include coins sold in sets

4262

4262 **Two pounds** 500th Anniversary of Sovereign. For the obverse impression a representation Of
Ourself as at Our Coronation, seated in King Edward's Chair and having received the Sceptre
with the Cross and the Rod with the Dove, all within the circumscription 'ELIZABETH.
II.DEI.GRA.REG.FID.DEF' and for the reverse a Shield of Our Royal Arms ensigned by an
open Royal Crown, the whole superimposed upon a double Rose, and with the circumscription
'ANNIVERSARY OF THE GOLD SOVEREIGN 1489-1989' (Designs: Bernald Sindall)
1989 Proof *FDC* (Issued: 2,000) £900

Obverse portrait by Ian Rank-Broadley

4420

4420 **Two pounds.** R. St. George

1998 Proof *FDC* (see PGS28)* £500		2000 Proof *FDC* (see PGS32)* £500
2003 Proof *FDC* (see PGS38)* £500		2006 Proof *FDC* (see PGS44)* £500
2007 Proof *FDC* (see PGS46)* £500		2008 Proof *FDC* (see PGS49)* £500

4421

4421 **Two pounds.** R. The Shield of Arms of Our United Kingdom of Great Britain and
Northern Ireland within an open wreath of laurel and ensigned by Our Royal Crown and
beneath the date of the year. (Reverse design: Timothy Noad)
2002 Proof *FDC* (see PGS36)* £700

* Coins marked thus were originally issued in Royal Mint sets.

4422   4423

4422 **Two pounds.** R. A depiction of St George, carrying a shield and a sword, slaying the
dragon, with the date '2005' beneath the wing of the dragon.(Reverse design:
Timothy Noad)
2005 Proof *FDC* (see PGS42)* £700
4423 **Two pounds.** R. St George. Based on the original design of 1820 with greater detail on
the dragon.
2009 Proof *FDC* (see PGS52)* £600
2010 Proof *FDC* (Edition: 2,750 in sets)* £600
2011 Proof *FDC* (Edition: 2,950 in sets)* £1000
2013 BU (Issued: 124 in sets, see PGS70)
—   Proof *FDC* (Edition: 1,895 in sets)*
2014 BU (Edition: 1,300)..£650
—   Proof *FDC* (Edition:)
2015 Proof *FDC* (Edition: 1,100 including coins in sets)

4424

4424 **Two pounds.** R. The image of St George on horseback, attacking the dragon with a
lance, with date of the year to the left. (Reverse design: Paul Day)
2012 BU (Edition: 60 in three coin set, see PGS6)* £1000
—   Proof *FDC* (Edition: 1,944 including coins in sets)*

Obverse portrait by Jody Clark
4425 **Two pounds**.
2015 Proof (Edition: 1,100 including coins in sets)

* Coins marked thus were originally issued in Royal Mint sets.

Obverse portrait by Arnold Machin

4201

4201　Five pounds. R. The image of St George armed, sitting on horseback, attacking the dragon with a sword, and a broken spear upon the ground, and the date of the year.(Reverse design: Benedetto Pistrucci)

1980 Proof *FDC* (see PGS01)*... £1250	1982 Proof *FDC* (see PGS03)* £1250
1981 Proof *FDC* (Issued: 5,400) ** £1250	1984 Proof *FDC* (Issued: 905)...............£1250

4202　As 4201 but, 'U' in a circle to left of date

1984 (Issued: 15,104) *Unc* £1250

Obverse portrait by Raphael Maklouf

4251

4251　Five pounds. R. St. George (as 4201)

1985 Proof *FDC* (see PGS06)*... £1250	1990 Proof *FDC* (see PGS12)* £1250
1991 Proof *FDC* (see PGS14)*... £1250	1992 Proof *FDC* (see PGS16)* £1250
1993 Proof *FDC* (see PGS18)*... £1250	1994 Proof *FDC* (see PGS20)* £1250
1995 Proof *FDC* (see PGS22)*... £1250	1996 Proof *FDC* (see PGS24)* £1250
1997 Proof *FDC* (see PGS26)*.. £1250	

4252　Five pounds R. St George, 'U' in a circle to left of date.

1985 (Issued: 13,626).................. £1250	1993 (Issued: 906)................................£1250
1986 (Issued: 7,723).................... £1250	1994 (Issued: 1,000).............................£1250
1990 (Issued: 1,226)................... £1250	1995 (Issued: 1,000).............................£1250
1991 (Issued: 976)...................... £1250	1996 (Issued: 901)................................£1250
1992 (Issued: 797)...................... £1250	1997 (Issued: 802)................................£1250

* Coins marked thus were originally issued in Royal Mint sets.

4253

4253 **Five pounds** Uncouped portrait of Queen Elizabeth II. As illustration. R. St. George, 'U' in a circle to left of date.

1987 (Issued: 5,694).................... £1250   1988 (Issued: 3,315)............................. £1250

4254

4254 **Five pounds** 500th Anniversary of Sovereign. For the obverse impression a representation Of Ourself as at Our Coronation, seated in King Edward's Chair and having received the Sceptre with the Cross and the Rod with the Dove, all within the circumscription 'ELIZABETH.II.DEI.GRA.REG.FID.DEF' and for the reverse a Shield of Our Royal Arms ensigned by an open Royal Crown, the whole superimposed upon a double Rose, and with the circumscription 'ANNIVERSARY OF THE GOLD SOVEREIGN 1489-1989' (Designs: Bernald Sindall)

1989 (Issued: 2,937).. £1650
—   Proof *FDC* (see PGS10)*... £2000

* Coins marked thus were originally issued in Royal Mint sets.

Obverse portrait by Ian Rank-Broadley

4400

4400 Five pounds. R. St.George

1998 Proof *FDC* (see PGS28)* ... £1250	2004 Unc (Issued: 1,000) £1250
1999 Proof *FDC* (see PGS30)* ... £1250	— Proof *FDC* (see PGS40)* £1250
2000 Bullion type £1250	2006 Unc (Issued: 731) £1250
— Proof *FDC* (see PGS32)* £1250	— Proof *FDC* (see PGS44)* £1250
2001 Proof *FDC* (see PGS34)* ... £1250	2007 Unc (Issued: 768) £1250
2003 Unc (Issued: 812) £1250	— Proof *FDC* (see PGS46)* £1250
— Proof *FDC* (see PGS38)* £1250	2008 Unc (Issued: 750) £1250
	— Proof *FDC* (see PGS49)* £1250

4401   4402

4401 Five pounds. R. The Shield of Arms of Our United Kingdom of Great Britain and
Northern Ireland within an open wreath of laurel and ensigned by Our Royal Crown and
beneath the date of the year. (Reverse design: Timothy Noad)

2002 Unc (Issued: 1,370) £1300
—   Proof *FDC* (see PGS36)* £1500

4402 Five pounds. R. A depiction of St George, carrying a shield and a sword, slaying the dragon,
with the date '2005' beneath the wing of the dragon.(Reverse design: Timothy Noad)

2005 Unc (Issued: 936) £1300
—   Proof *FDC* (see PGS42)* £1500

* Coins marked thus were originally issued in Royal Mint sets.

4403   4404

4403 Five pounds. R. St George. Based on the original pattern piece of 1820 with the designer's
name, 'PISTRUCCI', shown in full in the exergue, and with a broader rim.

2009 BU (Issued: 1,000) ....£1550   —   Proof *FDC* (see PGS52)*.................£1550

2010 BU (Issued: 1,000) ....£1550   —   Proof *FDC* (Edition: 2,000 in sets)* £1550

2011 BU (Issued: 657) ....£2100   —   Proof *FDC* (Edition: 2,000 in sets)* £2100

2013 BU (Issued: 262) ....£1900   —   Proof *FDC* (Issued: 388 in sets)*

2014 BU (Edition 1,000)................£1450   —   Proof *FDC* (Edition:)

2015 Proof *FDC* (Edition: 600 including coins in sets)

4404 Five pounds. R. The image of St George on horseback, attacking the dragon with a lance,
with date of the year to the left. (Reverse design: Paul Day)

2012 BU (Issued: 496) £2000

—   Proof *FDC* (Issued: 956 coins in sets)*

4410 Five pounds. R. St. George, 'U' in a circle to left of date

1998 (Issued: 825) .... £1250   2000 (Issued: 994) £1250

1999 (Issued: 970) .... £1250   2001 (Issued: 1,000) £1250

* *Coins marked thus were originally issued in Royal Mint sets.*

Obverse portrait by Jody Clark
4411 Five pounds.

2015 BU (Edition : 750)............. £1450

—   Proof (Edition :600 including coins in sets)

BRITANNIA COIN ISSUES

In 1987 the Mint decided to enter the market for bullion coins and launched a series of four gold coins with weights that corresponded to those already issued by a number of gold producing countries such as Canada, South Africa and China. The plan was to sell bullion quality coins in quantity to trade customers and investors at modest premiums over the ruling gold market price, and also to sell proof versions in limited editions to collectors.

Due to market reaction, particularly from the Far East, silver rather than copper was alloyed with the gold in 1990 in an effort to increase demand but in the absence of sales figures, it appears that the major interest is now to be found among collectors of the proof collector versions.

To mark the 10th anniversary of the first design, silver coins struck in Britannia silver (0.958) were introduced in the same four weights. Again the main interest seems to have been among collectors of the proof versions although the one ounce silver bullion coin of £2 face value has proved popular as silver prices have risen.

There are some attractive and different interpretations of Britannia with the gold and silver issues sharing the same designs as they are changed. The range of designs thus far are shown below, and the complete sets are listed in the appropriate sections towards the end of the catalogue.

BRITANNIA SILVER

Obverse portrait by Ian Rank-Broadley

4675

4675 Britannia. Five pence. R. (1/40 oz of fine silver) A design of the standing figure of Britannia baring a trident and shield, with a lion at her feet, set against the backdrop of a globe, and with the inscription 'BRITANNIA 999 1/40 OZ FINE SILVER 2014' (Reverse design: Jody Clark)
2014 — Proof in silver *FDC* (0.999) (Edition: 2,750 including coins in sets)*
Illustration shown larger than actual coin diameter of 8mm

Obverse portrait by Jody Clark

5000

5000 Britannia. Five pence. R. (1/40 oz of fine silver) A figure of Britannia baring a trident and shield, set against a backdrop of a sailing ship, cliffs and a lighthouse with the inscription 'BRITANNIA 999 1/40 OZ FINE SILVER 2015' (Reverse design: Antony Dufort)
2015 — Proof in silver *FDC* (0.999) (Edition: 1,750 including coins in sets)*
Illustration shown larger than actual coin diameter of 8mm

---

* *Coins marked thus were originally issued in Royal Mint sets.*

Obverse portrait by Ian Rank-Broadley

4680

4680 Britannia. Ten pence. (1/20 oz of fine silver) (Previously listed as 4550) R. Seated
figure of Britannia holding a trident with a shield at her side and an owl upon her knee
with the word 'BRITANNIA' and the date of the year above and the inscription '1/20
OUNCE FINE SILVER' below the figure of Britannia. (Reverse design: Robert Hunt)
2013 — Proof in silver *FDC* (0.999) (Edition: 12,000 including coins in sets)*

4681

4681 Britannia. Ten pence. (1/20 oz of fine silver) R. A design of the standing figure of
Britannia baring a trident and shield, with a lion at her feet, set against the backdrop of a
globe, and with the inscription ' BRITANNIA 999 1/20 OZ FINE SILVER 2014'
(Reverse design: Jody Clark)
2014 — Proof in silver *FDC* (0.999) (Edition: 3,300 including coins in sets)*

Obverse portrait by Jody Clark

5005

5005 Britannia. Ten pence. (1/20 oz of fine silver) A figure of Britannia baring a trident and
shield, set against a backdrop of a sailing ship, cliffs and a lighthouse with the inscription
'BRITANNIA 999 1/20 OZ FINE SILVER 2015' (Reverse design: Antony Dufort)
2015 — Proof in silver *FDC* (0.999) (Edition: 3,300 including coins in sets)*

Obverse portrait by Raphael Maklouf

4300C

4300CBritannia. Twenty pence. (1/10 oz of fine silver) 10th Anniversary of Britannia issue R.
The figure of Britannia standing in a chariot drawn along the seashore by two horses,
with the word 'BRITANNIA', the inscription. '1/10 OUNCE FINE SILVER' and the
date of the year. (Reverse design: Philip Nathan).
1997 Proof *FDC* (Issued: 8,686, plus coins issued in sets, see PSB01)........................£20

* *Coins marked thus were originally issued in Royal Mint sets.*

Obverse portrait by Ian Rank-Broadley

4530   4531

4530 Britannia. Twenty pence. (1/10 oz of fine silver) R. The figure of Britannia standing upon a rock in the sea, her right hand grasping a trident and her left hand resting on a shield and holding an olive branch, with the word 'BRITANNIA', the date of the year, and the inscription '1/10 OUNCE FINE SILVER'. (Reverse design: Philip Nathan). (See 4500)

1998 — Proof *FDC* (Issued: 2,724, plus coins issued in sets, see PSB02)....................£20
2006 BU version...£15
2012 — Proof *FDC* (Issued: 2,595 in sets see PBS14)*

4531 Britannia. Twenty pence. (1/10 oz of fine silver) R. The figure of Britannia, as guardian, with a shield in her left hand and a trident in her right hand, accompanied by a lion and, against the background of a wave motif, the words '1/10 OUNCE FINE SILVER' to the left and 'BRITANNIA' and the date of the year to the right. (Reverse design: Philip Nathan).

2001 — Proof *FDC* (Issued: 826, plus coins issued in sets, see PSB03).......................£20

4532   4534   4536

4532 Britannia. Twenty pence. (1/10 oz fine silver) R. Helmeted head of Britannia with, to the left, the word 'BRITANNIA' and, to the right, the inscription '1/10 OUNCE FINE SILVER' and the date of the year, the whole being overlaid with a wave pattern. (Reverse design: Philip Nathan)

2003 — Proof *FDC* (Issued: 1,179, plus coins issued in sets, see PBS04)....................£20

4533 Britannia. Twenty pence. (Previously listed as 4515) (1/10 oz of fine silver) R. Seated figure of Britannia facing to the left holding a trident with a shield at her side, with the word 'BRITANNIA', the inscription '1/10 OUNCE FINE SILVER' and the date of the year. (Reverse design: Philip Nathan)

2005 — Proof *FDC** (Issued: 913, plus coins issued in sets, see PBS06)....................£20

4534 Britannia. Twenty pence. (1/10 oz of fine silver) R. Seated figure of Britannia facing right holding a trident in her right hand and a sprig of olive in the left hand with a lion at her feet with the inscription '1/10 OUNCE FINE SILVER' and the word 'BRITANNIA' and the date of the year (Reverse design: Christopher Le Brun)

2007 — Proof *FDC* (Issued: 901, plus coins issued in sets, see PBS08).......................£20

4535 Britannia. Twenty pence. (1/10 oz of fine silver) R. A Standing figure of Britannia holding a trident with a shield at her side, the folds of her dress transforming into a wave, with the word 'BRITANNIA' and the date of the year and the inscription '1/10 OUNCE FINE SILVER' (Reverse design: John Bergdahl). (See 4506)

2008 — Proof *FDC* (Edition: 2,500, plus coins issued in sets, see PBS1010) £20

4536 Britannia. Twenty pence. (1/10 oz fine silver) R. Standing figure of Britannia in horse drawn chariot. (See 4501)

2009 — Proof *FDC* (Edition; 3,500 including coins in sets)..£25

* Coins marked thus were originally issued in Royal Mint sets.

4537   4539

4537 Britannia. Twenty pence. (1/10 oz fine silver) R. A design depicting a profile bust of
Britannia wearing a helmet, accompanied by the name 'BRITANNIA', the inscription
'1/10 OUNCE FINE SILVER' and the date '2010'. (Reverse design: Suzie Zamit)
2010 Proof *FDC* (Edition: 8,000 including coins in sets)..£25

4538 Britannia. Twenty pence. (1/10 oz fine silver) R. A design depicting a seated figure of
Britannia set against a background of a rippling Union Flag accompanied by the words '1/10
OUNCE FINE SILVER BRITANNIA' and the date '2011'. (Reverse design: David Mach)
2011 — Proof *FDC* (Edition: 6,000 including coins in sets)

4539 Britannia. Twenty pence. (1/10 oz of fine silver).R. Seated figure of Britannia holding
a trident with a shield at her side and an owl upon her knee with the word 'BRITANNIA'
and the date of the year above and the inscription '1/10 OUNCE FINE SILVER' below
the figure of Britannia. (Reverse design: Robert Hunt)
2013 — Proof in silver *FDC* (0.999) (Edition: 12,000 including coins in sets)*

4540 Britannia. Twenty pence. (1/10 oz of fine silver) R. A design of the standing figure
of Britannia baring a trident and shield, with a lion at her feet, set against the backdrop
of a globe , and with the inscription ' BRITANNIA 999 1/10 OZ FINE SILVER 2014'
(Reverse design: Jody Clark)
2014— Proof in silver *FDC* (0.999) (Edition: 3,300 including coins in sets)*

Obverse portrait by Jody Clark

5010

5010 Britannia. Twenty pence. (1/10 oz of fine silver) R. A figure of Britannia baring a
trident and shield, set against a backdrop of a sailing ship, cliffs and a lighthouse with
the inscription 'BRITANNIA 999 1/10 OZ FINE SILVER 2015'
(Reverse design: Antony Dufort)
2015 – Proof in silver *FDC* (0.999) (Edition: 3,300 including coins in sets)*

* Coins marked thus were originally issued in Royal Mint sets.

Obverse portrait by Raphael Maklouf

4300B

4300B Britannia. Fifty pence. (1/4 oz of fine silver) 10th Anniversary of Britannia issue R. The figure of Britannia standing in a chariot drawn along the seashore by two horses, with the word 'BRITANNIA', the inscription. '1/4 OUNCE FINE SILVER' and the date of the year. (Reverse design: Philip Nathan).
1997 Proof *FDC* (in 1997 sets, see PSB01)* £30

Obverse portrait by Ian Rank-Broadley

4520   4521

4520 Britannia. Fifty pence. (1/4 oz of fine silver) R. The figure of Britannia standing upon a rock in the sea, her right hand grasping a trident and her left hand resting on a shield and holding an olive branch, the word 'BRITANNIA', the date of the year, and the inscription '1/4 OUNCE FINE SILVER'. (Reverse design: Philip Nathan). (See 4500)
1998 — Proof *FDC* (in 1998 set, see PSB02)* £25
2012 — Proof *FDC* (Issued: 2,595 in sets see PBS14)*

4520A Britannia. Fifty pence. (1/4 oz of fine silver, 0.999 fine) R. The figure of Britannia standing upon a rock in the sea, her .right hand grasping a trident and her left hand resting on a shield and holding an olive branch, with the word 'BRITANNIA', the date of the year, and the inscription' ¼ OUNCE FINE SILVER'. With the edge inscription 'SS Gairsoppa' (Reverse design: Philip Nathan)
2013
2014 (Edition: 20,000) £20

4521 Britannia. Fifty pence. (1/4 oz of fine silver) R. The figure of Britannia, as guardian, with a shield in her left hand and a trident in her right hand, accompanied by a lion and, against the background of a wave motif, the words '(1/4 OUNCE FINE SILVER' to the left and 'BRITANNIA' and the date of the year to the right. . (Reverse design: Philip Nathan).
2001 — Proof *FDC* (in 2001 set, see PSB03)* £25

* Coins marked thus were originally issued in Royal Mint sets.

4522   4524   4525

4522 **Britannia. Fifty pence.** (1/4 oz fine silver) R. Helmeted head of Britannia with, to the left, the word 'BRITANNIA' and, to the right, the inscription '1/4 OUNCE FINE SILVER' and the date of the year, the whole being overlaid with a wave pattern. (Reverse design: Philip Nathan)
2003 — Proof *FDC** £25

4523 **Britannia. Fifty pence.** (Previously listed as 4514) (1/4 oz of fine silver) R. Seated figure of Britannia facing to the left holding a trident with a shield at her side, with the word 'BRITANNIA', the inscription '1/4 OUNCE FINE SILVER' and the date of the year. (Reverse design: Philip Nathan). (See 4504)
2005 — Proof *FDC** £25

4524 **Britannia. Fifty pence.** (1/4 oz of fine silver) R. Seated figure of Britannia facing right holding a trident in her right hand and a sprig of olive in the left hand with a lion at her feet with the inscription '1/4 OUNCE FINE SILVER' and the word 'BRITANNIA' and the date of the year (See 4505) (Reverse design: Christopher Le Brun)
2007 — Proof *FDC** £25

4525 **Britannia. Fifty pence.** (1/4 oz of fine silver) R. A Standing figure of Britannia holding a trident with a shield at her side, the folds of her dress transforming into a wave, with the word 'BRITANNIA' and the date of the year and the inscription '1/4 OUNCE FINE SILVER' (Reverse design: John Bergdahl)
2008 — Proof *FDC** £25

4526 **Britannia. Fifty pence.** (1/4 oz fine silver) R. Standing figure of Britannia in horse drawn chariot. (see 4300B above)
2009 — Proof *FDC** £30

4527   4529

4527 **Britannia. Fifty pence.** (1/4 oz fine silver) R. A design depicting a profile bust of Britannia wearing a helmet, accompanied by the name 'BRITANNIA', the inscription '1/4 OUNCE FINE SILVER' and the date '2010'. (Reverse design: Suzie Zamit)
2010 Proof *FDC* * £30

4528 **Britannia. Fifty pence.** (1/4 oz fine silver) R. A design depicting a seated figure of Britannia set against a background of a rippling Union Flag accompanied by the words '1/4 OUNCE FINE SILVER BRITANNIA' and the date '2011'. (Reverse design: David Mach)
2011 Proof *FDC* (Edition: 5,000 including coins in sets)......................................£30

4529 **Britannia. Fifty pence.** (1/4 oz of fine silver).R. . Seated figure of Britannia holding a trident with a shield at her side and an owl upon her knee with the word 'BRITANNIA' and the date of the year above and the inscription '1/4 OUNCE FINE SILVER' below the figure of Britannia. (Reverse design: Robert Hunt)
2013 — Proof in silver *FDC* (0.999) (Issued: 3,087 including coins in sets)*

* *Coins marked thus were originally issued in Royal Mint sets.*

5015

5015 Britannia. Fifty pence. (Previously listed as 4530). (1/4 oz of fine silver) R. A design
of the standing figure of Britannia baring a trident and shield, with a lion at her feet, set
against the backdrop of a globe, and with the inscription 'BRITANNIA 999 1/4 OZ FINE
SILVER 2014' (Reverse design: Jody Clark)
2014 — Proof in silver *FDC* (0.999) (Edition: 2,300 including coins in sets)*

Obverse portrait by Jody Clark

5016

5016 Britannia. Fifty pence. (1/4 oz of fine silver) R. A figure of Britannia baring a trident and
shield, set against a backdrop of a sailing ship, cliffs and a lighthouse with the inscription
'BRITANNIA 999 1/4 OZ FINE SILVER 2015' (Reverse design: Antony Dufort)
2015 – Proof in silver *FDC* (0.999) (Edition: 2,300 including coins in sets)*

Obverse portrait by Raphael Maklouf

4300A

4300A Britannia. One pound. (1/2 oz of fine silver) 10th Anniversary of Britannia issue. R. The
figure of Britannia standing in a chariot drawn along the seashore by two horses, with the
word 'BRITANNIA', the inscription. '1/2 OUNCE FINE SILVER' and the date of the year.
(Reverse design: Philip Nathan).
1997 Proof *FDC** £40

* Coins marked thus were originally issued in Royal Mint sets.

Obverse portrait by Ian Rank-Broadley

4510

4510 Britannia. One pound. (1/2 oz of fine silver) R. The figure of Britannia standing upon a rock in the sea, her right hand grasping a trident and her left hand resting on a shield and holding an olive branch, with the word 'BRITANNIA', the date of the year, and the inscription '1/2 OUNCE FINE SILVER' (Reverse design: Philip Nathan).
1998 — Proof *FDC**..£40
2012 — Proof *FDC* (Issued: 4,251 in sets see PBS14 and PBS15)*
4510A 2007 Proof with satin finish on reverse (see 2007 set, PBS09) * £40

4511   4512   4514

4511 Britannia. One pound. (1/2oz of fine silver) R The figure of Britannia, as guardian, with a shield in her left hand and a trident in her right hand, accompanied by a lion and, against the background of a wave motif, the words '1/2 OUNCE FINE SILVER' to the left and 'BRITANNIA' and the date of the year to the right. (Reverse design: Philip Nathan).
2001 — Proof *FDC**..£40
2012 — Proof *FDC* (Issued: 1,656 in sets see PBS15)*
4511A 2007 Proof with satin finish on reverse (see 2007 set, PBS09) * £40
4512 Britannia. One pound. (1/2 oz fine silver) R. Helmeted head of Britannia with, to the left, the word 'BRITANNIA' and, to the right, the inscription '1/2 OUNCE FINE SILVER' and the date of the year, the whole being overlaid with a wave pattern. (Reverse design: Philip Nathan)
2003 — Proof *FDC**..£40
2012 — Proof *FDC* (Issued: 1,656 in sets see PBS15)*
4512A 2007 Proof with satin finish on reverse (see 2007 set, PBS09) * £40
4513 Britannia. One pound. (1/2 oz of fine silver) R. Seated figure of Britannia facing to the left holding a trident with a shield at her side, with the word 'BRITANNIA', the inscription '1/2 OUNCE FINE SILVER' and the date of the year. (Reverse design: Philip Nathan). (See 4504)
2005 — Proof *FDC**..£40
2012 — Proof *FDC* (Issued: 1,656 in sets see PBS15)*
4513A 2007 Proof with satin finish on reverse (see 2007 set, PBS09) * £40

* Coins marked thus were originally issued in Royal Mint sets.

4514 Britannia. One pound. (1/2 oz of fine silver) R. Seated figure of Britannia facing
right holding a trident in her right hand and a sprig of olive in the left hand with a lion
at her feet with the inscription '1/2 OUNCE FINE SILVER' and the word
'BRITANNIA' and the date of the year. (Reverse design: Christopher Le Brun)
2007 Proof *FDC* * £40
2012 — Proof *FDC* (Issued: 1,656 in sets see PBS15)*

4514A 2007 Proof with satin finish on reverse (see 2007 set, PBS09) * £40

4515 Britannia. One pound. (1/2 oz of fine silver) R. Standing figure of Britannia in
horse drawn chariot. (See 4300A)
2007 Proof with satin finish on reverse (see 2007 set, PBS09) * £40

4516   4517

4516 Britannia. One pound. (1/2 oz of fine silver) R. A Standing figure of Britannia holding
a trident with a shield at her side, the folds of her dress transforming into a wave, with
the word 'BRITANNIA' and the date of the year and the inscription '1/2 OUNCE FINE
SILVER' (Reverse design: John Bergdahl)
2008 Proof *FDC* * £40
2012 — Proof *FDC* (Issued: 1,656 in sets see PBS15)*

4517 Britannia. One pound. (1/2 oz fine silver) R. Standing figure of Britannia in horse
drawn chariot. (Reverse design: Philip Nathan) (See 4300A above)
2009 — Proof *FDC** £40
2012 — Proof *FDC* (Issued: 1,656 in sets see PBS15)*

4518   4519

4518 Britannia. One pound. (1/2 oz fine silver) R. A design depicting a profile bust of
Britannia wearing a helmet, accompanied by the name 'BRITANNIA', the inscription
'1/2 OUNCE FINE SILVER' and the date '2010'. (Reverse design: Suzie Zamit)
2010 Proof *FDC* * £40
2012 — Proof *FDC* (Issued: 1,656 in sets see PBS15)*

4519 Britannia. One pound. (1/2 oz fine silver) R. A design depicting a seated figure of
Britannia set against a background of a rippling Union Flag accompanied by the words
'1/2 OUNCE FINE SILVER BRITANNIA' and the date '2011'. (Reverse design: David
Mach)
2011 Proof *FDC* (Edition: 5,000 including coins in sets) £40
2012 — Proof *FDC* (Issued: 1,656 in sets see PBS15)*

* *Coins marked thus were originally issued in Royal Mint sets.*

4700

4700 Britannia. One pound. (1/2 oz of fine silver) R. Seated figure of Britannia holding
a trident with a shield at her side and an owl upon her knee with the word
'BRITANNIA' and the date of the year above and the inscription '1/2 OUNCE FINE
SILVER' below the figure of Britannia. (Reverse design: Robert Hunt)
2013 — Proof in silver *FDC* (0.999) (Issued: 3,087 including coins in sets)*

4701

4701 Britannia. One pound. (1/2 oz of fine silver) R. A design of the standing figure of
Britannia baring a trident and shield, with a lion at her feet, set against the backdrop
of a globe , and with the inscription ' BRITANNIA 999 1/2 OZ FINE SILVER 2014'
(Reverse design: Jody Clark)
2014 — Proof in silver *FDC* (0.999) (Edition: 2,300 including coins in sets)*

Obverse portrait by Jody Clark

5020

5020 Britannia. One pound. (1/2 oz of fine silver) R. A figure of Britannia baring a trident and
shield, set against a backdrop of a sailing ship, cliffs and a lighthouse with the inscription
'BRITANNIA 999 1/2 OZ FINE SILVER 2015' (Reverse design: Antony Dufort)
2015 — Proof in silver *FDC* (0.999) (Edition: 2,300 including coins in sets)*

* Coins marked thus were originally issued in Royal Mint sets.

Obverse portrait by Raphael Maklouf

4300

4300 Britannia. Two pounds. (1 oz fine silver) 10th Anniversary of Britannia issue R. The figure of Britannia standing in a chariot drawn along the seashore by two horses, with the word 'BRITANNIA', the inscription. 'ONE OUNCE FINE SILVER' and the date of the year. (Reverse design: Philip Nathan)
1997 Proof *FDC* (Issued: 4,173)..£120

Obverse portrait by Ian Rank-Broadley

4500

4500 Britannia. Two pounds. (1 oz of fine silver) R. The figure of Britannia standing upon a rock in the sea, her right hand grasping a trident and her left hand resting on a shield and holding an olive branch, with the word 'BRITANNIA', the date of the year, and the inscription' ONE OUNCE FINE SILVER'. (Reverse design: Philip Nathan)

1998 (Issued: 88,909).....................£40	2006 (Edition 100,000)............................£40
— Proof *FDC* (Issued: 2,168)......£80	— Proof *FDC* (Issued: 2,529) £65
2000 (Issued: 81,301).....................£40	2012 (Edition 100,000)............................£58
2002 (Issued: 36,543).....................£40	— Proof *FDC* (Issued 5,532 including coins
2004 (Edition: 100,000) £40	in sets) £93
— Proof *FDC* (Issued: 2,174)......£65	

4500A Britannia. Two pounds. (1 oz of fine silver) R. Standing figure of Britannia
2006 – Proof *FDC** with selected gold plating of obverse and reverse (See PBS07) £70
4500B Britannia. Two pounds. (1 oz. of fine silver – 0.999) R. Reverse as 4500 above.
2013 (Issued: 2,387)

* Coins marked thus were originally issued in Royal Mint sets.

4500C Britannia. Two pounds. (1 oz. of fine silver – 0.999) R. As 4500 above but with revised inscription 'BRITANNIA 2014 1 oz. 999 FINE SILVER'
2014
  — (Edition: 10,000) £58
2015 As 2014 but dated 2015
  — (Edition: 10,000) £58
4500D Britannia. Two pounds. (Previously listed as 4500B). (1 oz. of fine silver – 0.999)
2013
  — As 4500 above but with edge decoration of snake design symbolising the Year of the Snake.
4500E Britannia. Two pounds. (1 oz. of fine silver – 0.999)
2014
  — As 4500 above but with edge decoration of horse design symbolising Year of the Horse
4500F Two pounds. Error obverse – known as a Mule. The obverse design of The Queen used for the Year of the Horse £2 Silver coin was paired with the reverse design of the Britannia £2 silver coin.
2014

4501   4502

4501 Britannia. Two pounds. (1oz fine silver) R. Standing figure of Britannia in horse drawn chariot.(Reverse design: Philip Nathan)
1999 (Issued: 69,394)..£40
2009 (Issued: 100,000)..£40
  — Proof *FDC* (Edition: 12,000 including coins in sets)...£65
4501A Britannia. Two pounds. (1 oz of fine silver) R. Standing figure of Britannia in horse drawn chariot
2006 — Proof *FDC** with selected gold plating of obverse and reverse (See PBS07)....£70
4502 Britannia. Two pounds. (1 oz of fine silver) R. The figure of Britannia, as guardian, with a shield in her left hand and a trident in her right hand, accompanied by a lion and, against the background of a wave motif, the words 'ONE OUNCE FINE SILVER' to the left and 'BRITANNIA' and the date of the year to the right. (Reverse design: Philip Nathan)
2001 (Issued: 44,816)..£40
  — Proof *FDC* (Issued: 3,047)..£60
4502A Britannia. Two pounds. (1 oz of fine silver) R. Helmeted figure of Britannia holding a trident and a shield with a lion in the background
2006 — Proof *FDC** with selected gold plating of obverse and reverse (See PBS07)....£70

* Coins marked thus were originally issued in Royal Mint sets.

4503   4504

4503 Britannia. Two pounds. (1oz fine silver) R. Helmeted head of Britannia with, to the left,
the word 'BRITANNIA' and, to the right, the inscription 'ONE OUNCE FINE SILVER'
and the date of the year, ... the whole being overlaid with a wave pattern. (Reverse design:
Philip Nathan)
2003 (Issued: 73,271) £40
— Proof *FDC* (Issued: 2,016) £65
4503A Britannia. Two pounds. (1oz fine silver) R. Helmeted figure of Britannia with stylised waves
2006 — Proof *FDC** with selected gold plating of obverse and reverse (See PBS07) £70
4504 Britannia. Two pounds. (1 oz of fine silver) R. Seated figure of Britannia facing to the
left holding a trident with a shield at her side, with the word 'BRITANNIA', the inscription
'ONE OUNCE FINE SILVER' and the date of the year. (Reverse design: Philip Nathan)
2005 (Edition: 100,000) £40
— Proof *FDC* (Issued: 1,539) £65
4504A Britannia. Two pounds. (1 oz of fine silver) R. Seated figure of Britannia facing left
2006 — Proof *FDC** with selected gold plating of obverse and reverse (See PBS07) £70

4505   4506

4505 Britannia. Two pounds. (1 oz of fine silver) R. Seated figure of Britannia facing right
holding a trident in her right hand and a sprig of olive in the left hand with a lion at her feet
with the inscription 'ONE OUNCE FINE SILVER' and the word 'BRITANNIA' and the
date of the year (See 4505) (Reverse design: Christopher Le Brun)
2007 (Edition: 100,000) £40
— Proof *FDC* (Issued: 5,157 ....£65
4506 Britannia. Two pounds. (1 oz of fine silver) R. A Standing figure of Britannia holding a
trident with a shield at her side, the folds of her dress transforming into a wave, with the word
'BRITANNIA' and the date of the year and the inscription 'ONE OUNCE FINE SILVER'
(Reverse design: John Bergdahl)
2008 (Edition: 100,000) £40
— Proof *FDC* (Edition: 2,500) £65

* Coins marked thus were originally issued in Royal Mint sets.

4507

4507 Britannia. Two pounds. (1 oz fine silver) R. A design depicting a profile bust of Britannia wearing a helmet, accompanied by the name 'BRITANNIA', the inscription 'ONE OUNCE FINE SILVER' and the date '2010'. (Reverse design: Suzie Zamit)
2010 (Edition: 100,000) £40
— Proof *FDC* (Edition: 8,000 including coins in sets)...£65

4508

4508 Britannia. Two pounds. (1 oz fine silver) R. A design depicting a seated figure of Britannia set against a background of a rippling Union Flag accompanied by the words 'ONE OUNCE FINE SILVER BRITANNIA' and the date '2011'.
(Reverse design: David Mach)
2011 (Edition: 500,000) £58
— Proof *FDC* (Edition: 10,000) £90

4509

4509 Britannia. Two pounds. (1 oz of fine silver) R. Seated figure of Britannia holding a trident with a shield at her side and an owl upon her knee with the word 'BRITANNIA' and the date of the year above and the inscription 'ONE OUNCE FINE SILVER' below the figure of Britannia. (Reverse design: Robert Hunt)

2013 — Proof in silver *FDC* (0.999) (Issued: 7,555 including coins in sets) £93

5025

5025 Britannia. Two pounds. (Previously listed as 4540). (1 oz of fine silver) R. A design of the standing figure of Britannia baring a trident and shield, with a lion at her feet, set against the backdrop of a globe, and with the inscription 'BRITANNIA 999 ONE OZ FINE SILVER 2014' (Reverse design: Jody Clark)

2014 — Proof in silver *FDC* (0.999) (Edition: 5,300 including coins in sets) £83

Obverse portrait by Jody Clark

5026

5026 Britannia. Two pounds. (1 oz of fine silver) R. A figure of Britannia baring a
trident and shield, set against a backdrop of a sailing ship, cliffs and a lighthouse
with the inscription 'BRITANNIA 999 1 OZ FINE SILVER 2015'
(Reverse design: Antony Dufort)
2015 — Proof in silver *FDC* (0.999) (Edition: 6,550 including coins in sets) £83

Obverse portrait by Ian Rank-Broadley

4810

4810 Britannia. Ten pounds. (5 oz of fine silver).R. . Seated figure of Britannia holding a
trident with a shield at her side and an owl upon her knee with the word 'BRITANNIA'
and the date of the year above and the inscription 'FIVE OUNCES FINE SILVER'
below the figure of Britannia. (Reverse design: Robert Hunt)
2013 — Proof in silver FDC (0.999) (Issued: 4,054)..£450
Illustration shown at a reduced size - actual coin diameter 63mm

4811

4811 Britannia. Ten pounds. (5 oz. of fine silver) R. A design of the standing figure of
Britannia baring a trident and shield, with a lion at her feet, set against the backdrop
of a globe, and with the inscription 'BRITANNIA 999.9 FIVE OZ FINE SILVER 2014'
(Reverse design: Jody Clark)
2014 — Proof in silver *FDC* (0.999) (Edition: 1,350) £395
Illustration shown at a reduced size - actual coin diameter 63mm

Obverse portrait by Jody Clark

4812

4812 Britannia. Ten pounds. (5 oz. of fine silver). R. A figure of Britannia baring a trident and
shield, set against a backdrop of a sailing ship, cliffs and a lighthouse with the inscription
'BRITANNIA 999 FIVE OZ FINE SILVER 2015' (Reverse design: Antony Dufort)
2015 — Proof in silver *FDC* (0.999) (Edition: 1,150) £395
Illustration shown at reduced size – actual coin diameter 63mm

Obverse portrait by Ian Rank-Broadley
4820 Britannia. Fifty pounds. (1 kilo of fine silver). R. A design of the figure of Britannia
on a textured background standing upon a rock in the sea, her right hand grasping a
trident and her left hand on a shield and holding an olive branch, with the inscription
'BRITANNIA' (and the date of the year) 1KILO OF 999 FINE SILVER' (Original
reverse design: Philip Nathan)
2014

Obverse portrait by Ian Rank-Broadley

4740

4740 **Britannia. 50 pence.** (1/40 oz. of fine gold) R. A design of the standing figure of Britannia baring a trident and shield, with a lion at her feet, set against the backdrop of a globe, and with the inscription 'BRITANNIA 999.9 1/40 OZ FINE GOLD 2014' (Reverse design: Jody Clark)

2014 — Proof in gold *FDC* (0.9999) (Edition: 10,000 including coins in sets)*

Illustration shown larger than actual coin diameter of 8mm

Obverse portrait by Jody Clark

5030

5030 **Britannia. 50 pence.** (1/40 oz. of fine gold)..R. A figure of Britannia baring a trident and shield, set against a backdrop of a sailing ship, cliffs and a lighthouse with the inscription 'BRITANNIA 999 1/40 OZ FINE GOLD 2015' (Reverse design: Antony Dufort)

2015 — Proof in gold *FDC* (0.9999) (Edition: 8,000 including coins in sets)* £50

Illustration shown larger than actual coin diameter of 8mm

Obverse portrait by Ian Rank-Broadley

4775   4776

4775 **Britannia. One pound.** (1/20 oz of fine gold) R. Seated figure of Britannia holding a trident with a shield at her side and an owl upon her knee with the word 'BRITANNIA' and the date of the year above and the inscription '1/20 OUNCE FINE GOLD' below the figure of Britannia. (Reverse design: Robert Hunt)

2013 — Proof in gold *FDC* (0.9999) (Issued: 2,496 including coins in sets)

4776 **Britannia. One pound.** (1/20 oz of fine gold) R. A design of the standing figure of Britannia baring a trident and shield, with a lion at her feet, set against the backdrop of a globe , and with the inscription ' BRITANNIA 999.9 1/20 OZ FINE GOLD 2014' (Reverse design: Jody Clark)

2014 — Proof in gold *FDC* (0.9999) (Edition: 1,550 including coins in sets)* £100

Obverse portrait by Jody Clark

5035

5035 **Britannia. One pound.**(1/20 oz of fine gold)..R. A figure of Britannia baring a trident and shield, set against a backdrop of a sailing ship, cliffs and a lighthouse with the inscription 'BRITANNIA 999 1/20 OZ FINE GOLD 2015' (Reverse design: Antony Dufort)

2015 — Proof in gold *FDC* (0.9999) (Edition: 1,550 including coins in sets)* £100

* Coins marked thus were originally issued in Royal Mint sets.

NB. The spot price of gold at the time of going to press was £720 per oz.

Obverse portrait by Raphael Maklouf

4296   4298

4296 Britannia. Ten pounds. (1/10oz of fine gold alloyed with copper). R. The figure of
Britannia standing upon a rock in the sea, her right hand grasping a trident and her left
hand resting on a shield and holding an olive branch, with the inscription '1/10 OUNCE
FINE GOLD BRITANNIA' and the year of the date. (Reverse design: Philip Nathan)

1987.. £130   1989 ....£130
— Proof *FDC* (Issued: 3,500).... £150   — Proof *FDC* (Issued: 1,609) £150
1988.. £130
— Proof *FDC* (Issued: 2,694).... £150

4297 Britannia. Ten pounds. (1/10oz of fine gold alloyed with silver). R. Britannia standing.

1990.. £130   1994 ....£130
— Proof *FDC* (Issued: 1,571).... £150   — Proof *FDC* (Issued: 994) £150
1991.. £130   1995 ....£130
— Proof *FDC* (Issued: 954)....... £150   — Proof *FDC* (Issued: 1,500) £150
1992.. £130   1996 ....£130
— Proof *FDC* (Issued: 1,000).... £150   — Proof *FDC* (Issued: 2,379) £150
1993.. £130
— Proof *FDC* (Issued: 997)....... £150

4298 Britannia. Ten pounds. (1/10 oz fine gold, alloyed with silver) 10th Anniversary of
Britannia issue. R. The figure of Britannia standing in a chariot drawn along the seashore
by two horses, with the word 'BRITANNIA', .the inscription '1/10 OUNCE FINE GOLD'
and the date of the year. (Reverse design: Philip Nathan)

1997 Proof *FDC* (Issued: 1,821)..£180

Obverse portrait by Ian Rank-Broadley

4480

4480 Britannia. Ten pounds. (1/10 oz fine gold alloyed with silver) R. The figure of Britannia
standing upon a rock in the sea, Her right hand grasping a trident and her left hand resting
on a shield and holding an olive branch, with the word 'BRITANNIA', the date of the year,
and the inscription '1/10 OUNCE FINE GOLD'. (Reverse design: Philip Nathan)

1998 Proof *FDC* (Issued: 392)...... £150   2002 Proof *FDC* (Issued: 1,500) £150
1999.. £130   2004 ....£130
1999 Proof *FDC* (Issued: 1,058)... £150   2004 Proof *FDC* (Issued: 929) £150
2000.. £130   2006 Proof *FDC* (issued: 700).................£150
2000 Proof *FDC* (Issued: 659)...... £150   2012 ....£150
2002.. £130   2012 Proof *FDC* (Issued: 1,249) £225

* Coins marked thus were originally issued in Royal Mint sets.
NB. The spot price of gold at the time of going to press was £720 per oz.

4481   4482   4483   4484

4481 **Britannia. Ten pounds.** (1/10 oz fine gold alloyed with silver) R. The figure of Britannia, as guardian, with a shield in her left hand and a trident in her right hand, accompanied by a lion and, against the background of a wave motif, and the words '1/10 OUNCE FINE GOLD' to the left and 'BRITANNIA' and the date of the year to the right. (Reverse design: Philip Nathan)
2001 .... £130   2001 Proof *FDC* (Issued: 1,557) £150

4482 **Britannia. Ten pounds.** (1/10 oz fine gold alloyed with silver) R. . Helmeted head of Britannia with, to the left, the word 'BRITANNIA' and, to the right, the inscription '1/10 OUNCE FINE GOLD' and the date of the year, the whole being overlaid with a wave pattern. (Reverse design: Philip Nathan)
2003 .... £130   2003 Proof *FDC* (Issued: 1,382) £150

4483 **Britannia. Ten pounds.** (1/10 oz fine gold alloyed with silver) R. Seated figure of Britannia facing to the left holding a trident with a shield at her side, with the word 'BRITANNIA', the inscription '1/10 OUNCE FINE GOLD' and the date of the year. (Reverse design: Philip Nathan)
2005 Proof *FDC* (issued: 1,225) £150

4484 **Britannia. Ten pounds.** (1/10 oz fine gold alloyed with silver) R. Seated figure of Britannia facing right holding a trident in her right hand and a sprig of olive in the left hand with a lion at her feet with the inscription '1/10 OUNCE FINE GOLD' and the word 'BRITANNIA' and the date of the year. (Reverse design: Christopher Le Brun)
2007 .... £130   2007 Proof *FDC* (Issued: 893) £150

4484A (1/10 oz platinum)
2007 Proof *FDC* (Issued: 691) £225

4485   4486   4487

4485 **Britannia. Ten pounds.** (1/10 oz fine gold alloyed with silver) R. A Standing figure of Britannia holding a trident with a shield at her side, the folds of her dress transforming into a wave, with the word 'BRITANNIA' and the date of the year and the inscription '1/10 OUNCE FINE GOLD' (Reverse design: John Bergdahl)
2008 Proof *FDC* (Issued: 748 plus coins issued in sets, see PBS30) £150

4485A (1/10 oz platinum)
2008 Proof *FDC* (Issued: 268 plus coins issued in sets, see PPBCS2) £225

4486 **Britannia. Ten pounds.** (1/10 oz fine gold alloyed with silver) R. Standing figure of Britannia in horse drawn chariot.
2009 .... £130   2009 Proof *FDC* (Edition: 750) £160

4487 **Britannia. Ten pounds.** (1/10 oz fine gold alloyed with silver) R. A design depicting a profile bust of Britannia wearing a helmet, accompanied by the name 'BRITANNIA', the inscription '1/10 OUNCE FINE GOLD' and the date '2010'. (Reverse design: Suzie Zamit)
2010 Proof *FDC* (Edition: 3,000 including coins in sets) £160

4488 **Britannia. Ten pounds.** (1/10 oz fine gold alloyed with silver) R. A design depicting a seated figure of Britannia set against a background of a rippling Union Flag accompanied by the words '1/10 OUNCE FINE GOLD BRITANNIA, and the date '2011'. (Reverse design: David Mach)
2011 Proof *FDC* (Edition: 8,000 including coins in sets) £225

* Coins marked thus were originally issued in Royal Mint sets.
NB. The spot price of gold at the time of going to press was £720 per oz.

4489   4490

4489 Britannia. Ten pounds. (1/10 oz of fine gold) R. Seated figure of Britannia holding a trident with a shield at her side and an owl upon her knee with the word 'BRITANNIA' and the date of the year above and the inscription '1/10 OUNCE FINE GOLD' below the figure of Britannia. (Reverse design: Robert Hunt)

2013 — Proof in gold *FDC* (0.9999) (Issued: 1,150 including coins in sets)*

4490 Britannia. Ten pounds. (1/10 oz of fine gold) R. A design of the standing figure of Britannia baring a trident and shield, with a lion at her feet, set against the backdrop of a globe, and with the inscription 'BRITANNIA 999.9 1/10 OZ FINE GOLD 2014' (Reverse design: Jody Clark)

2014 — Proof in gold *FDC* (0.9999) (Edition: 650 including coins in sets)*

Obverse portrait by Jody Clark

5040

5040 Britannia. Ten pounds. (1/10 oz of fine gold)..R. A figure of Britannia baring a trident and shield, set against a backdrop of a sailing ship, cliffs and a lighthouse with the inscription 'BRITANNIA 999 1/10 OZ FINE GOLD 2015' (Reverse design: Antony Dufort)

2015 — Proof in gold *FDC* (0.9999)

Obverse portrait by Raphael Maklouf

4291

4291 Britannia. Twenty five pounds. (1/4oz of fine gold alloyed with copper). R. The figure of Britannia standing upon a rock in the sea, her right hand grasping a trident and her left hand resting on a shield and holding an olive branch, with the inscription '1/4 OUNCE FINE GOLD BRITANNIA' and the year of the date. (Reverse design: Philip Nathan)

1987	£325	1989	£325
— Proof *FDC* (Issued: 3,500)	£350	— Proof *FDC* (see PBS05)*	£350
1988	£325		
— Proof *FDC* (see PBS03)*	£350		

* Coins marked thus were originally issued in Royal Mint sets.
NB. The spot price of gold at the time of going to press was £720 per oz.

4292 Britannia. Twenty five pounds. (1/4oz of fine gold alloyed with silver). R. Britannia standing.

1990 .... £325	1994 .... £325
— Proof *FDC* (see PBS07)* £350	— Proof *FDC* (see PBS11)* £350
1991 .... £325	1995 .... £325
— Proof *FDC* (see PBS08)* £350	— Proof *FDC* (see PBS12)* £350
1992 .... £325	1996 .... £325
— Proof *FDC* (see PBS09)* £350	— Proof *FDC* (see PBS13 .... £350
1993 .... £325	
— Proof *FDC* (see PBS10)* £350	

4293

4293 Britannia. Twenty five pounds. (1/4 oz fine gold, alloyed with silver) 10th Anniversary of Britannia issue. R. The figure of Britannia standing in a chariot drawn along the seashore by two horses, with the word 'BRITANNIA', ..the inscription. '1/4 OUNCE FINE GOLD' and the date of the year. (Reverse design: Philip Nathan)

1997 Proof *FDC* (Issued: 923) £350

Obverse portrait by Ian Rank-Broadley

4470

4470 Britannia. Twenty five pounds. (1/4 oz fine gold alloyed with silver) R. The figure of Britannia standing upon a rock in the sea, her right hand grasping a trident and her left hand resting on a shield and holding an olive branch, with the word 'BRITANNIA', the date of the year, and the inscription' 1/4 OUNCE FINE GOLD'. (Reverse design: Philip Nathan)

1998 Proof *FDC* (Issued: 560) £350	2002 Proof *FDC* (Issued: 750) £350
1999 .... £325	2004 Proof *FDC* (Issued: 750) £350
1999 Proof *FDC* (Issued: 1,000)... £350	2006 Proof *FDC* (Edition: 1,000)............ £350
2000 .... £325	2012 Proof *FDC* (Issued: 316) £500
2000 Proof *FDC* (Issued: 500) £350	

* *Coins marked thus were originally issued in Royal Mint sets.*
NB. The spot price of gold at the time of going to press was £720 per oz.

4471   4472

4471 Britannia. Twenty five pounds. (1/4 oz fine gold alloyed with silver) R. The figure of Britannia, as guardian, with a shield in her left hand and a trident in her right hand, accompanied by a lion and, against the background of a wave motif, the words '1/4 OUNCE FINE GOLD' to the left and 'BRITANNIA' and the date of the year to the right. (Reverse design: Philip Nathan)

2001 .... £325   2006 Proof *FDC* (see PBS28)* £350
2001 Proof *FDC* (Issued: 500)...... £350

4472 Britannia. Twenty five pounds. (1/4 oz fine gold alloyed with silver) R. Helmeted head of Britannia with, to the left, the word 'BRITANNIA' and, to the right, the inscription '1/4 OUNCE FINE GOLD' and the date of the year, the whole being overlaid with a wave pattern. (Reverse design: Philip Nathan)

2003 Proof *FDC* (Issued: 609)...... £325   2006 Proof *FDC* (see PBS28)* £350

4473 Britannia. Twenty five pounds. (1/4 oz fine gold alloyed with silver) R. Seated figure of Britannia facing to the left holding a trident with a shield at her side, with the word 'BRITANNIA', the inscription '1/4 OUNCE FINE GOLD' and the date of the year. (Reverse design: Philip Nathan)

2005 Proof *FDC* (Issued: 750) .....£325   2006 Proof *FDC* (seePBS28)* £350

4474 Britannia. Twenty five pounds. (1/4 oz fine gold alloyed with silver) R. Standing figure of Britannia in horse drawn chariot. (See 4293)

2006 Proof *FDC* (see PBS28)* ....£325   2009 Proof *FDC* (Edition: 1,000) £350

4475 Britannia. Twenty five pounds. (Previously listed as 4474) (1/4 oz fine gold alloyed with silver) R. Seated figure of Britannia facing right holding a trident in her right hand and a sprig of olive in the left hand with a lion at her feet with the inscription '1/4 OUNCE FINE GOLD' and the word 'BRITANNIA' and the date of the year. (Reverse design: Christopher Le Brun)

2007 ....£325   2007 Proof *FDC* (Issued: 1,000) £350

4475A (1/4 oz platinum)
2007 Proof *FDC* (Issued: 210) £450

4475   4476

4476 Britannia. Twenty five pounds. (1/4 oz fine gold alloyed with silver) R. A Standing figure of Britannia holding a trident with a shield at her side, the folds of her dress transforming into a wave, with the word 'BRITANNIA' and the date of the year and the inscription '1/4 OUNCE FINE GOLD' (Reverse design: John Bergdahl)

2008 Proof *FDC* (Edition: 1,000) £350

4476A (1/4 oz platinum)
2008 Proof *FDC* (Edition: 500) £450

4477   4479

4477 **Britannia. Twenty five pounds.** (1/4 oz fine gold alloyed with silver) R. A design
depicting a profile bust of Britannia wearing a helmet, accompanied by the name
'BRITANNIA', the inscription '1/4 OUNCE FINE GOLD' and the date '2010'. (Reverse
design: Suzie Zamit)
2010 Proof *FDC* (Edition: 3,000 including coins in sets)..£350

4478 **Britannia. Twenty Five pounds.** (1/4 oz fine gold alloyed with silver) R. A design
depicting a seated figure of Britannia set against a background of a rippling Union Flag
accompanied by the words ' 1/4 OUNCE FINE GOLD BRITANNIA, and the date
'2011'. (Reverse design: David Mach)
2011 Proof *FDC* (Edition: 7,000 including coins in sets) £500

4479 **Britannia. Twenty five pounds.** (1/4 oz of fine gold) R. Seated figure of Britannia
holding a trident with a shield at her side and an owl upon her knee with the word
'BRITANNIA' and the date of the year above and the inscription '1/4 OUNCE FINE
GOLD' below the figure of Britannia. (Reverse design: Robert Hunt)
2013 — Proof in gold *FDC* (0.9999) (Edition: 875 including coins in sets)*

5045

5045 Britannia. Twenty five pounds. (Previously listed as 4480). (1/4 oz of fine gold) R. A
design of the standing figure of Britannia baring a trident and shield, with a lion at her
feet, set against the backdrop of a globe , and with the inscription ' BRITANNIA 999.9
1/4 OZ FINE GOLD 2014' (Reverse design: Jody Clark) ....
2014 — Proof in gold *FDC* (0.9999) (Edition: 650 including coins in sets)*

5046

5046 Britannia. Twenty five pounds.(1/4 oz of fine gold). R. A figure of Britannia baring a
trident and shield, set against a backdrop of a sailing ship, cliffs and a lighthouse
with the inscription 'BRITANNIA 999 1/4 OZ FINE GOLD 2015' (Reverse design:
Antony Dufort) ....
2015 – Proof in gold *FDC* (0.9999) (Edition: 450 including coins in sets)*

* Coins marked thus were originally issued in Royal Mint sets.
NB. The spot price of gold at the time of going to press was £720 per oz.

Obverse portrait by Raphael Maklouf

4286

4286 Britannia. Fifty pounds. (1/2oz of fine gold alloyed with copper). R. The figure of
Britannia standing upon a rock in the sea, her right hand grasping a trident and her left
hand resting on a shield and holding an olive branch, with the inscription '1/2 OUNCE
FINE GOLD BRITANNIA' and the year of the date. (Reverse design: Philip Nathan)

1987... £650	1989 ....£650	
— Proof *FDC* (Issued: 2,486).... £700	— Proof *FDC* (see PBS05)* £700	
1988.. £650		
— Proof *FDC* (see PBS03)* £700		

4288

4287 Britannia. Fifty pounds. (1/2oz of fine gold, alloyed with Silver). R. Britannia standing.

1990.. £650	1994 ....£650	
— Proof *FDC* (see PBS07)* £700	— Proof *FDC* (see PBS11)*................£700	
1991.. £650	1995 ....£650	
— Proof *FDC* (see PBS08)* £700	— Proof *FDC* (see PBS12)* £700	
1992.. £650	1996 ....£650	
— Proof *FDC* (see PBS09)* £700	— Proof *FDC* (see PBS13)* £700	
1993.. £650		
— Proof *FDC* (see PBS10)* £700		

4288 Britannia. Fifty pounds. (1/2 oz fine gold, alloyed with silver) 10th Anniversary of
Britannia issue. R.The figure of Britannia standing in a chariot drawn along the seashore
by two horses, with the word 'BRITANNIA', the inscription. '1/2 FINE GOLD' and the
date of the year. (Reverse design: Philip Nathan)
1997 Proof *FDC* (see PBS14)* £700

* Coins marked thus were originally issued in Royal Mint sets.
NB. The spot price of gold at the time of going to press was £720 per oz.

Obverse portrait by Ian Rank-Broadley

4460   4461

4460 **Britannia. Fifty pounds.** (1/2 oz fine gold alloyed with silver). R̟. The figure of Britannia standing upon a rock in the sea, her right hand grasping a trident and her left hand resting on a shield and holding an olive branch, with the word 'BRITANNIA', the date of the year, and the inscription' 1/2 OUNCE FINE GOLD'. (Reverse design: Philip Nathan)

1998 Proof *FDC* (see PBS15)* £700	2002 Proof *FDC* (see PBS19)* £700
1999..£650	2004 Proof *FDC* (see PBS23)* £700
1999 Proof *FDC* (see PBS16)* £700	2006 Proof *FDC* (see PBS27)* £700
2000..£650	2012 Proof *FDC* (Edition: 1,000) £700
— Proof *FDC* (see PBS17)* £700	

4461 **Britannia. Fifty pounds.** (1/2 oz fine gold alloyed with silver). R̟. The figure of Britannia, as guardian, with a shield in her left hand and a trident in her right hand, accompanied by a lion and, against the background of a wave motif, the words '1/2 OUNCE FINE GOLD' to the left and 'BRITANNIA' and the date of the year to the right. (Reverse design: Philip Nathan)

2001 ....£650   2001 Proof *FDC* (see PBS18)* £700

4463   4464

4462 **Britannia. Fifty pounds.** (1/2 oz fine gold alloyed with silver) R. Helmeted head of Britannia with, to the left, the word 'BRITANNIA' and, to the right, the inscription '1/2 OUNCE FINE GOLD' and the date of the year, ...the whole being overlaid with a wave pattern. (Reverse design: Philip Nathan)

2003 ....£650   2003 Proof *FDC* (see PBS20)* £700

4463 **Britannia. Fifty pounds.** (1/2 oz fine gold alloyed with silver) R. Seated figure of Britannia facing to the left holding a trident with a shield at her side, with the word 'BRITANNIA', the inscription '1/2 OUNCE FINE GOLD' and the date of the year. (Reverse design: Philip Nathan)

2005 Proof *FDC* * £700

4464 **Britannia. Fifty pounds.** (1/2 oz fine gold alloyed with silver) R. Seated figure of Britannia facing right holding a trident in her right hand and a sprig of olive in the left hand with a lion at her feet with the inscription '1/2 OUNCE FINE GOLD' and the word 'BRITANNIA' and the date of the year (See 4505) (Reverse design: Christopher Le Brun)

2007 ....£650   2007 Proof *FDC* (see PBS29)* £700

4464A (½ oz platinum)

2007 Proof *FDC* * (see 2007 set, PPBCS1)...£800

* Coins marked thus were originally issued in Royal Mint sets.
NB. The spot price of gold at the time of going to press was £720 per oz.

4465   4466   4467

4465 Britannia. Fifty pounds. (1/2 oz fine gold alloyed with silver) R. A Standing figure of
       Britannia holding a trident with a shield at her side, the folds of her dress transforming
       into a wave, with the word 'BRITANNIA' and the date of the year and the inscription '1/2
       OUNCE FINE GOLD' (Reverse design: John Bergdahl)
       2008 Proof *FDC* * £700

4465A (1/2 oz platinum)
       2008 Proof *FDC* (see PPBCS2)* £800

4466 Britannia. Fifty pounds. (1/2oz fine gold alloyed with silver) R.Standing figure of
       Britannia in horse drawn chariot.(see 4288 above)
       2009.. £650   2009 Proof *FDC* (see PBS31)* £700

4467 Britannia. Fifty pounds. (1/2 oz fine gold alloyed with silver) R. A design depicting a
       profile bust of Britannia wearing a helmet, accompanied by the name 'BRITANNIA', the
       inscription '1/2 OUNCE FINE GOLD' and the date '2010' (Reverse design: Suzie Zamit)
       2010 Proof *FDC* (Edition: 1,750 in sets)* £700

4468 Britannia. Fifty pounds. (1/2 oz fine gold alloyed with silver) R. A design depicting a
       seated figure of Britannia set against a background of a rippling Union Flag accompanied
       by the words ' 1/2 OUNCE FINE GOLD BRITANNIA, and the date '2011'. (Reverse
       design: David Mach)
       2011 Proof *FDC* (Edition: 2,000 including coins in sets)*... £700

4469   5050

4469 Britannia. Fifty pounds. (1/2 oz of fine gold) R. Seated figure of Britannia holding a trident
      with a shield at her side and an owl upon her knee with the word 'BRITANNIA' and the and
      the inscription '1/2 OUNCE FINE GOLD' and the date '2013' below the figure of Britannia.
      (Reverse design: Robert Hunt)
      2013 — Proof in gold *FDC* (0.9999) (Edition: 525 including coins in sets)*

5050 Britannia. Fifty pounds. (Previously listed as 4470). (1/2 oz of fine gold)..R. A design of
      the standing figure of Britannia baring a trident and shield, with a lion at her feet, set against
      the backdrop of a globe, and with the inscription 'BRITANNIA 999.9 1/2 OZ FINE GOLD
      2014'. (Reverse design: Jody Clark)
      2014 — Proof in gold *FDC* (0.9999) (Edition: 500 including coins in sets)*

* Coins marked thus were originally issued in Royal Mint sets.
NB. The spot price of gold at the time of going to press was £720 per oz.

Obverse portrait by Jody Clark

5051

5051 Britannia. Fifty pounds. (1/2 oz. of fine gold). R. A figure of Britannia baring a trident and shield, set against a backdrop of a sailing ship, cliffs and a lighthouse with the inscription 'BRITANNIA 999 1/2 OZ FINE GOLD 2015' (Reverse design: Antony Dufort)
2015 – Proof in gold *FDC* (0.9999) (Edition: 450 including coins in sets)*

Obverse portrait by Raphael Maklouf

4281

4281 Britannia. One hundred pounds. (1oz of fine gold alloyed with copper) R. The figure of Britannia standing upon a rock in the sea, her right hand grasping a trident and her left hand resting on a shield and holding an olive branch, with the inscription ...'ONE OUNCE FINE GOLD BRITANNIA' and the year of the date. (Reverse design: Philip Nathan)

1987... £1300	1989 ....£1300
— Proof *FDC* (Issued: 2,485)..£1350	— Proof *FDC* (Issued: 338) £1350
1988... £1300	
— Proof *FDC* (Issued: 626)..... £1350	

4282 Britannia. One hundred pounds. (1oz of fine gold alloyed with silver) R. Britannia standing.

1990... £1300	1994 ....£1300
— Proof *FDC* (Issued: 262)**. £1350	— Proof *FDC* (see PBS11)*...............£1350
1991... £1300	1995 ....£1300
— Proof *FDC* (Issued: 143)**. £1350	— Proof *FDC* (see PBS12)* £1350
1992... £1300	1996 ....£1300
— Proof *FDC* (see PBS09)* £1350	— Proof *FDC* (see PBS13)* £1350
1993... £1300	
— Proof *FDC* (see PBS10)* £1350	

* *Coins marked thus were originally issued in Royal Mint sets.*
** *Where numbers of coins are quoted, these refer to individual coins. Additional coins were included in sets which are listed in the appropriate section.*
NB. The spot price of gold at the time of going to press was £720 per oz.

4283

4283 Britannia. One Hundred pounds. (1 oz of fine gold, alloyed with silver) 10th
Anniversary of Britannia issue. ℞. The figure of Britannia standing in a chariot drawn
along the seashore by two horses, with the word 'BRITANNIA', the inscription. 'ONE
OUNCE FINE GOLD' and the date of the year. (Reverse design: Philip Nathan)
1997... £1400   1997 Proof *FDC* (Issued: 164) £1600

Obverse portrait by Ian Rank-Broadley

4450   4451

4450 Britannia. One Hundred pounds. (1oz fine gold alloyed with silver) ℞. The figure of
Britannia standing upon a rock in the sea, her right hand grasping a trident and her left hand
resting on a shield and holding an olive branch, with the word 'BRITANNIA', the date of the
year, and the inscription' ONE OUNCE FINE GOLD'. (Reverse design: Philip Nathan)

1998 Proof *FDC* (see PBS15)* ... £1350	2004 ....£1300
1999............................... £1300	2004 Proof *FDC* (see PBS23)* £1350
1999 Proof *FDC* (see PBS16)* ... £1350	2006 Proof *FDC* (see PBS27)* £1350
2000............................... £1300	2012 ....£1300
2000 Proof *FDC* (see PBS17)* ... £1350	2012 Proof *FDC* (see PBS36) £1500
2002 Proof *FDC* (see PBS19)* ... £1350	

4450A(1 oz fine gold – 0.9999) R. As 4450 above
2013
4450B(1 oz fine gold – 0.9999) R. As 4450 above but with revised inscription 'BRITANNIA
2014 1 oz 999.9 FINE GOLD'
4451 Britannia. One Hundred pounds. (1oz fine gold alloyed with silver) R. The figure of Britannia,
as guardian, with a shield in her left hand and a trident in her right hand, accompanied by a lion
and, against the background of a wave motif, the words 'ONE OUNCE FINE GOLD' to the left
and 'BRITANNIA' and the date of the year to the right. (Reverse design: Philip Nathan)
2001... £1300   2001 Proof *FDC* (see PBS18)* £1350

* Coins marked thus were originally issued in Royal Mint sets.
NB. The spot price of gold at the time of going to press was £720 per oz.

4452   4453

4452 Britannia. One Hundred pounds. (1oz fine gold alloyed with silver) ℞. Helmeted head
of Britannia with, to the left, the word 'BRITANNIA' and, to the right, the inscription
'ONE OUNCE FINE GOLD' and the date of the year, the whole being overlaid with a
wave pattern. (Reverse design: Philip Nathan)
2003..£1300   2003 Proof *FDC* (see PBS20)* £1350

4453 Britannia. One Hundred pounds. (1oz fine gold alloyed with silver) ℞. Seated figure
of Britannia facing to the left holding a trident with a shield at her side, with the word
'BRITANNIA', the inscription 'ONE OUNCE FINE GOLD' and the date of the year.
(Reverse design: Philip Nathan)
2005 Proof *FDC* (see PBS25)* £1350

4454   4455

4454 Britannia. One Hundred pounds. (1 oz fine gold alloyed with silver) ℞. Seated figure
of Britannia facing right holding a trident in her right hand and a sprig of olive in the left
hand with a lion at her feet with the inscription 'ONE OUNCE FINE GOLD' and the word
'BRITANNIA' and the date of the year (See 4505) (Reverse design: Christopher Le Brun)
2007..£1300   2007 Proof *FDC* (see PBS29)* £1350

4454A(1 oz platinum)
2007 Proof *FDC* (see 2007 set, PPBCS1)*..£1500

4455 Britannia. One Hundred pounds. (1oz fine gold alloyed with silver) ℞. A Standing figure
of Britannia holding a trident with a shield at her side, the folds of her dress transforming
into a wave, with the word 'BRITANNIA', and the date of the year, and the inscription
'ONE OUNCE FINE GOLD' (Reverse design: John Bergdahl)
2008..£1300   2008 Proof *FDC* (see PBS30)* £1350

4455A(1 oz platinum)
2008 Proof *FDC* (see 2008 set, PPBCS2)*..£1500

* Coins marked thus were originally issued in Royal Mint sets.
NB. The spot price of gold at the time of going to press was £720 per oz.

4456   4457

4456 Britannia. One Hundred pounds. (1oz fine gold alloyed with silver) ℞. Standing figure
of Britannia in horse drawn chariot.
2009...£1300   2009 Proof *FDC* (see PBS31)* £1350

4457 Britannia. One Hundred pounds. (1oz fine gold alloyed with silver) ℞. A design
depicting **a** profile bust of Britannia wearing a helmet, accompanied by the name
'BRITANNIA', the inscription 'ONE OUNCE FINE GOLD' and the date '2010'.
(Reverse design: Suzie Zamit)
2010 ....£1300   2010 Proof *FDC* (Edition: 1,250 in sets)*£1350

4458

4458 Britannia. One Hundred pounds. (1 oz fine gold alloyed with silver) ℞. A design
depicting a seated figure of Britannia set against a background of a rippling Union Flag
accompanied by the words 'ONE OUNCE FINE GOLD BRITANNIA, and the date
'2011'. (Reverse design: David Mach)
2011 Proof *FDC (*Edition: 3,000 including coins in sets) * £1500

* Coins marked thus were originally issued in Royal Mint sets.
NB. The spot price of gold at the time of going to press was £720 per oz.

4459

4459 **Britannia. One Hundred pounds.** (1 oz. of fine gold) R. Seated figure of Britannia holding a trident with a shield at her side and an owl upon her knee with the word 'BRITANNIA' and 'ONE OUNCE FINE GOLD' and the date '2013' below the figure of Britannia. (Reverse design: Robert Hunt)

2013 — Proof in gold *FDC* (0.9999) (Edition: 400 including coins in sets)*

5055

5055 **Britannia. One Hundred pounds.** (Previously listed as 4460). 1 oz of fine gold) R. A design of the standing figure of Britannia baring a trident and shield, with a lion at her feet, set against the backdrop of a globe, and with the inscription 'BRITANNIA 999.9 ONE OZ FINE GOLD 2014'.(Reverse design: Jody Clark)

2014 — Proof in gold *FDC* (0.9999) (Edition: 400 including coins in sets)*

Obverse portrait by Jody Clark

5056

5056 **Britannia. One Hundred pounds.** (1 oz of fine gold). R. A figure of Britannia baring a trident and shield, set against a backdrop of a sailing ship, cliffs and a lighthouse with the inscription 'BRITANNIA 999 ONE OZ FINE GOLD 2015' (Reverse design: Antony Dufort)

2015 – Proof in gold *FDC* (0.9999) (Edition: 400 including coins in sets)*

* *Coins marked thus were originally issued in Royal Mint sets.*
NB. The spot price of gold at the time of going to press was £720 per oz.

Obverse portrait by Ian Rank-Broadley

4800

4800 Britannia. Five Hundred pounds. (5 oz of fine gold) R. Seated figure of Britannia
holding a trident with a shield at her side and an owl upon her knee with the word
'BRITANNIA' and '5 oz. FINE GOLD' and the date '2013' below the figure of
Britannia. (Reverse design: Robert Hunt) (Reverse design: Robert Hunt)
2013 — Proof in gold *FDC* (0.9999) (Issued: 61) £8200

4801

4801 Britannia. Five Hundred pounds. (5 oz of fine gold) R A design of the standing figure
of Britannia baring a trident and shield, with a lion at her feet, set against the backdrop
of a globe, and with the inscription 'BRITANNIA 999.9 FIVE OZ FINE GOLD 2014'.
(Reverse design: Jody Clark)
2014 — Proof in gold *FDC* (0.9999) (Edition: 75)...£7500

4802 Britannia. Five Hundred pounds. (5 oz of fine gold).R A figure of Britannia baring
a trident and shield, set against a backdrop of a sailing ship, cliffs and a lighthouse
with the inscription 'BRITANNIA 999 FIVE OZ FINE GOLD 2015'
(Reverse design: Antony Dufort)
2015 — Proof in gold *FDC* (Edition: 60)..£7500
Illustration shown at reduced size – actual coin diameter 65mm

5100

5100 **Two pounds.** (Previously lisyed as 4830). (1 oz 0.999 fine silver). R. A design depicting a horse prancing past the Uffington chalk white horse, with the inscription 'YEAR OF THE HORSE. 2014' and the Chinese symbol for horse. (Reverse design: Wuon-Gean Ho)
2014 — Proof in silver *FDC* (Edition: 8,888) £83

5100A **Two pounds. Error obverse – known as a Mule.** The obverse design of The Queen used for the £2 Silver Britannia uncirculated coin was paired with the reverse design of the Year of the Horse £2 silver coin.
2014

5101

5101 **Two pounds.** (Previously listed as 4831). ((1 oz 0.999 fine silver). R. Design depicting two Swaledale sheep, with the inscription 'YEAR OF THE SHEEP 2015' and the Chinese symbol for sheep. (Reverse design: Wuon-Gean Ho)
2015
— Proof in silver *FDC* (Edition: 9,888) £83
— Proof in silver with gold plating *FDC* (Edition: 4,888) £110

5120

5120 **Ten pounds.** (Previously listed as 4840). (5 oz 0.999 fine silver). R. A design depicting a horse prancing past the Uffington chalk white horse, with the inscription 'YEAR OF THE HORSE. 2014' and the Chinese symbol for horse. (Reverse design: Wuon-Gean Ho)
2014 — Proof in silver *FDC* (Edition; 1,488) £450
Illustration shown at reduced size - actual coin diameter 65mm

5121

5121 **Ten pounds.** (Previously listed as 4841). (5 oz 0.999 fine silver). R. Design depicting two Swaledale sheep, with the inscription 'YEAR OF THE SHEEP 2015' and the Chinese symbol for sheep. (Reverse design: Wuon-Gean Ho)
2015
— Proof in silver *FDC* (Edition: 1,088) £395
Illustration shown at reduced size - actual coin diameter 65mm

5140

5140 **Ten pounds.** (Previously listed as 4860). (1/10 oz 0.9999 fine gold). R. A design depicting a horse prancing past the Uffington chalk white horse, with the inscription 'YEAR OF THE HORSE. 2014' and the Chinese symbol for horse. (Reverse design: Wuon-Gean Ho) 2014 — BU (Edition; 2,888) £225

5141

5141 **Ten pounds.** (Previously listed as 4861). (1/10 oz 0.9999 fine gold). R. Design depicting two Swaledale sheep, with the inscription 'YEAR OF THE SHEEP 2015' and the Chinese symbol for sheep. (Reverse design: Wuon-Gean Ho) 2015 — BU (Edition: 2,888) £225

5160

5160 **One hundred pounds.** (Previously listed as 4870). (1 oz 0.9999 fine gold). R. A design depicting a horse prancing past the Uffington chalk white horse, with the inscription 'YEAR OF THE HORSE . 2014' and the Chinese symbol for horse. (Reverse design: Wuon-Gean Ho)

2014

— Gold bullion type (Edition: 30,000)

— Proof in gold *FDC* (Edition; 888)...£1950

NB. The spot price of gold at the time of going to press was £720 per oz.

5161

5161 **One hundred pounds.** (Previously listed as 4871). (1 oz 0.999 fine gold). R. Design
depicting two Swaledale sheep, with the inscription 'YEAR OF THE SHEEP 2015' and
the Chinese symbol for sheep. (Reverse design: Wuon-Gean Ho)
2015
—   Proof in gold *FDC* (Edition: 888) £1950

5200 **Five hundred pounds.** (Previously listed as 4881). (5 oz. 0.9999 fine gold). R. A design
depicting a horse prancing past the Uffington chalk white horse, with the inscription
'YEAR OF THE HORSE . 2014' and the Chinese symbol for horse. (Reverse design:
Wuon-Gean Ho)
2014 — Proof in gold *FDC* (Edition:) £7500

5201

5201 **Five hundred pounds.** (Previously listed as 4882). (5 oz. 0.9999 fine gold). R. Design
depicting two Swaledale sheep, with the inscription 'YEAR OF THE SHEEP 2015' and
the Chinese symbol for sheep. (Reverse design: Wuon-Gean Ho)
2015
—   Proof in gold *FDC* (5 oz. fine gold) (Edition: 38) £7500
Illustration shown at reduced size - actual coin diameter 65mm

NB. The spot price of gold at the time of going to press was £720 per oz.

4850

4850 Five pound. (crown). (Previously listed as 4764). R. A design depicting British
troops waving to crowds as they embark on a ship with the inscription '1914 THE
FIRST WORLD WAR 1918. BEF' with the edge inscription 'SALUTE THE OLD
CONTEMPTIBLES'. (Reverse design: John Bergdahl)

2014 — Proof in silver *FDC* (Edition: 1,914 in sets, see PSS60)
— Proof in gold *FDC*

4851   4852

4851 Five pound. (crown). (Previously listed as 4765). R. A design depicting three Howitzers
with the inscription '1914 THE FIRST WORLD WAR 1918' and the edge inscription
'NEW AND FURIOUS BOMBARDMENT' (Reverse design: Edwina Ellis)

2014 — Proof in silver *FDC* (Edition: 1,914 in sets, see PSS60)
— Proof in gold *FDC*

4852 Five pound. (crown). (Previously listed as 4766). R. A design depicting an effigy of Walter
Tull in uniform with soldiers walking out over no man's land and the inscription '1914
THE FIRST WORLD WAR 1918' and 'WALTER TULL' around the coin, separated by
poppy flowers with barbed wire with the edge inscription' A HERO ON AND OFF THE
FIELD'. (Reverse design: David Cornell)

2014 — Proof in silver *FDC* (Edition: 1,914 in sets, see PSS60)
— Proof in gold *FDC*

4853   4854

4853 Five pound. (crown). (Previously listed as 4767). R. A design depicting a naval gun being
   loaded on board the deck of a battleship with the inscription '1914 THE FIRST WORLD
   WAR 1918. NAVY' and the edge inscription 'THE KING'S SHIPS WERE AT SEA'.
   (Reverse design: David Rowlands)

    2014 — Proof in silver *FDC* (Edition: 1,914 in sets, see PSS60)

        — Proof in gold *FDC*

4854 Five pound. (crown). (Previously listed as 4768). R. A design depicting a man putting up
   propaganda posters onto a brick wall with the inscription '1914 THE FIRST WORLD
   WAR 1918' and the edge inscription 'FOLLOW ME! YOUR COUNTRY NEEDS YOU'

    2014 — Proof in silver *FDC* (Edition: 1,914 in sets, see PSS60)

        — Proof in gold *FDC*

4855

4855 Five pound. (crown). (Previously listed as 4769). R. A design depicting a woman working
   fields with a plough with the inscription '1914 THE FIRST WORLD WAR 1918.
   HOMEFRONT' and the edge inscription 'SPEED THE PLOUGH AND THE WOMAN
   WHO DRIVES IT'. (Reverse design: David Rowlands)

    2014 — Proof in silver *FDC* (Edition: 1,914 in sets, see PSS60)

        — Proof in gold *FDC*

4856   4857

4856 **Five pounds.** (crown). R. A design of troops landing on the beaches below a map
showing the Gallipoli landings with the inscription '1914 THE FIRST WORLD
WAR 1918 – GALLIPOLI' with the edge inscription 'HEROES THAT SHED
THEIR BLOOD' (Reverse design : John Bergdahl)
2015 — Proof in silver *FDC* (Edition: 5,000 including coins in sets, see PSS66) *
  — Proof in gold *FDC*

4857 **Five pounds.** (crown). R. An effigy of Edith Cavell together with a nurse tending
a patient and the inscription '1914 THE FIRST WORLD WAS 1918' AND '
and 'EDITH CAVELL' around the coin, separated by poppy flowers attached
with barbed wire and the edge inscription 'SHE FACED THEM GENTLE AND
BOLD' (Reverse design: David Cornell)
2015 — Proof in silver *FDC* (Edition: 2,500 including coins in sets, see PSS69)..........£80
  — Proof in gold *FDC*

4858   4859

4858 **Five pounds.** (crown). R. An effigy of Albert Ball with First World War fighter
planes and the inscription '1914 THE FIRST WORLD WAR 1918' and 'ALBERT
BALL VC' around the coin , separated by poppy flowers attached with barbed wire
and with the edge inscription 'BY FAR THE BEST ENGLISH FLYING MAN'.
(Reverse design:
David Cornell)
2015 — Proof in silver *FDC* (Edition:2,500 including coins in sets in sets, see PSS66)
  — Proof in gold *FDC*

4859 **Five pounds.** (crown). R. A First World War submarine and the inscription '1914
THE FIRST WORLD WAR 1918'and the edge inscription 'IN LTTLE BOXES
MADE OF TIN' (Reverse design: David Rowlands)
2015 — Proof in silver *FDC* (Edition:2,500 including coins in sets in sets, see PSS66)
  — Proof in gold *FDC*

NB. The spot price of gold at the time of going to press was £720 per oz.

4860   4861

4860 Five pounds. (crown).R. A horse carrying munitions and a howitzer in the
background with the inscription '1914 THE FIRST WORLD WAR 1918' with the
edge inscription ' PATIENT EYES COURAGEOUS HEARTS'. (Reverse design:
David Lawrence)

   2015 — Proof in silver *FDC* (Edition: 2,500 including coins in sets in sets, see PSS66)
        — Proof in gold *FDC*

4861 Five pounds. (crown). R. A sailor standing on deck below a red ensign with a ship in the
background and the inscription '1914 THE FIRST WORLD WAR 1918 MERCHANT
NAVY' and the edge inscription 'SEPULCHRED IN THE HARBOUR OF THE DEEP'
(Reverse design: Edwina Ellis)

   2015 — Proof in silver *FDC* (Edition: 2,500 including coins in sets in sets, see PSS69)
        — Proof in gold *FDC*

NB. The spot price of gold at the time of going to press was £720 per oz.

The Royal Mint issued a considerable number of coins to mark the London 2012 Olympic and Paralympic Games. It was decided that it would be easier for collectors if these coins were grouped together rather than be included with other coins of the same denomination. As a consequence the £2 coins issued in 2008 (previously listed as 4585 and 4586) have been renumbered and are now part of the Olympic group.

As part of their Programme of Olympic commemorative issues the Royal Mint has struck and released into circulation a series of 29 different 50 pence coins and details are given below. In addition to the circulating coins there is a series of numbered coin packs each containing the cupro-nickel versions of the coins but of higher quality. There are also sterling silver brilliant uncirculating examples.

The artist for each coin in the series has received a gold version of their design and a further example has been placed in the Mint museum. No value is shown at the present time.

4960   4961

4960 **Fifty pence**. To commemorate the London 2012 Olympic and Paralympic Games. R. A design which depicts an athlete clearing a high jump bar, with the London 2012 logo above and the denomination '50 pence' below. (Reverse design: Florence Jackson) 2009
— Specimen in presentation folder (Edition: 100,000) £3
— Gold FDC – presented to the artist
2011 ....£1
— Specimen in card (3/29) £3
— Specimen in presentation folder signed by Daley Thompson (Edition: 500) £50
— Specimen in presentation folder signed by Dame Kelly Holmes (Edition: 500) £50
— Specimen in presentation folder signed by Lord Sebastian Coe (Edition: 500) £50
— Silver BU (Edition: 30,000) £35

4961 **Fifty pence**. To commemorate the London 2012 Olympic and Paralympic Games. R. A design which depicts a cyclist in a velodrome, with the London Olympic logo above and the denomination '50 PENCE' below. (Reverse design: Theo Crutchley- Mack) 2010
— Gold FDC – presented to the artist
2011 ....£1
Specimen in card (9/29) £3
— Silver BU (Edition: 30,000)...£35

4962   4963

4962 Fifty pence. To commemorate the London 2012 Olympic and Paralympic Games. R.
A design which depicts a swimmer submerged in water, with the London Olympic logo
above and the denomination '50 PENCE' below. (Reverse design: Jonathan Olliffe)
2011 ....£1   Specimen in card (1/29)................................£3
— Silver BU (Edition: 30,000).....£35   — Gold *FDC* – presented to the artist

4963 Fifty pence. To commemorate the London 2012 Olympic and Paralympic Games. R. A
design which depicts a bow being drawn, with the London Olympic logo above and the
denomination '50 PENCE' below. (Reverse design: Piotr Powaga)
2011 ....£1   Specimen in card (2/29)................................£3
— Silver BU (Edition: 30,000).....£35   — Gold *FDC* – presented to the artist

4964   4965

4964 Fifty pence. To commemorate the London 2012 Olympic and Paralympic Games. R. A
design which depicts a shuttlecock and a diagram of badminton actions, with the London
Olympic logo above and the denomination '50 PENCE' below. (Reverse design: Emma
Kelly)
2011 ....£1   Specimen in card (4/29)................................£3
— Silver BU (Edition: 30,000).....£35   — Gold *FDC* – presented to the artist

4965 Fifty pence. To commemorate the London 2012 Olympic and Paralympic Games. R. A
design which depicts basketball players against a textured background of a large basketball,
with the London Olympic logo above and the denomination '50 PENCE' below. (Reverse
design: Sarah Payne)
2011 ....£1   Specimen in card (5/29)................................£3
— Silver BU (Edition: 30,000).....£35   — Gold *FDC* – presented to the artist

          4966   4967

4966 Fifty pence. To commemorate the London 2012 Olympic and Paralympic Games. R. A design
which depicts a boccia player in a wheelchair throwing a ball, with the London Olympic logo
above and the denomination "50 PENCE" below. (Reverse design: Justin Chung)
2011 .... £1   Specimen in card (6/29) £3
—   Silver BU (Edition: 30,000) ..... £35   —   Gold *FDC* – presented to the artist

4967 Fifty pence. To commemorate the London 2012 Olympic and Paralympic Games. R. A design
which depicts a pair of boxing gloves against the background of a boxing ring, with the London
Olympic logo above and the denomination "50 PENCE" below. (Reverse design: Shane Abery)
2011 .... £1   Specimen in card (7/29) £3
—   Silver BU (Edition: 30,000) ..... £35   —   Gold *FDC* – presented to the artist

          4968   4969

4968 Fifty pence. To commemorate the London 2012 Olympic and Paralympic Games. R. A
design which depicts a figure in a canoe on a slalom course, with the London Olympic logo
above and the denomination "50 PENCE" below. (Reverse design: Timothy Lees)
2011 .... £1   Specimen in card (8/29) £3
—   Silver BU (Edition: 30,000) ..... £35   —   Gold *FDC* – presented to the artist

4969 Fifty pence. To commemorate the London 2012 Olympic and Paralympic Games. R. A
design which depicts a horse and rider jumping over a fence, with the London Olympic logo
above and the denomination "50 PENCE" below. (Reverse design: Thomas Babbage)
2011 .... £1   Specimen in card (10/29) £3
—   Silver BU (Edition: 30,000) ..... £35   —   Gold *FDC* – presented to the artist

4970   4971

4970 Fifty pence. To commemorate the London 2012 Olympic and Paralympic Games. R. A design which depicts two figures fencing, with the London Olympic logo above and the denomination "50 PENCE" below. (Reverse design: Ruth Summerfield)
2011 ....£1   Specimen in card (11/29) £3
— Silver BU (Edition: 30,000) ..... £35   — Gold *FDC* – presented to the artist

4971 Fifty pence. To commemorate the London 2012 Olympic and Paralympic Games. R. A diagrammatic explanation of the offside rule in football, with the London Olympic logo above and the denomination "50 PENCE" below. (Reverse design: Neil Wolfson)
2011 ....£1   Specimen in card (12/29) £3
— Silver BU (Edition: 30,000) ..... £35   — Gold *FDC* – presented to the artist

4972   4973

4972 Fifty pence. To commemorate the London 2012 Olympic and Paralympic Games. R. A design which depicts a goalball player throwing a ball, with the London Olympic logo above and the denomination "50 PENCE" below. (Reverse design: Jonathan Wren)
2011 ....£1   Specimen in card (13/29) £3
— Silver BU (Edition: 30,000) ..... £35   — Gold *FDC* – presented to the artist

4973 Fifty pence. To commemorate the London 2012 Olympic and Paralympic Games. R. A design which depicts a gymnast with a ribbon, with the London Olympic logo above and the denomination "50 PENCE" below. (Reverse design: Jonathan Olliffe)
2011 ....£1   Specimen in card (14/29) £3
— Silver BU (Edition: 30,000) ..... £35   — Gold *FDC* – presented to the artist

4974 4975

4974 Fifty pence. To commemorate the London 2012 Olympic and Paralympic Games. R. A
design which depicts a handball player throwing a ball against a background of a handball
court, with the London Olympic logo above and the denomination '50 PENCE' below.
(Reverse design: Natasha Ratcliffe)
2011 .... £1   Specimen in card (15/29) £3
—   Silver BU (Edition: 30,000) ..... £35   —   Gold *FDC* – presented to the artist

4975 Fifty pence. To commemorate the London 2012 Olympic and Paralympic Games. R. A design
which depicts two hockey players challenging for the ball, with the London Olympic logo
above and the denomination "50 PENCE" below. (Reverse design: Robert Evans)
2011 .... £1   Specimen in card (16/29) £3
—   Silver BU (Edition: 30,000) ..... £35   —   Gold *FDC* – presented to the artist

4976 4977

4976 Fifty pence. To commemorave the London 2012 Olympic and Paralympic Games. R. A
depiction of a judo throw, with the London Olympic logo above and the denomination '50
PENCE' below. (Reverse design: David Cornell)
2011 .... £1   Specimen in card (17/29) £3
—   Silver BU (Edition: 30,000) ..... £35   —   Gold *FDC* – presented to the artist

4977 Fifty pence. To commemorate the London 2012 Olympic and Paralympic Games. R. A
montage of the five sports which form the modern pentathlon, with the London Olympic logo
above and the denomination '50 PENCE' below. (Reverse design: Daniel Brittain)
2011 .... £1   Specimen in card (18/29) £3
—   Silver BU (Edition: 30,000) ..... £35   —   Gold *FDC* – presented to the artist

4978   4979

4978 Fifty pence. To commemorate the London 2012 Olympic and Paralympic Games. R. A design which depicts a rowing boat accompanied by a number of words associated with the Olympic movement, with the London Olympic logo above and the denomination '50 PENCE' below. (Reverse design: David Podmore)

2011 ....£1
— Specimen in card   (19/29) £3
— Specimen in presentation folder signed by Sir Steve Redgrave (Edition: 500)............£50
— Silver BU (Edition: 30,000) £35

4979 Fifty pence. To commemorate the London 2012 Olympic and Paralympic Games. R. A design which depicts three sailing boats accompanied by a map of the coast of Weymouth, with the London Olympic logo above and the denomination '50 PENCE' below. (Reverse design: Bruce Rushin)

2011 ....£1   Specimen in card (20/29) £3
— Silver BU (Edition: 30,000) ..... £35   — Gold *FDC* – presented to the artist

4980   4981

4980 Fifty pence. To commemorate the London 2012 Olympic and Paralympic Games. R. A design which depicts a figure shooting, with the London Olympic logo above and the denomination '50 PENCE' below. (Reverse design: Pravin Dewdhory)

2011 ....£1   Specimen in card (21/29) £3
— Silver BU (Edition: 30,000) ..... £35   — Gold *FDC* – presented to the artist

4981 Fifty pence. To commemorate the London 2012 Olympic and Paralympic Games. R. A design which depicts two table tennis bats against the background of a table and net, with the London Olympic logo above and the denomination "50 PENCE" below. (Reverse design: Alan Linsdell)

2011 ....£1   Specimen in card (22/29) £3
— Silver BU (Edition: 30,000) ..... £35   — Gold *FDC* – presented to the artist

4982   4983

4982 Fifty pence. To commemorate the London 2012 Olympic and Paralympic Games. R. A
design which depicts two athletes engaged in Taekwondo, with the London Olympic logo
above and the denomination "50 PENCE" below. (Reverse design: David Gibbons)
2011 ....£1   Specimen in card (23/29)..............................£3
—   Silver BU (Edition: 30,000)..... £35   —   Gold *FDC* – presented to the artist
4983 Fifty pence. To commemorate the London 2012 Olympic and Paralympic Games. R. A
design which depicts a tennis net and tennis ball, with the London Olympic logo above and
the denomination "50 PENCE" below. (Reverse design: Tracy Baines)
2011 ....£1   Specimen in card (24/29)..............................£3
—   Silver BU (Edition: 30,000)..... £35   —   Gold *FDC* – presented to the artist

4984   4985

4984 Fifty pence. To commemorate the London 2012 Olympic and Paralympic Games. R. A
montage of the three sports which form the triathlon, with the London Olympic logo above
and the denomination "50 PENCE" below. (Reverse design: Sarah Harvey)
2011 ....£1   Specimen in card (25/29)..............................£3
—   Silver BU (Edition: 30,000)..... £35   —   Gold *FDC* – presented to the artist
4985 Fifty pence. To commemorate the London 2012 Olympic and Paralympic Games. R. A
design which depicts three figures playing beach volleyball, with the London Olympic logo
above and the denomination "50 PENCE" below. (Reverse design: Daniela Boothman)
2011 ....£1   Specimen in card (26/29)..............................£3
—   Silver BU (Edition: 30,000)..... £35   —   Gold *FDC* – presented to the artist

4986   4987

4986 Fifty pence. To commemorate the London 2012 Olympic and Paralympic Games. ℞. A design which depicts the outline of a weightlifter starting a lift, with the London Olympic logo above and the denomination "50 PENCE" below. (Reverse design: Rob Shakespeare)

2011 ....£1   Specimen in card (27/29)...........................£3
—   Silver BU (Edition: 30,000)...£35   —   Gold *FDC* – presented to the artist

4987 Fifty pence. To commemorate the London 2012 Olympic and Paralympic Games. ℞. A design which depicts a wheelchair rugby player in action, with the London Olympic logo above and the denomination "50 PENCE" below. (Reverse design: Natasha Ratcliffe)

2011 ....£1   Specimen in card (28/29)...........................£3
—   Silver BU (Edition: 30,000)...£35   —   Gold *FDC* – presented to the artist

4988

4988 Fifty pence. To commemorate the London 2012 Olympic and Paralympic Games. ℞. A design which depicts two figures wrestling in a stadium, with the London Olympic logo above and the denomination "50 PENCE" below. (Reverse design: Roderick Enriquez)

2011 ....£1   Specimen in card (29/29)...........................£3
—   Silver BU (Edition: 30,000)...£35   —   Gold *FDC* – presented to the artist

4951   4952

4951 **Two pounds.** (Previously listed as 4585) Centenary of the Olympic Games of 1908 held in London. R. A running track on which is superimposed the date '1908' accompanied by the denomination 'TWO POUNDS' and the date '2008', the whole design being encircled by the inscription 'LONDON OLYMPIC CENTENARY' with the edge inscription 'THE 4TH OLYMPIAD LONDON' (Reverse design: Thomas T Docherty)

2008 .... £5
— Specimen in presentation folder (Issued: 29,594) £10
— Proof *FDC* (in 2008 set, see PS93)* £15
— Proof in Silver *FDC* (Issued: 8,023) £35
— Proof piedfort in silver *FDC* (Edition: 5,000) £55
— Proof in gold *FDC* (Issued: 1,908 including coins in sets) £700

4952 **Two pounds.** (Previously listed as 4586) London Olympic Handover Ceremony. R. The Olympic flag being passed from one hand to another, encircled by the inscription 'BEIJING 2008 LONDON 2012' and with the London 2012 logo below with the edge inscription 'I CALL UPON THE YOUTH OF THE WORLD' (Reverse design: Royal Mint Engraving Team)

2008 .... £5
— Specimen in presentation folder (Edition: 250,000) £10
— Proof in Silver *FDC* (Issued: 30,000) £38
— Proof piedfort in silver *FDC* (Issued: 3,000) £60
— Proof in gold *FDC* (Edition: 3,250 including coins in sets)................................£700

4953

4953 **Two pounds.** London to Rio Olympic Handover coin. R. A design which depicts a baton being passed from one hand to another, accompanied by the conjoined Union and Brazilian Flags. The reverse design is set against the background of a running track motif, with the London 2012 logo above and the surrounding inscription 'LONDON 2012 RIO 2016'. With the edge inscription 'I CALL UPON THE YOUTH OF THE WORLD'. (Reverse design: Jonathan Olliffe)

2012
— Specimen in presentation card (Issued: 28,356)..£10
— Proof in silver *FDC* (Issued: 3,781) £60
— Proof piedfort in silver *FDC* (Issued: 2,000) £105
— Proof in gold *FDC* (Issued: 771)...£1195

4920

4920 Five pounds. (crown) UK countdown to 2012 Olympic Games. R. In the centre a
depiction of two swimmers as faceted figures accompanied by the number '3' with
a section of a clock face to the right and the London 2012 logo to the left printed in
coloured ink on the precious metal versions and surrounded by a plan view of the main
Olympic Stadium incorporating the date '2009' with the words 'COUNTDOWN' above
and the inscription 'XXX OLYMPIAD' below. (Reverse design: Claire Aldridge) (Obv.
as 4556)

2009 (Edition: 500,000) £8
—   Specimen in presentation folder (Edition: 500,000) £10
—   Proof in silver *FDC* (Issued: 30,000) £95
—   Proof piedfort in silver *FDC* (Issued: 6,000) £175
—   Proof in gold *FDC* (Edition: 4,000) £2000

4921

4921 Five pounds. (crown) UK countdown to 2012 Olympic Games. R. In the centre a
depiction of two runners as faceted figures accompanied by the number '2' with a section
of a clock face to the right and the London 2012 logo to the left printed in coloured
ink on the precious meta versions and surrounded by a plan view of the main Olympic
Stadium incorporating the date '2010' with the words 'COUNTDOWN' above and the
inscription 'XXX OLYMPIAD' below.(Reverse design: Claire Aldridge) (Obv. as 4556)

2010
—   Specimen in presentation card   (Edition: 250,000) £8
—   Specimen in presentation folder (Edition: 250,000) £10
—   Proof in silver *FDC* (Edition: 30,000) £80
—   Proof piedfort in silver *FDC* (Edition: 4,000)..£200
—   Proof in gold *FDC* (Edition: 3,000) £2000

4922

4922 Five pounds. (crown) UK countdown to 2012 Olympic Games. R. In the centre a
depiction of a cyclist as a faceted figure, accompanied by the number '1' with a section
of a clock face to the right, below and to the left, and the London 2012 logo to the right
printed in coloured ink on the precious metal versions and surrounded by a plan view of
the main Olympic Stadium incorporating the date '2011' with the words
'COUNTDOWN' above and the inscription '**XXX OLYMPIAD**' below. (Reverse design:
Claire Aldridge)

2011
— Specimen in presentation card   (Edition: 250,000) £8
— Specimen in presentation folder (Edition: 250,000)..£10
— Proof in silver *FDC* (Edition: 30,000) £100
— Proof piedfort in silver *FDC* (Edition: 4,000) £175
— Proof in gold *FDC* (Edition: 3,000)...£2880

4923

4923 Five pounds. (crown) UK countdown to 2012 Olympic Games. R. A depiction of three
athletes as faceted figures standing on a victory podium, with a section of a clock-face to
the right, to the left and above, and the London 2012 logo to the right. The reverse design
is surrounded by a plan view of the main Olympic Stadium, incorporating the date '2012'
at the top, and the word 'COUNTDOWN' above and the inscription '**XXX OLYMPIAD**'
below. (Reverse design: Claire Aldridge)

2012
— Specimen in presentation card   (Edition: 250,000) £8
— Specimen in presentation folder (Edition: 250,000) £13
— Proof in silver *FDC* (Issued: 12,670) £100
— Proof piedfort in silver *FDC* (Issued: 2,324) £175
— Proof in gold *FDC* (Issued: 1,007)..£2880

4924

4924 **Five pounds.** (crown) The London 2012 Olympic Games. ℞. An image of the skyline of some of the most well-known landmarks and buildings in London reflected in the River Thames, with the inscription 'LONDON 2012' above. Surrounding the skyline image is a selection of sports from the London 2012 Games with the London 2012 logo at the top. (Reverse design: Saiman Miah)

2012

—	Specimen in presentation folder	£15
—	Proof in silver *FDC* (Edition: 100,000)	£100
—	Proof in silver with gold plating *FDC* (Edition: 12,500)	£125
—	Proof piedfort in silver *FDC* (Edition: 7,000)	£175
—	Proof in gold *FDC* (Edition: 5,000)	£2880

4925

4925 **Five pounds.** (crown) The London 2012 Paralympic Games. ℞. A design showing segments of a target, a spoked wheel, a stopwatch and the clock face of the Palace of Westminster. The inscription 'LONDON 2012' appears on the target and the London 2012 Paralympic logo appears on the stopwatch. On the gold and silver coins the London Paralympic logo will be printed in coloured ink , while on the cupro-nickel coin the logo will be struck into the surface. (Reverse design: Pippa Anderson)

2012

—	Specimen in presentation folder (Edition: 250,000)	£15
—	Proof in silver *FDC* (Edition: 10,000)	£100
—	Proof in silver with gold plating *FDC* (Edition: 3,000)	£125
—	Proof piedfort in silver *FDC* (Edition: 2,012)	£175
—	Proof in gold *FDC* (Edition: 2,012)	£2880

4930

4930 Five pounds. (crown) The Mind of Britain. ℞. A depiction of the clock-face of the Palace of Westminster accompanied by the London 2012 logo, printed in coloured ink and a quotation From Walter Bagehot, 'NATIONS TOUCH AT THEIR SUMMITS'. (Reverse design: Shane Greeves and the Royal Mint Engraving Department)
2009
— Proof *FDC* (Edition: 100,000)£20   — Proof silver *FDC* (Edition: 95,000) £100

4931

4931 Five pounds. (crown). The Mind of Britain. ℞. A depiction of Stonehenge accompanied by the London 2012 logo, printed in coloured ink on the silver version and a quotation from William Blake 'GREAT THINGS ARE DONE WHEN MEN AND MOUNTAINS MEET' (Reverse design: Shane Greeves and the Royal Mint Engraving Department)
2009
— Proof silver *FDC* (Edition: 95,000) £100

4932   4933

4932   Five pounds. (crown). The Mind of Britain. R. A depiction of the Angel of the North
accompanied   by the London 2012 logo printed in coloured ink on the silver version and a
quotation from William Shakespeare 'I HAVE TOUCHED THE HIGHEST POINT OF MY
GREATNESS' (Reverse design: Shane Greeves and the Royal Mint Engraving Department)
2009
  —   Proof silver *FDC* (Edition: 95,000) £100

4933   Five pounds. (crown). The Mind of Britain. R. A depiction of the Flying Scotsman
accompanied   by the London 2012 logo printed in coloured ink on the silver version and
a quotation from William Shakespeare 'TRUE HOPE IS SWIFT' (Reverse design:
Shane Greeves and the Royal Mint Engraving Department)
2009
  —   Proof silver *FDC* (Edition: 95,000) £100

4934

4934   Five pounds. (crown). The Mind of Britain. R. A depiction of Eduardo Paolozzi's
sculpture of Isaac Newton North accompanied   by the London 2012 logo printed in
coloured ink on the silver version and a quotation from William Shakespeare 'MAKE
NOT YOUR THOUGHTS YOUR PRISONS' (Reverse design: Shane Greeves and the
Royal Mint Engraving Department)
2009
  —   Proof silver *FDC* (Edition: 95,000) £100

4935

4935 Five pounds. (crown). The Mind of Britain. ℞. A depiction of the Globe Theatre
accompanied by the London 2012 logo printed in coloured ink on the silver version and a
quotation from William Shakespeare 'WE ARE SUCH STUFF AS DREAMS ARE MADE
ON' (Reverse design: Shane Greeves and the Royal Mint Engraving Department)
2009
— Proof silver *FDC* (Edition: 95,000) £100

4936   4937

4936 Five pounds. (crown). The Body of Britain. ℞. A depiction of Rhossili Bay accompanied
by the London 2012 logo printed in coloured ink, and a quotation from William Blake
'TO SEE A WORLD IN A GRAIN OF SAND' (Reverse design: Shane Greeves and the
Royal Mint Engraving Department)
2010
— Proof silver *FDC* (Edition: 95,000) £100

4937 Five pounds. (crown). The Body of Britain ℞. A depiction of Giant's Causeway
accompanied by the London 2012 logo printed in coloured ink, and a quotation from
Alice Oswald 'WHEN THE STONE BEGAN TO DREAM' (Reverse design: Shane
Greeves and the Royal Mint Engraving Department)
2010
— Proof silver *FDC* (Edition: 95,000) £100

4938   4939

4938   **Five pounds.** (crown). The Body of Britain R. A depiction of the River Thames accompanied by the London 2012 logo printed in coloured ink, and a quotation from Percy Bysshe Shelley, 'TAMELESS, AND SWIFT AND PROUD' (Reverse design: Shane Greeves and the Royal Mint Engraving Department)
2010
—   Proof silver *FDC* (Edition: 95,000)...£100

4939   **Five pounds.** (crown). The Body of Britain. R. A depiction of a barn owl accompanied by the London 2012 logo printed in coloured ink, and a quotation from Samuel Johnson 'THE NATURAL FLIGHTS OF THE HUMAN MIND' (Reverse design: Shane Greeves and the Royal Mint Engraving Department)
2010
—   Proof silver *FDC* (Edition: 95,000)...£100

4940   4941

4940   **Five pounds.** (crown). The Body of Britain. R. A depiction of oak leaves and an acorn accompanied by the London 2012 logo printed in coloured ink, and a quotation from Alfred, Lord Tennyson, 'TO STRIVE, TO SEEK......AND NOT TO YIELD' (Reverse design: Shane Greeves and the Royal Mint Engraving Department)
2010
—   Proof silver *FDC* (Edition: 95,000)...£100

4941   **Five pounds.** (crown). The Body of Britain. R. A depiction of a weather-vane accompanied by the London 2012 logo printed in coloured ink, and a quotation from Charlotte Bronte, NEVER MAY A CLOUD COME O'ER THE SUNSHINE OF YOUR MIND' (Reverse design: Shane Greeves and the Royal Mint Engraving Department)
2010
—   Proof silver *FDC* (Edition: 95,000)...£100

4942 4943

4942 **Five pounds.** (crown). The Spirit of Britain. R. A depiction of the intertwined national emblems of England, Scotland, Wales and Northern Ireland accompanied by the London 2012 logo, printed in coloured ink, and a quotation from John Lennon, 'AND THE WORLD WILL BE ONE' (Reverse design: Shane Greeves and the Royal Mint Engraving Department) 2010
— Proof silver *FDC* (Edition: 95,000)..£100

4943 **Five pounds.** (crown).The Spirit of Britain. R. A depiction of the White Rabbit from Lewis Carroll's *Alice in Wonderland* accompanied by the London 2012 logo, printed in coloured ink, and a quotation from T S Eliot, 'ALL TOUCHED BY A COMMON GENIUS' (Reverse design: Shane Greeves and the Royal Mint Engraving Department) 2010
— Proof silver *FDC* (Edition: 95,000)..£100

4944 4945

4944 **Five pounds.** (crown).The Spirit of Britain. R. A view down the Mall of cheering crowds accompanied by the London 2012 logo, printed in coloured ink, and a quotation from Alfred, Lord Tennyson, 'KIND HEARTS ARE MORE THAN CORONETS' (Reverse design: Shane Greeves and the Royal Mint Engraving Department) 2010
— Proof *FDC* (Edition; 100,000)...£20
— Proof silver *FDC* (Edition: 95,000)...£100

4945 **Five pounds.** (crown).The Spirit of Britain. R. A DEPICTION OF THE STATUE OF Winston Churchill in Parliament Square accompanied by the London 2012 logo, printed in coloured ink, and a quotation from Anita Roddick, 'BE DARING, BE FIRST, BE DIFFERENT, BE JUST' (Reverse design: Shane Greeves and the Royal Mint Engraving Department) 2010
— Proof *FDC* (Edition; 100,000)...£20
— Proof silver *FDC* (Edition: 95,000)...£100

4946

4946   Five pounds. (crown).The Spirit of Britain. R An arrangement of musical instruments
based on a well known sculpture accompanied by the London 2012 logo, printed in
coloured ink, and a quotation from John Lennon and Paul McCartney, 'ALL YOU NEED
IS LOVE'. (Reverse design: Shane Greeves and the Royal Mint Engraving Department)
2010
—   Proof silver *FDC* (Edition: 95,000) £100

4947

4947   Five pounds. (crown).The Spirit of Britain. R. An image of the nineteenth-century anti-
slavery campaigner Equiano accompanied by the London 2012 logo, printed in coloured
ink, and a quotation from William Shakespeare, 'TO THINE OWN SELF BE TRUE'.
(Reverse design: Shane Greeves and the Royal Mint Engraving Department)
2010
—   Proof silver *FDC* (Edition: 95,000) £100

4950

4950 Ten pounds. (Five ounce). R. A design of the winged horse Pegasus rearing on its hind
legs surrounded by the inscription 'LONDON OLYMPIC GAMES', and the London 2012
logo and the date '2012'.(Reverse design: Christopher Le Brun)
2012
— Proof in 0.999 fine silver *FDC* (Issued: 5,056) £525
— Proof in 0.999 fine gold *FDC* (Issued: 193)...£11500
Illustration shown at reduced size – actual coin diameter 65 mm.

4905

4905 Twenty five pounds. Faster. R. An image of Diana accompanied by a depiction of the
sport of cycling, specifically pursuit racing ,with Olympic Rings above, the name 'DIANA'
to the left, the Latin word for faster 'CITIUS', to the right, and the inscription 'LONDON
2012' below. (Reverse design: John Bergdahl)
2010
— Proof in gold *FDC* (Edition: 20,000) £600

4906

4906 Twenty five pounds. Faster. R. An image of Mercury accompanied by a depiction of
the sport of running, with Olympic Rings above, the name 'MERCURY' to the left, the
Latin word for faster 'CITIUS', to the right, and the inscription 'LONDON 2012' below.
(Reverse design: John Bergdahl)
2010
— Proof in gold *FDC* (Edition: 20,000)...£600

4907

4907 Twenty five pounds. Higher. R̄. An image of Apollo accompanied by a depiction of the
sport of rhythmic gymnastics, with Olympic Rings above, the name 'APOLLO' to the
left, the Latin word for higher 'ALTIUS', to the right, and the inscription 'LONDON
2012' below. (Reverse design: John Bergdahl)
2011
— Proof in gold *FDC* (Edition: 20,000 including coins in sets) £600

4908   4909   4910

4908 Twenty five pounds. Higher. R̄. An image of Juno accompanied by a depiction of the
sport of pole vaulting, with Olympic Rings above, the name 'JUNO' to the left, the Latin
word for higher 'ALTIUS', to the right, and the inscription 'LONDON 2012' below.
(Reverse design: John Bergdahl)
2011
— Proof in gold *FDC* (Edition: 20,000 including coins in sets) £600

4909 Twenty five pounds. Stronger. R̄. An image of Vulcan accompanied by a depiction of
the sport of hammer throwing, with the Olympic Rings above, the name 'VULCAN'
to the left, and the Latin word for stronger 'FORTIUS', to the right, and the inscription
'LONDON 2012' below. (Reverse design: John Bergdahl)
2012
— Proof in gold *FDC* (Edition: 20,000 including coins in sets) £600

4910 Twenty five pounds. Stronger. R̄. An image of Minerva accompanied by a depiction
Of the sport of javelin throwing, with the Olympic Rings above, the name 'MINERVA'
to the left , the Latin word for stronger, 'FORTIUS', to the right, and the inscription
'LONDON 2012@ below. (Reverse design: John Bergdahl)
2012
— Proof in gold *FDC* (Edition: 20,000 including coins in sets) £600

4915

4915 One hundred pounds. Faster. R. An image of Neptune, accompanied by a depiction of the sport of sailing, with the Olympic Rings above, the name 'NEPTUNE' to the left, the Latin word for faster 'CITIUS' to the right, and the inscription 'LONDON 2012' below. (Reverse design: John Bergdahl)
2010
— Proof in gold *FDC* (Edition: 7,500 including coins in sets)..............................£2300

4916

4916 One hundred pounds. Higher. R. An image of Jupiter, accompanied by a depiction of the sport of diving, with the Olympic Rings above, the name 'JUPITER' to the left, the Latin word for higher 'ALTIUS' to the right, and the inscription 'LONDON 2012' below. (Reverse design: John Bergdahl)
2011
— Proof in gold *FDC** (Edition: 7,500 including coins in sets)............................£2300

4917

4917 One hundred pounds. Stronger. R. An image of Mars accompanied by a depiction of the sport of boxing, with the Olympic Rings above, the name 'MARS' to the left, the Latin word for stronger, 'FORTIUS', to the right, and the inscription 'LONDON 2012' below. (Reverse design: John Bergdahl)
2012
— Proof in gold *FDC* (Edition: 7,500 including coins in sets) £2300

4920

4918 Five hundred pounds. (One kilo). R. A design consisting of celebratory pennants and the inscription 'XXX OLYMPIAD' surrounded by the epigram 'UNITE OUR DREAMS TO MAKE THE WORLD A TEAM OF TEAMS' (Reverse design: Tom Phillips) 2012

—   Proof in silver (Issued: 910) £3000

Illustration shown at reduced size – actual coin diameter 100 mm

4921

4919 One thousand pounds. (One kilo). R. A design depicting individual pieces of sporting equipment encircled by a laurel of victory. (Reverse design: Sir Anthony Caro) 2012

—   Proof in gold (Issued: 20)..£100000

Illustration shown at reduced size – actual coin diameter 100 mm

The practice of issuing annual sets of coins was started by the Royal Mint in 1970 when a set of the £SD coins was issued as a souvenir prior to Decimalisation. There are now regular issues of brilliant uncirculated coin sets as well as proofs in base metal, and issues in gold and silver. In order to simplify the numbering system, and to allow for the continuation of the various issues in the future, the Prefix letters have been changed. The base metal proof sets will continue the series of numbers from the 1970 set, PS20. Other sets, such as those of uncirculated coins, silver and gold now have their numbering series commencing with number 01 in each case.

In addition to the annual sets of uncirculated and proofs coins sold by the Royal Mint to collectors and dealers, the Mint has produced specially packaged sets and single coins for companies. No details are made available of these issues and therefore no attempt has been made to include them in the listings below. The Mint also sells 'Christening' and 'Wedding' sets in distinctive packaging but the numbers circulating in the market are relatively modest and of limited appeal after the year of issue.

The Mint has recently offered sets of coins to collectors that consist of coins obtained from the market e.g. silver proofs, crowns and gold sovereigns showing different portraits. Although these are available in limited numbers from the Mint, it has been decided not to list them in the section devoted to sets.

Following the comprehensive review of the layout, it has been decided to move the folder containing the two 50 pence coins of 1992 to the list below of uncirculated coins. This was formerly included as 4352A, and is now US13 with all subsequent numbers adjusted by one.

Uncirculated Sets

			£
US01–**1982**	Uncirculated (specimen) set in Royal Mint folder, 50p to ½p, new reverse type, including 20 pence (Issued: 205,000)	(7)	9
US02–**1983**	'U.K.' £1 (4221) to ½p (Issued: 637,100)	(8)	15
US03–**1984**	'Scottish' £1 (4222) to ½p (Issued: 158,820)	(8)	15
US04–**1985**	'Welsh' £1 (4331) to 1p, new portrait of The Queen (Issued: 102,015)	(7)	15
US05–**1986**	'Commonwealth Games' £2 (4311) plus 'Northern Irish' £1 (4332) to 1p, (Issued: 167,224)	(8)	18
US06–**1987**	'English' £1 (4333) to 1p, (Issued: 172,425)	(7)	15
US07–**1988**	'Arms' £1 (4334) to 1p, (Issued: 134,067)	(7)	15
US08–**1989**	'Scottish' £1 (4335) to 1p, (Issued: 77,569)	(7)	20
US09–**1989**	'Bill of Rights' and 'Claim of Right' £2s (4312 and 4313) in Royal Mint folder (Issued: not known)	(2)	25
US10–**1990**	'Welsh' £1 (4331) to 1p plus new smaller 5p, (Issued: 102,606)	(8)	20
US11–**1991**	'Northern Irish' £1 (4332) to 1p, (Issued: 74,975)	(7)	20
US12–**1992**	'English' £1 (4333), 'European Community' 50p (4352) and 'Britannia' 50p, 20p to 1p plus new smaller 10p (Issued: 78,421)	(9)	25
US13-**1992**	'European Community' 50p (4352) and 'Britannia' 50p (4351) in presentation folder previously listed as 4352A	(2)	20
US14–**1993**	'UK' £1 (4336), 'European Community' 50p (4352) to 1p ((Issued: 56,945)	(8)	25
US15–**1994**	'Bank of England' £2 (4314), 'Scottish' £1 (4337) and 'D-Day' 50p (4353) to 1p, (Issued: 177,971)	(8)	15
US16–**1995**	'Peace' £2 (4315) and 'Welsh' £1 (4338) to 1p (Issued: 105, 647)	(8)	15
US17–**1996**	'Football' £2 (4317) and 'Northern Irish' £1 (4339) to 1p (Issued: 86,501)	(8)	15
US18–**1997**	'Bimetallic' £2 (4318), 'English' £1 (4340) to 1p plus new smaller 50p (Issued: 109,557)	(9)	15
US19–**1998**	'Bimetallic' £2 (4570), 'UK' £1 (4590) and 'EU' 50 pence (4611) to1 pence (Issued: 96,192)	(9)	25
US20–**1998**	'EU' and 'Britannia' 50 pence (4611 and 4610) in Royal Mint folder	(2)	6
US21–**1999**	'Bimetallic' 'Rugby' £2 (4571), 'Scottish' £1 (4591) to 1p (Issued: 136,696)	(8)	18
US22–**2000**	'Bimetallic' £2 (4570), 'Welsh' £1 (4592) to 1p plus 'Library' 50 pence (4613) (Issued: 117,750)	(9)	18
US23–**2001**	'Bimetallic' £2 (4570), 'Bimetallic' 'Marconi' £2 (4572), 'Irish' £1 (4594) to 1p (Issued: 57,741)	(9)	18

£

£

US46–**2011**	'Bimetallic' £2 (4570), 'Royal Shield' £1 (4604), 50 pence to 1 pence (4620, 4631, 4651, 4671, 4691 4711)	(8)	21
US47–**2011**	'Edinburgh' £1 (4607) and 'Cardiff' £1 (4608) (Edition: 10,000)	(2)	14
US48–**2012**	Diamond Jubilee £5, struck in c/n (4569), 'Bimetallic' 'Charles Dickens' £2 (4730), 'Bimetallic' £2 (4570) 'Royal Shield' £1 (4604), 50 pence to 1 pence (4620, 4631, 4652, 4672, 4691 and 4711)	(10)	39
US49–**2012**	'Bimetallic' £2 (4570) 'Royal Shield '£1(4604), 50 pence to 1 pence (4620, 4631, 4652, 4672, 4691 and 4711)	(8)	21
US50–**2013**	Coronation £5, struck in c/n (4751), 'Bimetallic' 'Guinea' £2 (4731), 'Bimetallic' 'Roundel' £2 (4732), 'Bimetallic' 'Train' £2 (4733),'Bimetallic' £2 (4570) 'Royal Shield' £1 (4604), 'England' £1 (4720), 'Wales' £1 (4721), 50 pence 'Ironside' (4628), 50 pence to 1 pence (4620, 4631, 4652, 4672, 4691 and 4711)	(15)	50
US51–**2013**	'Bimetallic' £2 (4570) 'Royal Shield '£1 (4604), 50 pence to 1 pence (4620, 4631, 4652, 4672, 4691 and 4711)	(8)	£25
US52–**2014**	Queen Anne £5, struck in c/n (4758), 'Bimetallic' 'Trinity House' £2 (4734), 'Bimetallic' 'World War I' £2 (4735), 'Bimetallic' £2 (4570) 'Royal Shield' £1 (4604), 'Northern Ireland' £1 (4722), 'Scotland' £1(4723.), 50 pence 'Commonwealth Games' (4630), 50 pence to 1 pence (4620, 4636, 4652, 4672, 4691 and 4711)	(14)	£50
US53–**2014**	'Bimetallic' £2 (4570) 'Royal Shield '£1(4604), 50 pence to 1 pence (4620, 4631, 4652, 4672, 4691 and 4711)	(8)	£25
US54–**2015**	Churchill £5, struck in c/n (4764), Waterloo £5, struck in c/n (4765) 'Bimetallic' 'Magna Carta' £2 (4737), 'Bimetallic' 'Royal Navy' £2 (4738), 'Bimetallic' £2 (4570) 'Royal Shield' £1 (4604), 50 pence 'Battle of Britain' (4632) 50 pence to 1 pence (4620, 4636, 4652, 4672, 4691 and 4711)	(13)	£50
US55–**2015**	Fourth Portrait 'Bimetallic' £2 (4570) 'Royal Shield' £1 (4604), 50 pence to 1 pence (4632, 4636, 4652, 4672, 4691 and 4711) (Edition: 75,000)	(8)	£25
US56–**2015**	Fifth Portrait 'Bimetallic' £2 (4736) 'Royal Shield' £1 (4604), 50 pence to 1 pence (4632, 4636, 4652, 4672, 4691 and 4711) (Edition: 75,000)	(8)	£25

Proof Sets

PS21–**1971**	Decimal coinage set, 50 new pence 'Britannia' to ¹/₂ new pence, in sealed plastic case with card wrapper (Issued: 350,000)	(6)	18
PS22–**1972**	Proof 'Silver Wedding' Crown struck in c/n (4226) plus 50p to ½p (Issued: 150,000)	(7)	20
PS23–**1973**	'EEC' 50p (4224) plus 10p to ½p, (Issued: 100,000)	(6)	15
PS24–**1974**	'Britannia' 50p to ½p, as 1971 (Issued: 100,000)	(6)	15
PS25–**1975**	'Britannia'50p to ½p (as 1974), (Issued: 100,000)	(6)	12
PS26–**1976**	'Britannia' 50p to ½p, as 1975, (Issued: 100,000)	(6)	12
PS27–**1977**	Proof 'Silver Jubilee' Crown struck in c/n (4227) plus 50p to ½p, (Issued: 193,000)	(7)	12
PS28–**1978**	'Britannia' 50p to ½p, as 1976, (Issued: 86,100)	(6)	12
PS29–**1979**	'Britannia' 50p to ½p, as 1978, (Issued: 81,000)	(6)	12
PS30–**1980**	'Britannia' 50p to ½p, as 1979, (Issued: 143,000)	(6)	15
PS31–**1981**	'Britannia' 50p to ½p, as 1980, (Issued: 100,300)	(6)	15
PS32–**1982**	'Britannia' 50p to ½p including 20 pence (Issued: 106,800)	(7)	15
PS33–**1983**	'U.K.' £1 (4221) to ½p in new packaging (Issued: 107,800)	(8)	20
PS34–**1984**	'Scottish' £1 (4222) to ½p, (Issued: 106,520)	(8)	20
PS35–**1985**	'Welsh' £1 (4331) to 1p, (Issued: 102,015)	(7)	20
PS36–**1985**	As last but packed in deluxe red leather case (Included above)	(7)	20
PS37–**1986**	'Commonwealth Games' £2 (4311) plus 'Northern Irish' £1 (4332) to 1p, (Issued: 104,597)	(8)	20

				£
PS38–**1986**	As last but packed in deluxe red leather case (Included above)......................	(8)		23
PS39–**1987**	'English' £1 (4333) to 1p, (Issued: 88,659)...	(7)		20
PS40–**1987**	As last but packed in deluxe leather case (Included above)............................	(7)		23
PS41–**1988**	'Arms' £1 (4334) to 1p, (Issued: 79,314)...	(7)		25
PS42–**1988**	As last but packed in deluxe leather case (Included above)............................	(7)		29
PS43–**1989**	'Bill of Rights' and 'Claim of Right' £2s (4312 and 4313), 'Scottish' £1 (4335) to 1p, (Issued: 85,704)...	(9)		30
PS44–**1989**	As last but packed in red leather case, (Included above)	(9)		35
PS45–**1990**	'Welsh' £1 (4331) to 1p plus new smaller 5p, (Issued: 79,052).....................	(8)		27
PS46–**1990**	As last but packed in red leather case (Included above)	(8)		32
PS47–**1991**	'Northern Irish' £1 (4332) to 1p, (Issued: 55,144).....................................	(7)		27
PS48–**1991**	As last but packed in red leather case (Included above)	(7)		33
PS49–**1992**	'English' £1 (4333), 'European community' 50p (4352) and 'Britannia' 50p, 20p to 1p plus new smaller 10p, (Issued: 44,337).....................................	(9)		28
PS50–**1992**	As last but packed in red leather case (Issued: 17,989)................................	(9)		33
PS51–**1993**	Proof 'Coronation Anniversary' £5 struck in c/n (4302), 'U.K.' £1 (4336), 50p to 1p, (Issued: 43,509)...	(8)		30
PS52–**1993**	As last but packed in red leather case (Issued: 22,571)................................	(8)		35
PS53–**1994**	'Bank' £2 (4314), 'Scottish' £1 (4337), 'D-Day' 50p (4353) to 1p, (Issued: 44,643)	(8)		30
PS54–**1994**	As last but packed in red leather case (Issued: 22,078)................................	(8)		35
PS55–**1995**	'Peace' £2 (4315), 'Welsh' £1 (4338) to 1p, (Issued: 42,842)......................	(8)		32
PS56–**1995**	As last but packed in red leather case (Issued: 17,797)................................	(8)		35
PS57–**1996**	Proof '70th Birthday' £5 struck in c/n (4303), 'Football' £2 (4317), 'Northern Irish' £1 (4339) to 1p, (Issued: 46,295)...	(9)		32
PS58–**1996**	As last but packed in red leather case (Issued: 21,286)................................	(9)		37
PS59–**1997**	Proof 'Golden Wedding' £5 struck in c/n (4304), 'Bimetallic' £2 (4318), 'English' £1 (4340) to 1p plus new smaller 50p (Issued: 48,761)	(10)		33
PS60–**1997**	As last but packed in red leather case (Issued: 31,987)................................	(10)		40
PS61–**1998**	Proof 'Prince of Wales 50th Birthday' £5 struck in c/n (4550), 'Bimetallic' £2 (4570), 'UK'. £1 (4590), 'EU' 50 pence (4611) to 1p. (Issued: 36,907).........	(10)		33
PS62–**1998**	As last, but packed in red leather case. (Issued: 26,763)............................	(10)		40
PS63–**1999**	Proof 'Diana, Princess of Wales' £5 struck in c/n (4551), 'Bimetallic' 'Rugby' £2 (4571), 'Scottish' £1 (4591) to 1p. (Issued: 40,317)...........................	(9)		34
PS64–**1999**	As last, but packed in red leather case. (Issued: 39,827)............................	(9)		40
PS65–**2000**	Proof 'Millennium' £5 struck in c/n (4552), 'Bimetallic' £2 (4570), 'Welsh' £1 (4592), 'Library' 50 pence (4613) and 'Britannia' 50 pence (4610) to 1p.Standard Set, (Issued: 41,379)...	(10)		30
PS66–**2000**	As last, but Deluxe set (Issued: 21,573 above)	(10)		30
PS67–**2000**	As last, but Executive set (Issued: 9,517)	(10)		60
PS68–**2001**	Proof 'Victoria' £5 struck in c/n (4554), 'Bimetallic' £2 (4570), 'Bimetallic' 'Marconi' £2 (4572), 'Irish' £1 (4593) to 1p. Standard Set. (Issued: 28,244).	(10)		34
PS69–**2001**	As last, but Gift Set (Issued: 1,351)	(10)		30
PS70–**2001**	As last, but packed in red leather case (Issued: 16,022)...............................	(10)		48
PS71–**2001**	As last, but Executive Set (Issued: 3,755)...	(10)		60
PS72–**2002**	Proof 'Golden Jubilee' £5 struck in c/n (4555), 'Bimetallic' £2 (4570), 'English' £1 (4594) to 1p. Standard set. (Issued: 30,884)...........................	(9)		32
PS73–**2002**	As last, but Gift Set (Issued: 1,544)	(9)		30
PS74–**2002**	As last, but packed in red leather case (Issued: 23,342)...............................	(9)		46
PS75–**2002**	As last, but Executive Set (Issued: 5,000)...	(9)		70
PS76–**2002**	'Bimetallic' 'Commonwealth Games'£2 (4573, 4574, 4575 and 4576) (Issued: 3,358)...	(4)		36
PS77–**2002**	As last, but Display Set (Issued: 673)	(4)		33

£

PS78–**2003**	Proof 'Coronation'£5 struck in c/n (4557), 'Bimetallic' 'DNA' £2 (4577), 'Bimetallic' £2 (4570), 'UK' £1 (4590), 'Suffragette' 50 pence (4614) and 'Britannia' 50 pence (4610) to 1p. Standard set. (Issued: 23,650)	(11)	34
PS79–**2003**	As last, but packed in red leather case (Issued: 14,863)	(11)	47
PS80–**2003**	As last, but Executive Set (Issued: 5,000)	(11)	70
PS81–**2004**	'Bimetallic' 'Penydarren engine' £2 (4578), 'Bimetallic' £2 (4570), 'Forth Rail Bridge' £1 (4595), 'Sub four-minute mile' 50 pence (4615) and 'Britannia' 50 pence (4610) to 1p. Standard set. (Issued: 17,951)	(10)	35
PS82–**2004**	As last, but packed in red leather case (Issued: 12,968)	(10)	45
PS83–**2004**	As last, but Executive Set (Issued: 4,101)	(10)	65
PS84–**2005**	Proof 'Trafalgar'£5 struck in c/n (4559), Proof 'Nelson'£5 struck in c/n (4560) 'Bimetallic' 'Gunpowder Plot' £2 (4579), 'Bimetallic' £2 (4570), 'Menai Straits Bridge' £1 (4596), 'Samuel Johnson's Dictionary' 50 pence (4616) and 'Britannia' 50 pence (4610) to 1p. (Issued: 21,374)	(12)	40
PS85–**2005**	As last, but packed in red leather case (Issued: 14,899)	(12)	50
PS86–**2005**	As last, but Executive Set (Issued: 4,290)	(12)	75
PS87–**2006**	Proof '80th Birthday'£5 struck in c/n (4561), 'Bimetallic' 'Isambard Brunel' £2 (4581), 'Bimetallic' 'Paddington Station' £2 (4582), 'Bimetallic' £2 (4570), 'MacNeill's Egyptian Arch' £1 (4597), 'Victoria Cross' 50 pence (4617), 'Wounded soldier' 50 pence (4618) and 'Britannia' 50 pence (4610) to 1p (Issued: 17,689)	(13)	42
PS88 –**2006**	As last, but packed in red leather case (Issued: 15,000)	(13)	50
PS89 –**2006**	As last, but Executive Set (Issued: 5,000)	(13)	78
PS90 –**2007**	Proof 'Diamond Wedding'£5 struck in c/n (4562), 'Bimetallic' 'Act of Union' £2 (4583), 'Bimetallic' 'Abolition of Slave Trade' £2 (4584), 'Gateshead Millennium Bridge' £1 (4598), 'Scouting Movement' 50 pence (4619), and 'Britannia' 50p (4610) to 1p (Issued: 18,215)	(12)	40
PS91 –**2007**	As last, but packed in red leather case (Issued: 15,000)	(12)	50
PS92 –**2007**	As last, but Executive Set (Issued: 5,000)	(12)	78
PS93 –**2008**	Proof 'Prince Charles 60th Birthday' £5 struck in c/n (4564), Proof 'Elizabeth I Anniversary' struck in c/n (4563), 'Bimetallic' 'London Olympics Centenary' £2 (4951), 'Bimetallic' £2 (4570) 'UK' £1 (4590), and 'Britannia' 50p (4610) to 1p (Issued: 17,719)	(11)	40
PS94 – **2008**	As last, but packed in black leather case (Issued: 13,614)	(11)	50
PS95 – **2008**	As last, but Executive Set (Issued: 5,000)	(11)	80
PS96 – **2008**	'The Royal Shield of Arms', 'Royal Shield' £1 (4604) to 1p (4611, 4631, 4651, 4671, 4691, 4711) (Issued: 20,000)	(7)	45
PS97 – **2009**	Proof 'Henry VIII' £5 struck in c/n (4565), 'Bimetallic' 'Charles Darwin' £2 (4586), 'Bimetallic' 'Robert Burns' £2 (4585) 'Bimetallic' £2 (4570), 'Royal Shield' £1 (4604), 'Kew Gardens' 50 pence (4621) 50 pence (4620), 20 pence (4631), 10 pence (4651), 5 pence (4671), 2 pence (4691) and 1 pence (4711) (Edition: 20,000)	(12)	40
PS98 – **2009**	As last, but packed in black leather case (Edition: 15,000)	(12)	50
PS99 – **2009**	As last, but Executive Set (Edition: 5,000)	(12)	80
PS100–**2009**	Set of sixteen 50 pence reverse designs marking the 40th Anniversary of the introduction of the 50 pence denomination (4610- 4625) (Edition: 5,000)	(16)	195
PS101–**2010**	Proof 'Restoration of the Monarchy' £5 struck in c/n (4566), 'Bimetallic' 'Florence Nightingale' £2 (4587), 'Bimetallic'£2 (4570), 'London' £1 (4605), 'Belfast' £1 (4606), Royal Shield £1 (4604), 'Girl Guiding' 50 pence (4626), and 50 pence to 1 pence (4620, 4631, 4651, 4671, 4691and 4711) (Edition: 20,000)	(13)	40
PS102–**2010**	As last, but packed in black leather case (Edition: 15,000)	(13)	50

£

PS103–**2010**	As last, but Executive Set (Edition: 5,000)	(13)	80
PS104–**2011**	Proof 'Prince Philip 90th Birthday' £5 struck in c/n (4568),'Bimetallic' 'Mary Rose' £2 (4588), 'Bimetallic' King James Bible'£2 (4589), 'Bimetallic' £2 (4570) 'Edinburgh' £1 (4607), 'Cardiff' £1 (4608), 'Royal Shield '£1(4604), 50 pence, 'WWF' (4627), 50 pence to 1 pence (4620, 4631, 4651, 4671, 4691, and 4711) (Edition: 20,000)..	(14)	45
PS105–**2011**	As last, but packed in black leather case (Edition: 15,000)..........................	(14)	52
PS106–**2011**	As last, but Executive Set (Edition: 5,000)......................................…….	(14)	82
PS107–**2012**	Diamond Jubilee £5, struck in c/n (4569), 'Bimetallic' 'Charles Dickens' £2 (4730), 'Bimetallic' £2 (4570) 'Royal Shield '£1(4604), 50 pence to 1 pence (4620, 4631, 4652, 4672, 4691 and 4711) (Issued: 21,614)	(10)	55
PS108–**2012**	Premium Proof set, Proof Diamond Jubilee £5, struck in c/n (4569), 'Bimetallic' 'Charles Dickens' £2 (4730), 'Bimetallic' £2 (4570) 'Royal Shield '£1(4604), 50 pence to 1 pence (4620, 4631, 4652, 4672, 4691, 4711) and Mint medal (Issued:.3,463)	(10)	99
PS109–**2013**	Premium Proof set, Coronation £5, struck in c/n (4751), 'Bimetallic' 'Guinea' £2 (4731) 'Bimetallic' 'Roundel' £2 (4732), 'Bimetallic' 'Train' £2 (4733),'Bimetallic' £2 (4570) 'Royal Shield' £1 (4604), 'England' £1 (4720), 'Wales' £1(4721), 50 pence 'Ironside' (4628), 50 pence to 1 pence (4620, 4631, 4652, 4672, 4691 and 4711) (Issued:3,965)..	(15)	150
PS109–**2013**	Collector Proof set, Coronation £5, struck in c/n (4751), 'Bimetallic' 'Guinea' £2 (4731) 'Bimetallic' 'Roundel' £2 (4732), 'Bimetallic' 'Train' £2 (4733), 'Bimetallic' £2 (4570) 'Royal Shield' £1 (4604), 'England' £1 (4720), 'Wales' £1 (4721), 50 pence 'Ironside' (4628), 50 pence to 1 pence (4620, 4631, 4652, 4672, 4691 and 4711) (Issued:8,493)...	(15)	110
PS111–**2013**	Commemorative Proof set, Coronation £5, struck in c/n (4751), 'Bimetallic' 'Guinea' £2 (4731) 'Bimetallic' 'Roundel' £2 (4732), 'Bimetallic' 'Train'£2 (4733), 'England' £1 (4720), 'Wales' £1(4721)and 50 pence 'Ironside' (4628) (Issued: 6,121)...	(7)	65
PS112–**2014**	Premium Proof set, Queen Anne £5, struck in c/n (4758), 'Bimetallic' 'Trinity House' £2 (4734), 'Bimetallic' 'World War I' £2 (4735), 'Bimetallic' £2 (4570) 'Royal Shield' £1 (4604), 'Northern Ireland' £1 (4722), 'Scotland' £1(4723.), 50 pence 'Commonwealth Games' (4630), 50 pence to 1 pence (4620, 4636, 4652, 4672, 4691 and 4711) (Edition: 4,500)............................	(14)	155
PS113–**2014**	Collector Proof set, Queen Anne £5, struck in c/n (4758), 'Bimetallic' 'Trinity House' £2 (4734), 'Bimetallic' 'World War I' £2 (4735), 'Bimetallic' £2 (4570) 'Royal Shield' £1 (4604), 'Northern Ireland' £1 (4722), 'Scotland' £1 (4723.), 50 pence 'Commonwealth Games' (4630), 50 pence to 1 pence (4620, 4636, 4652, 4672, 4691 and 4711) (Edition: 30,000)..........................	(14)	110
PS114–**2014**	Commemorative Proof set, Queen Anne £5, struck in c/n (4758), 'Bimetallic' 'Trinity House' £2 (4734), Bimetallic' 'World War I' £2 (4735), 'Northern Ireland' £1 (4722), 'Scotland' £1(4723.), and 50 pence 'Commonwealth Games' (4630), (Edition: 7,500)	(6)	65
PS115–**2015**	Fourth Portrait 'Bimetallic' £2 (4570) 'Royal Shield' , £1 (4604), 50 pence to 1 pence (4620, 4636, 4652, 4672, 4691 and 4711) (Edition: 15,000)	(8)	60
PS116–**2015**	Fifth Portrait 'Bimetallic' £2 (4736) 'Royal Shield', £1 (4604), 50 pence to 1 pence (4632, 4636, 4652, 4672, 4691 and 4711) (Edition: 15,000)	(8)	60
PS117–**2015**	Premium Proof set, Churchill £5, struck in c/n (4764), Waterloo £5, struck in c/n (4765) 'Bimetallic' 'Magna Carta' £2 (4737), 'Bimetallic' 'Royal Navy' £2 (4738), 'Bimetallic' £2 (4736) 'Royal Shield' £1 (4604), 50 pence ' Battle of Britain' (4632) 50 pence to 1 pence (4620, 4636, 4652, 4672, 4691 and 4711) (Edition: 5,000)	(13)	155

£

PS118–**2015**   Collector Proof set, Churchill £5, struck in c/n (4764), Waterloo £5, struck
in c/n (4765) 'Bimetallic' 'Magna Carta' £2 (4737), 'Bimetallic' 'Royal
Navy' £2 (4738), 'Bimetallic' £2 (4570) 'Royal Shield' £1 (4604),
50 pence 'Battle of Britain' (4632), 50 pence to 1 pence (4620, 4636, 4652,
4672, 4691 and 4711) (Edition: 20,000) .... (13) 110

PS118–**2015**   Commemorative Proof set, Churchill £5, struck in c/n (4764), Waterloo £5,
struck in c/n (4765) 'Bimetallic' 'Magna Carta' £2 (4737), 'Bimetallic' 'Royal
Navy' £2 (4738), 50 pence 'Battle of Britain' (4632) (Edition: 10,000) .... (5)   65

Silver Maundy Sets   *FDC* £   *FDC* £

4211   Maundy Set (4p, 3p, 2p and 1p). Uniform dates. Types as 4131

1971 *Tewkesbury Abbey*	225	1989 *Birmingham Cathedral*	200
1972 *York Minster*	200	1990 *Newcastle Cathedral*	200
1973 *Westminster Abbey*	200	1991 *Westminster Abbey*	225
1974 *Salisbury Cathedral*	200	1992 *Chester Cathedral*	200
1975 *Peterborough Cathedral*	200	1993 *Wells Cathedral*	200
1976 *Hereford Cathedral*	200	1994 *Truro Cathedral*	200
1977 *Westminster Abbey*	200	1995 *Coventry Cathedral*	200
1978 *Carlisle Cathedral*	200	1996 *Norwich Cathedral*	200
1979 *Winchester Cathedral*	200	1997 *Bradford Cathedral*	200
1980 *Worcester Cathedral*	200	1998 *Portsmouth Cathedral*	200
1981 *Westminster Abbey*	225	1999 *Bristol Cathedral*	200
1982 *St. Davidís Cathedral*	200	2000 *Lincoln Cathedral*	200
1983 *Exeter Cathedral*	200	2001 *Westminster Abbey*	225
1984 *Southwell Minster*	200	2002 *Canterbury Cathedral*	200
1985 *Ripon Cathedral*	200	2002 *Proof in gold from set *(see PCGS1)	1850
1986 *Chichester Cathedral*	200	2003 *Gloucester Cathedral*	200
1987 *Ely Cathedral*	200	2004 *Liverpool Cathedral*	200
1988 *Lichfield Cathedral*	200	2005 *Wakefield Cathedral*	200

£

4212   — fourpence, 1971-2010 .... *from* 50
4213   — threepence, 1971-2010 .... *from* 50
4214   — twopence, 1971-2010 .... *from* 50
4215   — penny, 1971-2010 .... *from* 75

The place of distribution is shown after each date.

Silver Sets   £

PSS01–**1989**   'Bill of Rights' and 'Claim of Right' £2s (4312 and 4313), Silver piedfort proofs
(Issued: 10,000) .... (2)   85

PSS02–**1989**   As last but Silver proofs (Not known) .... (2)   65

PSS03–**1990**   2 x 5p Silver proofs (4371 and 4372), (Issued: 35,000) .... (2)   30

PSS04–**1992**   2 x 10p Silver proofs (4366 and 4367), (Not known) … .... (2)   34

PSS05–**1996**   25th Anniversary of Decimal Currency (4339, 4351, 4361, 4367, 4372, 4386,
4391) in Silver proof (Edition: 15,000) .... (7) 125

PSS06–**1997**   2 x 50p silver proofs (4351 and 4354) (Issued: 10,304) .... (2)   45

PSS07–**1998**   'EU' and 'NHS' Silver proofs (4611 and 4612) .... (2)   60

PSS08–**2000**   'Millennium' £5, 'Bimetallic' £2, 'Welsh' £1, 50p to 1p, and Maundy coins,
4p-1p, in silver proof (4552, 4570, 4592, 4610, 4630, 4650, 4670, 4212-4215)
(Issued: 13,180) .... (13) 275

£

			£
PSS09–**2002**	'Commonwealth Games' 'Bimetallic' £2 (4573, 4574, 4575 and 4576) in silver (Issued: 2,553)	(4)	140
PSS10–**2002**	As above with the addition of colour and piedfort in silver. (4573A, 4574A, 4575A and 4576A) (Issued: 3,497)	(4)	240
PSS11–**MD**	'Golden Jubilee' £5 (4555) and 'Coronation' £5 (4557) silver proofs	(2)	110
PSS12–**2003**	'Coronation' £5 (4557), 'Britannia' £2 (4503), 'Bimetallic' 'DNA' £2 (4577), 'UK' £1 (4590) and 'Suffragette' 50 pence (4614) silver proofs (Edition:)	(5)	165
PSS13–**2004**	'Entente Cordiale' £5 (4558), 'Britannia' £2 (4500), 'Bimetallic' 'Penydarren engine' £2 (4578) 'Forth Rail Bridge' £1 (4595) and 'Sub four-minute mile' 50 pence (4615) silver proofs (Edition:)	(5)	165
PSS14–**2004**	'Bimetallic' 'Penydarren engine' £2 (4578), 'Forth Rail Bridge' £1 (4595), 'Sub four-minute mile' 50 pence (4615) Silver piedfort proofs	(3)	145
PSS15–**2005**	'Bimetallic' 'Gunpowder Plot' £2 (4579), Bimetallic' 'World War II' £2 (4580), 'Menai Straits Bridge' £1 (4596), 'Samuel Johnson's Dictionary' 50 pence Silver piedfort proofs	(4)	190
PSS16–**2005**	'Trafalgar' £5 (4559) and 'Nelson' £5 (4560) silver piedfort proofs, (Issued: 2,818)	(2)	175
PSS17–**2006**	'H M The Queen's 80th Birthday' £5, 'Bimetallic' £2, 'Northern Ireland' £1, 50p to 1p,(4561, 4570, 4597, 4610, 4630, 4650, 4670, and Maundy Coins, 4p – 1p, in silver proof, (4212 – 4215) (Edition: 8,000)	(13)	275
PSS18–**2006**	'Bimetallic' 'Isambard Brunel' £2 (4581) and 'Bimetallic' 'Paddington Station' £2 (4582) silver proofs (Edition: taken from individual coin limits)	(2)	70
PSS19–**2006**	As last but silver piedforts (Edition: 5,000)	(2)	130
PSS20–**2006**	'Victoria Cross' 50 pence (4617) and 'Wounded soldier' 50 pence (4618) silver proofs (Edition: taken from individual coin limits)	(2)	65
PSS21–**2006**	As last but silver piedforts (Edition: 5,000)	(2)	115
PSS22–**2006**	'80th Birthday' £5 (4561), 'Bimetallic' 'Isambard Brunel' £2 (4581) and 'Bimetallic' 'Paddington Station' £2 (4582), 'MacNeill's Egyptian Arch' £1 (4597), 'Victoria Cross' 50 pence (4617), 'Wounded soldier' 50 pence (4618) silver piedforts (Edition: taken from individual coin limits)	(6)	325
PSS23–**2007**	'Diamond Wedding' £5, Britannia £2, 'Bimetallic' 'Act of Union' £2, 'Bimetallic' 'Abolition of Slavery' £2, 'Millennium Bridge' £1 and 'Scout Movement'50p in silver proof (4562, 4505, 4583, 4584, 4598 and 4619) (Edition: taken from individual coin limits)	(6)	200
PSS24–**2007**	'Diamond Wedding' £5, 'Bimetallic' 'Act of Union'£2, 'Bimetallic' 'Abolition of Slavery' £2, 'Millennium Bridge' £1 and 'Scout Movement'50p in silver piedfort (4562, 4583, 4584, 4598 and 4619) (Edition: taken from individual coin limits	(5)	250
PSS25–**MD**	Set of four £1 coins 'Forth Rail Bridge' (4595), 'Menai Straits Bridge' (4596) 'MacNiell's Egyptian Arch' (4597) and 'Gateshead Millennium Bridge' (4598) in silver proof (Edition: taken from individual coin limits)	(4)	115
PSS26–**MD**	As above but in silver piedfort (Edition: 1,400 taken from individual coin limits)	(4)	200
PSS27–**2008**	'Emblems of Britain', 'UK' £1 (4590), 'Britannia' 50 pence (4610), 20 pence to 1p silver proofs (Issued: 8,168)	(7)	150
PSS28–**2008**	'The Royal Shield of Arms', 'Royal Shield' £1 (4604) to 1p (4611, 4631, 4651, 4671, 4691, 4711) silver proof (Issued: 10,000)	(7)	160
PSS29–**2008**	As above but silver piedforts (Issued: 3,000)	(7)	295

£

			£
PSS30–**2008**	Set of 14 different £1 with selected gold plating to the reverse designs (4590 to 4603) (Edition: 15,000 collections)	(14)	395
PSS31–**2008**	Set of 3 £1 Regional designs for Scotland with selected gold plating to the reverse designs (4591B, 4595C and 4599A) (Edition: 750, taken from above)	(3)	95

£

PSS32–**2008** Set of 3 £1 Regional designs for Wales with selected gold plating to the reverse designs (4592B, 4596C and 4600A) (Edition: 750, taken from above) .... (3) 95

PSS33–**2008** Set of 3 £1 Regional designs for Northern Ireland with selected gold plating to the reverse designs (4593B, 4597C and 4601A) (Edition: 750, taken from above) .... (3) 95

PSS34–**2008** Set of 3 £1 Regional designs for England with selected gold plating to the reverse designs (4594B, 4598C and 4602A) (Edition: 750, taken from above) (3) 95

PSS35–**2008** 'Prince Charles 60th Birthday' £5 (4563), 'Elizabeth I Anniversary' £5 (4564), Britannia £2 (4506), 'London Olympic Centenary' £2 (4951) and 'UK' £1 (4590) silver proofs (Edition; 5,000) .... (5) 180

PSS36–**2008** 'Prince Charles 60th Birthday' £5 (4563), 'Elizabeth I Anniversary' £5 (4564), 'London Olympic Centenary' £2 (4951) and 'Royal Shield' £1 (4604) silver piedforts (Edition: 3,000) .... (4) 250

PSS37–**2009** 'Henry VIII' £5 (4565), 'Bimetallic' 'Charles Darwin' £2 (4586), Bimetallic 'Robert Burns' £2 (4585) 'Bimetallic'£2 (4570), 'Royal Shield' £1 (4604), 'Kew Gardens' 50 pence (4621), 50 pence (4620), 20 pence (4631), 10 pence (4651), 5 pence (4671), 2 pence (4691) and 1 pence (4711) silver proofs (Edition: 7,500 .... (12) 270

PSS38–**2009** 'Henry VIII' £5 (4565), Britannia £2 (4501), 'Charles Darwin' £2 (4586), 'Robert Burns' £2 (4585), 'Royal Shield' £1 (4604) and 50 pence 'Kew Gardens' (4621) silver proofs (Edition; 1,500) .... (6) 200

PSS39–**2009** 'Henry VIII' £5 (4565), 'Charles Darwin' £2 (4586), 'Robert Burns' £2 (4585) and 50 pence 'Kew Gardens' (4621) silver piedforts (Edition: 2,500) .... (4) 255

PSS40–**2009** Set of sixteen 50 pence reverse designs marking 40th Anniversary of the introduction of the 50 pence denomination (4610- 4625) silver proofs (Edition: 2,500) .... (16) 425

PSS41–**2010** 'Restoration of the Monarchy' £5 (4566), 'Bimetallic 'Florence Nightingale' £2 (4587), 'Bimetallic'£2 (4570), 'London' £1 (4605), 'Belfast' £1 (4606), Royal Shield £1 (4604), 'Girl Guiding' 50 pence (4626), and 50 pence to 1p (4620, 4631, 4651, 4671, 4691and 4711) silver proofs (Edition: 3,500) .... (13) 300

PSS42–**2010** 'Restoration of the Monarchy' £5 (4566), 'Bimetallic 'Florence Nightingale' £2 (4587), 'London' £1 (4605), 'Belfast' £1 (4606), and 'Girl Guiding' 50 pence (4626) silver proofs (Edition: 2,500) .... (5) 180

PSS43–**2010** 'Restoration of the Monarchy'£5 (4566), 'Bimetallic 'Florence Nightingale' £2 (4587), 'London' £1 (4605), 'Belfast' £1 (4606), and 'Girl Guiding' 50 pence (4626) silver piedforts (Edition: 2,500) .... (5) 300

PSS44-**2011** Proof 'Prince Philip 90th Birthday' £5 (4568),'Bimetallic' 'Mary Rose' £2 (4588), 'Bimetallic' King James Bible'£2 (4589),'Bimetallic' £2 (4570) 'Edinburgh' £1 (4607), 'Cardiff' £1 (4608), 'Royal Shield '£1(4604), 50 pence,' WWF' (4627), 50 pence to 1 pence (4620, 4631, 4651, 4671, 4691 and 4711) silver proofs (Edition: 2,500) .... (14) 450

PSS45-**2011** Proof 'Prince Philip 90th Birthday' £5 (4568),'Bimetallic' 'Mary Rose' £2 (4588), 'Bimetallic' King James Bible'£2 (4590), 'Edinburgh' £1 (4607), 'Cardiff' £1 (4608), 50 pence,' WWF' (4627), silver proofs (Edition: 1,500) .... (6) 285

PSS46-**2011** Proof 'Prince Philip 90th Birthday' £5 (4568),'Bimetallic' 'Mary Rose' £2 (4589), 'Bimetallic' King James Bible'£2 (4589), 'Edinburgh' £1 (4607), 'Cardiff' £1 (4608), 'WWF' (4627), silver piedforts (Edition: 2,000) .... (6) 455

PSS47–**2012** Proof Diamond Jubilee £5, (4569), 50 pence to 1 pence (4620, 4631, 4652, 4672, 4691 and 4711) silver proofs, (Edition: 995) .... (7) 395

PSS48–**2012** Proof Diamond Jubilee £5, (4569), 'Bimetallic' 'Charles Dickens' £2 (4730), 'Bimetallic' £2 (4570) 'Royal Shield '£1(4604), 50 pence to 1 pence (4620, 4631, 4652, 4672, 4691 and 4711) silver proofs, the £2s to 1 pence with selected gold plating (Edition: 2,012) .... (10) 490

£

PSS49–**MD** Proof Silver Wedding Crown, 25pence, Golden Wedding Crown, £5 and
Diamond Wedding Crown, £5 (4226, 4304 and 4562) silver proofs (Edition:
250 taken from the original sales and obtained from the secondary market). (3) 150

PSS50–**2013** Proof 'Coronation' £5, (4751), 'Bimetallic' 'Guinea' £2 (4731) 'Bimetallic'
'Roundel' (4732), 'Bimetallic' 'Train' £2 (4733), 'Bimetallic' £2 (4570)
'Royal Shield' £1 (4604), 'England' £1 (4720), 'Wales' £1 (4721),
50 pence 'Ironside' (4628), 50 pence to 1 pence (4620, 4631, 4652, 4672,
4691 and 4711) silver proofs (Issued: 985) .... (15) 600

PSS51–**2013** Proof 'Coronation' £5, (4751), 'Bimetallic' 'Guinea' £2 (4731) 'Bimetallic'
'Roundel' £2 (4732), 'Bimetallic' 'Train'£2 (4733), 'England' £1 (4720),
'Wales' £1 (4721) and 50 pence 'Ironside' (4628) silver piedfort
(Issued: 486) .... (7) 650

PSS52–**2013** 'Bimetallic' 'Roundel' £2 (4732) and 'Bimetallic' 'Train'£2 (4733) silver
proofs (Issued: 2,204) .... (2) 100

PSS53–**2013** Queen's Portrait set of £5 coins, (4754 – 4757) silver proofs (Issued: 1,465)...... (4) 400

PSS54–**2013** Queen's Portrait set of £5 coins, (4754 – 4757) silver piedfort (Issued: 697) ..... (4) 800

PSS55–**2013** Thirtieth Anniversary set of three £1 coins, (4590, 4603 and 4604) silver
proofs (Issued: 1,311) .... (3) 150

PSS56–**2014** Proof 'Queen Anne' £5, (4758), 'Bimetallic' 'Trinity House' £2 (4734),
'Bimetallic' 'World War I' £2 (4735), 'Bimetallic' £2 (4570) 'Royal Shield'
£1 (4604), 'Northern Ireland' £1 (4722), 'Scotland' £1 (4723.), 50 pence
'Commonwealth Games' (4630), 50 pence to 1 pence (4620, 4636, 4652,
4672, 4691 and 4711) silver proofs (Edition: 2,014) .... (14) 560

PSS57–**2014** Proof 'Queen Anne' £5, (4758), 'Bimetallic' 'Trinity House' £2 (4734),
'Bimetallic' 'World War I' £2 (4735), 'Bimetallic' £2 (4570) 'Royal Shield'
£1 (4604), 'Northern Ireland' £1 (4722), 'Scotland' £1 (4723.), and 50 pence
'Commonwealth Games' (4630), silver proofs (Edition: 1,000).................. (6) 295

PSS58–**2014** Proof 'Queen Anne' £5, (4758), 'Bimetallic' 'Trinity House' £2 (4734),
'Bimetallic' 'World War I' £2 (4735), 'Bimetallic' £2 (4570) 'Royal Shield'
£1 (4604), 'Northern Ireland' £1 (4722), 'Scotland' £1 (4723.), and 50 pence
'Commonwealth Games' (4630), silver piedforts (Edition: 2,014)............... (6) 570

PSS59–**2014** Celebrating British Landmarks. Set of four £5, (4760 – 4763), silver proofs
(Edition: 3,500) .... (4) 360

PSS60–**2014** World War 1. Set of six £5, Renumbered (4850 – 4855), silver proofs
(Edition: 1,914) .... (6) 450

PSS61–**2015** Fourth Portrait 'Bimetallic' £2 (4570) 'Royal Shield', £1 (4604), 50 pence
to 1 pence (4620, 4636, 4652, 4672, 4691 and 4711), silver proofs,
(Edition: 7,500) .... (8) 240

PSS62–**2015** Fifth Portrait 'Bimetallic' £2 (4736) 'Royal Shield', £1 (4604), 50 pence to
1 pence (4632, 4636, 4652, 4672, 4691 and 4711), silver proofs,
(Edition: 7,500) .... (8) 240

PSS63–**2015** Churchill £5 (4764), Waterloo £5, (4765) 'Bimetallic' 'Magna Carta' £2
(4737), 'Bimetallic' 'Royal Navy' £2 (4738), 'Bimetallic' £2 (4736) 'Royal
Shield' £1 (4604), 50 pence 'Battle of Britain' (4621) 50 pence to 1 pence
(4620, 4636, 4652, 4672, 4691 and 4711) silver proofs (Edition: 1,500) ..... (13) 560

PSS64–**2015** Churchill £5, (4764), Waterloo £5, (4765) 'Bimetallic' 'Magna Carta' £2
(4737), 'Bimetallic' 'Royal Navy' £2 (4738), 50 pence 'Battle of Britain'
(4632), silver proofs (Edition: 1,500).. (5) 295

PSS65–**2015** Churchill £5, (4764), Waterloo £5, (4765) 'Bimetallic' 'Magna Carta' £2
(4737), 'Bimetallic' 'Royal Navy' £2 (4738), 50 pence 'Battle of Britain'
(4632), silver piedforts (Edition: 1,500)... (5) 570

PSS66–**2015** World War 1. Second Set of six £5, (4856 – 4861), silver proofs (Edition: 1,915) (6) 450

Britannia Silver Proof Set

			£
PBS01–**1997**	£2 – 20 pence (4300, 4300A, 4300B, 4300C) (Issued: 11,832)	(4)	175
PBS02–**1998**	£2 – 20 pence (4500, 4510, 4520, 4530) (Issued: 3,044)	(4)	160
PBS03–**2001**	£2 – 20 pence (4502, 4511, 4521, 4531) (Issued: 4,596)	(4)	150
PBS04–**2003**	£2 – 20 pence (4503, 4512, 4522, 4532) (Issued: 3,669)	(4)	150
PBS05–**MD**	Britannia set of four different £2 designs, 1999- 2003 (4500, 4501,4502, 4503) (Edition: 5,000)	(4)	160
PBS06–**2005**	Britannia proofs, £2 – 20 pence (4504, 4513, 4523, 4533) (Issued: 2,360)	(4)	150
PBS07–**2006**	Britannia set of five different £2 designs with selected gold Plating of obverse and reverse (4500A, 4501A, 4502A, 4503A, 4504A) (Issued: 3,000)	(5)	350
PBS08–**2007**	Britannia proofs, £2 - 20 pence, (4505, 4514, 4524, 4534) (Issued: 2,500)	(4)	150
PBS09–**2007**	Britannia set of six different proof £1 designs with satin finish on reverse (4510A, 4511A, 4512A, 4513A, 4514A, 4515) (Issued: 2,000)	(6)	225
PBS10–**2008**	Britannia proofs, £2 – 20p (4506, 4516, 4525, 4535) (Issued: 2,500)	(4)	150
PBS11–**2009**	Britannia proofs, £2 – 20p (4501, 4517, 4526, 4536) (Issued: 2,500)	(4)	150
PBS12–**2010**	Britannia proofs, £2 – 20p (4502, 4518, 4527, 4537) (Edition: 3,500)	(4)	150
PBS13–**2011**	Britannia proofs, £2 – 20p (4508, 4519, 4528, 45387) (Edition: 3,500)	(4)	195
PBS14–**2012**	Britannia proofs, £2 – 20p, (As PB02) (Issued: 2,595)	(4)	195
PBS15–**2012**	Britannia £1 proofs, set of nine different reverse designs (4510 to 4514, and 4516 to 4519) (Issued: 1,656)	(9)	400
PBS16–**2013**	Britannia proofs, £2 – 10p, (0.999 silver) (4509,4560,4529,4539 and 4550) (Issued: 3,087)	(5)	450
PBS17–**2013**	Britannia proofs, 20p and 10p (0.999 silver) (4539 and 4550)	(2)	39
PBS18–**2014**	Britannia proofs, £2 – 50 pence, (0.999 silver) (5025, 4702, 5015, 4540, 4681 and 4675) (Edition: 1,750)	(6)	200
PBS19–**2014**	Britannia proofs, 20p – 50 pence, (0.999 silver) (Edition: 1,000)	(3)	45
PBS20–**2015**	Britannia proofs, £2 – 50 pence, (0.999 silver) (5026, 5020, 5016, 5010, 5005 and 5000) (Edition: 1,750)	(6)	200
PBS21–**2015**	Britannia proofs, 20p – 50 pence, (0.999 silver) (Edition: 1,000)	(3)	45

Gold Sovereign Proof Sets

Many of the coins that appear in the Gold proof sets were also offered for sale as individual coins in presentation cases with appropriate certificates. There are collectors of particular denominations such as £2 pieces, sovereigns and half sovereigns who request coins as issued i.e. in their cases with certificates rather than buying coins taken from sets. As a consequence, many of these individual coins command a premium over those that might have come from cased sets. As a result the prices for sets are often less than the sum of the individual coins.

PGS01–**1980**	Gold £5 to half-sovereign (4201, 4203-4205) (Issued: 10,000)	(4)	2000
PGS02–**1981**	U.K. Proof coin Commemorative collection. (Consists of £5, sovereign, 'Royal Wedding' Crown (4229) in silver, plus base metal proofs 50p to ½p), (Not known)	(9)	1500
PGS03–**1982**	Gold £5 to half-sovereign (as 1980 issue) (Issued: 2,500)	(4)	2000
PGS04–**1983**	Gold £2, sovereign and half-sovereign, (4203 – 4205) (Not known)	(3)	900
PGS05–**1984**	Gold £5, sovereign and half-sovereign, (4201, 4204 and 4205) (Issued: 7,095)	(3)	1600
PGS06–**1985**	Gold £5 to half-sovereign (4251, 4261, 4271, 4276) (Issued: 5,849)	(4)	2000
PGS07–**1986**	Gold Commonwealth games £2, sovereign and half-sovereign (4311, 4271 and 4276) (Issued: 12,500)	(3)	900
PGS08–**1987**	Gold £2, sovereign and half-sovereign (4261, 4271 and 4276) (Issued: 12,500)	(3)	900
PGS09–**1988**	Gold £2 to half-sovereign, (as 1987 issue) (Issued: 11,192)	(3)	900
PGS10–**1989**	Sovereign Anniversary Gold £5 to half-sovereign (4254, 4263, 4272, 4277), (Issued: 5,000)	(4)	4000

			£
PGS11–**1989**	Gold £2 to half-sovereign (4263, 4272 and 4277) (Issued: 7,936)	(3)	2000
PGS12–**1990**	Gold £5 to half-sovereign (as 1985 issue), (Issued: 1,721).............................	(4)	2000
PGS13–**1990**	Gold £2 to half-sovereign (as 1988 issue), (Issued: 1,937)............................	(3)	950
PGS14–**1991**	Gold £5 to half-sovereign (as 1985 issue) (Issued: 1,336).............................	(4)	2000
PGS15–**1991**	Gold £2 to half-sovereign (as 1987 issue (Issued: 1,152)..............................	(3)	950
PGS16–**1992**	Gold £5 to half-sovereign (as 1985 issue) (Issued: 1,165).............................	(4)	2000
PGS17–**1992**	Gold £2 to half-sovereign (as 1987 issue) (Issued: 967)................................	(3)	950
PGS18–**1993**	Gold £5 to half-sovereign with silver Pistrucci medal in case (Issued: 1,078)	(5)	2200
PGS19–**1993**	Gold £2 to half-sovereign (as 1985 issue) (Issued: 663)................................	(3)	1000
PGS20–**1994**	Gold £5, £2, sovereign and half-sovereign (4251, 4314, 4271 and 4276) (Issued: 918)..	(4)	2300
PGS21–**1994**	Gold £2, sovereign and half-sovereign (4314, 4271 and 4276) (Issued: 1,249)	(3)	950
PGS22–**1995**	Gold £5,£2,sovereign and half-sovereign (4251,4315,4271and 4276) (Issued: 718)..	(4)	2000
PGS23–**1995**	Gold £2, sovereign and half-sovereign (4315, 4271 and 4276) (Issued: 1,112)	(3)	950
PGS24–**1996**	Gold £5 to half-sovereign (as 1985 issue) (Issued: 742)................................	(4)	2000
PGS25–**1996**	Gold £2 to half-sovereign (as 1987 issue) (Issued: 868)................................	(3)	950
PGS26–**1997**	Gold £5,£2,sovereign and half-sovereign (4251,4318,4271 and 4276) (Issued: 860)..	(4)	2000
PGS27–**1997**	Gold £2 to half-sovereign (4318, 4271 and 4276) (Issued: 817)	(3)	950
PGS28–**1998**	Gold £5 to half sovereign (4400, 4420, 4430, 4440) (Issued: 789)	(4)	2000
PGS29–**1998**	Gold £2 to half sovereign (4420, 4430, 4440) (Issued: 560)	(3)	975
PGS30–**1999**	Gold £5, £2, sovereign and half sovereign (4400, 4571, 4430 and 4440) (Issued: 991)..	(4)	2000
PGS31–**1999**	Gold £2, sovereign and half sovereign (4571, 4430 and 4440) (Issued: 912) .	(3)	950
PGS32–**2000**	Gold £5 to half-sovereign (as 1998 issue) (Issued: 1,000).............................	(4)	2000
PGS33–**2000**	Gold £2 to half-sovereign (as 1998 issue) (Issued: 1,250).............................	(3)	900
PGS34–**2001**	Gold £5,£2,sovereign and half sovereign (4400, 4572, 4430 and 4440) (Issued: 1,000)..	(4)	2000
PGS35–**2001**	Gold £2 , sovereign and half sovereign (4572,4430 and 4440)(Issued: 891) ..	(3)	800
PGS36–**2002**	Gold £5 to half sovereign (4401, 4421, 4431, 4441) (Issued: 3,000)	(4)	2600
PGS37–**2002**	Gold £2 to half sovereign (4421, 4431, 4441) (Issued: 3,947)	(3)	1100
PGS38–**2003**	Gold £5 to half sovereign (as 1998 issue) (Issued: 2,050)	(4)	2000
PGS39–**2003**	Gold £2, sovereign and half sovereign (4577, 4430 and 4440) (Issued: 1,737)	(3)	900
PGS40–**2004**	Gold £5 to half sovereign (as 1998 issue) (Issued: 1,749)	(4)	2000
PGS41–**2004**	Gold £2, sovereign and half sovereign (4578, 4430 and 4440) (Issued: 761) .	(3)	900
PGS42–**2005**	Gold £5 to half sovereign (4402, 4422, 4432, 4442 (Issued: 2,161)...............	(4)	2600
PGS43–**2005**	Gold £2 to half sovereign (4422, 4432, 4442) (Issued: 797)	(3)	1100
PGS44–**2006**	Gold £5 to half sovereign (as 1998 issue) (Issued: 1,750)	(4)	2000
PGS45–**2006**	Gold £2 to half sovereign (as 1998 issue) (Issued: 540)	(3)	1100
PGS46–**2007**	Gold £5 to half sovereign (as 1998 issue) (Issued: 1,750)	(4)	2000
PGS47–**2007**	Gold £2 to half sovereign (as 1998 issue) (Issued: 651)	(3)	900
PGS48–**2007**	Gold sovereign and half sovereign (4430 and 4440) (Issued: 818)	(2)	500
PGS49–**2008**	Gold £5 to half sovereign (as 1998 issue) (Issued: 1,750)	(4)	2000
PGS50–**2008**	Gold £2 to half sovereign (as 1998 issue) (Issued: 583)	(3)	900
PGS51–**2008**	Gold sovereign and half sovereign (as 2007 issue) (Issued: 804, in addition to individual coin issues)...	(2)	500
PGS52–**2009**	Gold £5, £2, sovereign, half sovereign, and quarter sovereign (4403, 4423, 4433, 4443, and 4445) (Issued: 1,750)...	(5)	2500
PGS53–**2009**	Gold £2, sovereign and half sovereign (4423, 4433 and 4445) (Edition: 750)	(3)	950
PGS54–**2009**	Gold sovereign and half sovereign (4433 and 4443) (Edition: 1,000).............	(2)	500
PGS55–**2010**	Gold £5 to quarter sovereign (as 2009 issue) (Edition: 1,750) ....(5)		2500

£

PGS56–**2010**	Gold £2 to half sovereign (as 2009 issue) (Edition: 750)...................... ....(3)		975
PGS57–**2010**	Gold sovereign, half sovereign and quarter sovereign (4433, 4443 and 4445)		
	(Edition: 1,500)	(3)	600
PGS58–**2011**	Gold £5 to quarter sovereign (as 2010 issue) (Edition: 1,500)	(5)	3250
PGS59–**2011**	Gold £2 to quarter sovereign (4423, 4433, 4443 and 4445) (Edition: 200).....	(4)	1600
PGS60–**2011**	(Previously listed as PGS59) Gold £2 to half sovereign (as 2010 issue)		
	(Edition: 750)	(3)	1200
PGS61–**2011**	(Previously listed as PGS60) Gold sovereign, half sovereign and quarter		
	sovereign (4433, 4443 and 4445) (Edition: 1,000)	(3)	675
PGS62–**2012**	Gold £5, £2, sovereign, half sovereign and quarter sovereign (4404, 4424,		
	4434, 4444 and 4446) (Issued: 956)..	(5)	3250
PGS63–**2012**	Gold £2 to quarter sovereign (4424, 4434, 4444 and 4446) (Edition: 159).....	(4)	1600
PGS64–**2012**	Gold £2 to half sovereign (4424, 4434 and 4444) (Issued: 335)	(3)	1200
PGS65–**2012**	Gold sovereign, half sovereign and quarter sovereign (4433, 4443 and 4445)		
	(Issued: 701)...	(3)	675
PGS66–**2012**	BU Gold £2 to half sovereign (4424, 4434 and 4444) (Edition: 60)...............	(3)	2000
PGS67–**2013**	Gold £5, £2, sovereign, half sovereign and quarter sovereign (4403, 4423,		
	4433, 4443 and 4445) (Issued: 388)..	(5)	3600
PGS68–**2013**	Gold £2 to half sovereign (4423, 4433 and 4445) (Issued: 380)	(3)	1500
PGS69–**2013**	Gold sovereign, half sovereign and quarter sovereign (4433, 4443 and 4445)		
	(Issued: 652)	(3)	750
PGS70–**2013**	BU Gold £2 to half sovereign (4424, 4434 and 4444) (Issued: 124)...............	(3)	1550
PGS71–**2014**	Gold £5, £2, sovereign, half sovereign and quarter sovereign (4403, 4423,		
	4433, 4443 and 4445) (Edition: 750)	(5)	3300
PGS72–**2014**	Gold £2 to half sovereign (4423, 4433 and 4445) (Edition: 500)	(3)	1300
PGS73–**2014**	Gold sovereign, half sovereign and quarter sovereign (4433, 4443 and 4445)		
	(Edition: 750)	(3)	625
PGS73–**2015**	Gold £5, £2, sovereign, half sovereign and quarter sovereign (4403, 4423,		
	4433, 4443 and 4445) (Edition: 500)	(5)	2700
PGS74–**2015**	Gold £2 to half sovereign (4423, 4433 and 4445) (Edition: 500)	(3)	1200
PGS75–**2015**	Gold sovereign, half sovereign and quarter sovereign (4433, 4443 and 4445)		
	(Edition: 1,000)	(3)	625
PGS76–**2015**	New obverse portrait Gold £5, £2, sovereign, half sovereign and quarter		
	sovereign (4411, 4425, 4435, 4415 and 4447) (Edition: 350).........................	(5)	2700
PGS77–**2015**	New obverse portrait Gold £2 to half sovereign (4425, 4435 and 4415)		
	(Edition:500)	(3)	1200

Britannia Gold Proof Sets

PBG01–**1987**	Britannia Proofs £100, £50, £25, £10 (4281, 4286, 4291, and 4296), alloyed		
	with copper (Issued: 10,000)	(4)	2000
PBG02–**1987**	Britannia Proofs £25, £10 (4291 and 4296) (Issued: 11,100)	(2)	450
PBG03–**1988**	Britannia Proofs £100–£10 (as 1987 issue) (Issued: 3,505)............................	(4)	2000
PBG04–**1988**	Britannia Proofs £25, £10 (as 1987 issue) (Issued: 894)................................	(2)	450
PBG05–**1989**	Britannia Proofs £100–£10 (as 1987) (Issued: 2,268).....................................	(4)	2000
PBG06–**1989**	Britannia Proofs £25, £10 (as 1987 issue) (Issued: 451).................................	(2)	450
PBG07–**1990**	Britannia Proofs, £100–£10, gold with the addition of silver alloy (4282, 4287,		
	4292, 4297) (Issued: 527)..	(4)	2000
PBG08–**1991**	Britannia Proofs, as PBS07 (Issued: 509)	(4)	2000

£

PBG09–**1992** Britannia Proofs, as PBS07 (Issued: 500) .... (4) 2000

PBG10–**1993** Britannia Proofs, as PBS07 (Issued: 462) .... (4) 2000

PBG11–**1994** Britannia Proofs, as PBS07 ((Issued: 435) .... (4) 2000

PBG12–**1995** Britannia Proofs, as PBS07 (Issued: 500) .... (4) 2000

PBG13–**1996** Britannia Proofs, as PBS07 (Issued: 483) .... (4) 2000

PBG14–**1997** Britannia proofs £100, £50, £25, £10 (4283, 4288, 4293, 4298) (Issued: 892) (4) 2100

PBG15–**1998** Britannia proofs £100, £50, £25, £10 (4450, 4460, 4470, 4480) (Issued: 750) (4) 2000

PBG16–**1999** Britannia Proofs, as PBS15 (Issued: 740) .... (4) 2000

PBG17–**2000** Britannia Proofs, as PBS15 (Issued: 750) .... (4) 2000

PBG18–**2001** Britannia Proofs £100, £50, £25, £10 (4451, 4461, 4471, 4481) (Issued: 1,000) (4) 2000

PBG19–**2002** Britannia Proofs, as PBS15 (Issued: 945) .... (4) 2000

PBG20–**2003** Britannia Proofs £100, £50, £25, £10 (4452, 4462, 4472, 4482) (Issued: 1,250) (4) 2000

PBG21–**2003** Britannia Proofs £50, £25, £10 (4462, 4472, 4482) (Issued: 825) .... (3) 800

PBG22–**MD** Britannia BU £100 set of four different designs, 1987, 1997, 2001, 2003 (4281,
4283, 4451, 4452) (Edition: 2,500) .... (4) 4000

PBG23–**2004** Britannia Proofs, as PBS15 (Issued: 973) .... (4) 2000

PBG24–**2004** Britannia Proofs, £50, £25, £10 (4460, 4470, 4480) (Issued: 223) .... (3) 850

PBG25–**2005** Britannia Proofs, £100, £50, £25, £10 (4453, 4463, 4473, 4483) (Issued: 1,439) (4) 2000

PBG26–**2005** Britannia Proofs, £50, £25, £10 (4463, 4473, 4483) (Issued: 417) .... (3) 850

PBG27–**2006** Britannia Proofs, as PBS15 (Issued: 1,163) .... (4) 2000

PBG28–**2006** Britannia set of five different proof £25 designs (4470, 4471, 4472, 4473, 4474)
(Edition: 250) .... (5) 1500

PBG29–**2007** (Previously listed as **PBS28**) Britannia Proofs, £100, £50, £25, £10 (4454, 4464,
4475, 4484) (Issued: 1,250)... (4) 2000

PBG30–**2008** Britannia Proofs, £100, £50, £25, £10 (4455, 4465, 4476, 4485) (Issued: 1,250).. (4) 2000

PBG31–**2009** Britannia Proofs, £100, £50, £25, £10 (4456, 4466, 4474, 4486)
(Edition: 1,250) .... (4) 2000

PBG32–**2010** Britannia Proofs, £100, £50, £25, £10 (4457, 4467, 4477, 4487) (Edition: 1,250) (4) 2000

PBG33–**2010** Britannia Proofs, £50, £25, £10 (4467, 4475, 4487) (Edition: 500)................. (3) 950

PBG34–**2011** Britannia Proofs, £100, £50, £25, £10 (4458, 4468, 4478, 4488)
(Edition: 1,000) .... (4) 3000

PBG35–**2011** Britannia Proofs, £50, £25, £10 (4468, 4478, 4488) (Edition: 250) .... (3) 1500

PBG36–**2012** Britannia Proofs, as PBS15 (Issued: 352) .... (4) 3000

PBG37–**2012** Britannia Proofs, £50, £25 and £10 (4460, 4470 and 4480) (Issued: 99) .... (3) 1500

PBG38–**MD** Britannia Proof set of 1987 (£100 to £10, struck in copper alloyed gold, see
PBS01), and set of 2012 (£100 to £10, struck in silver alloyed gold, see
PBS36) (Issued: 13, sets of 1987 from the secondary market) .... (8) 5000

PBG39–**2013** Britannia Proofs, £100 - £1, (0.9999 gold), (4459, 4469, 4479, 4489 and 4760)
(Issued: 261) .... (5) 5750

PBG40–**2013** Britannia Proofs, Premium set, £50, £25 and £10, (0.9999 gold), (4469, 4479
and 4489) (Issued: 90)... (3) 1375

PBG41–**2013** Britannia Proofs, £25, £10 and £1, (0.9999 gold), (4479, 4489 and 4760)
(Issued 136) .... (3) 675

PBG42–**2014** Britannia Proofs, £100 – 50 pence, (0.9999 gold), (5055, 5050, 5045, 4490,
4776 and 4740) (Edition: 250) .... (6) 2600

PGB43–**2014** Britannia Proofs, £50 – £10, (0.9999 gold) (Edition: 100) .... (3) 1175

PGB44–**2014** Britannia Proofs, £25 – £1, (0.9999 gold) (Edition: 150) .... (3) 595

PBG45–**2015** Britannia Proofs, £100 - £1, (0.9999 gold), (5056, 5051, 5046, 5040, 5035
and 5030) (Edition: 250)... (6) 2600

PGB46–**2015** Britannia Proofs, £50 – £10, (0.9999 gold) (Edition: 100)............................. (3) 1175

PGB47–**2015** Britannia Proofs, £10 – 50 pence, (0.9999 gold) (Edition: 250) .... (3) 350

Gold Coin Proof Sets £

PCGS1–**2002**	Commonwealth Games 'Bimetallic' £2 (4573, 4574, 4575 and 4576) in gold (Issued: 315)..	(4) 2100
PGJS1–**2002**	'Golden Jubilee' £5, 'Bimetallic' £2, 'English' £1, 50p to 1p and Maundy coins, 4p-1p, in gold proof (4555, 4570, 4594, 4610, 4630, 4650, 4670, 4212-4215) (Issued: 2,002)	(13) 5250
PGBNS–**2006**	'Bimetallic' 'Isambard Brunel' £2 (4581) and 'Bimetallic' 'Paddington Station' £2 (4582) gold proofs (Edition: taken from individual coin limits)	(2) 1000
PGVCS–**2006**	'Victoria Cross' 50 pence (4617), 'Wounded Colleague' 50 pence (4618) gold proof (Edition: taken from individual coin limits).............................	(2) 975
PGBS1–**MD**	Set of four £1 coins 'Forth Rail Bridge' (4595), 'Menai Straits Bridge' (4596) 'MacNiell's Egyptian Arch' (4597) and 'Gateshead Millennium Bridge' (4598) in gold proof (Edition: 300 sets taken from individual coin limits)...........	(4) 2400
PGEBCS–**2008**	'Emblems of Britain', 'UK' £1 (4590), 'Britannia' 50 pence (4610), 20 pence to 1p gold proofs (Issued: 708)...	(7) 2600
PGRSAS–**2008**	'The Royal Shield of Arms', 'Royal Shield' £1 (4604) to 1p gold proof (4611, 4631, 4651, 4671, 4691, and 4711) (Issued: 886)	(7) 2600
PG1PCS–**2008**	Set of 14 different £1 reverse designs (4590 to 4603) (Issued: 150)	(14) 8500
PG50PCS–**2009**	Set of sixteen 50 pence reverse designs marking 40th Anniversary of the introduction of the 50 pence denomination (4610- 4625) gold proofs (Edition: 125)..	(16) 7500
PG50PPCS–**2009**	Set of sixteen 50 pence reverse designs marking 40th Anniversary of the introduction of the 50 pence denomination (4610- 4625) gold proof piedfort (Edition: 40)	(16) 20000
PGDJS–**2012**	Diamond Jubilee £5, (4569), 'Bimetallic' 'Charles Dickens' £2 (4730), 'Bimetallic' £2 (4570) 'Royal Shield '£1(4604), 50 pence to 1 pence (4620, 4631, 4652, 4672, 4691 and 4711) gold proofs (Edition: 150)....................	(10) 7000
PGCS–**2012**	Diamond Jubilee £5, (4569) and Golden Jubilee £5, (4555) (Edition: 60)..	(2) 3000
PGCS2–**2012**	Diamond Jubilee £5, (4569) and £2 (Sovereign design, 4424) set of two (Edition : 60, taken from individual coins limits)..	(2) 2600
PGCS3–**MD**	Set of six £2 with Sporting connections, Commonwealth Games 1986 (4311), European Football Championship 1996 (4317) and Commonwealth Games 2002 (4573 to 4576), coins obtained from the secondary market (Edition: 50)	(6) 3200
PGCAS–**2013**	Proof 'Coronation' £5, (4751), 'Bimetallic' 'Guinea' £2 (4731) 'Bimetallic' 'Roundel' £2 (4732), 'Bimetallic' 'Train' £2 (4733), 'Bimetallic' £2 (4570) 'Royal Shield' £1 (4604), 'England' £1 (4720), 'Wales' £1 (4721), 50 pence 'Ironside' (4628), 50 pence to 1 pence (4620, 4631, 4652, 4672, 4691 and 4711) gold proofs (Issued: 59)	(15) 11500
PGLUS–**2013**	Bimetallic' 'Roundel' £2 (4732) and 'Bimetallic' 'Train' £2 (4733) gold proofs (Issued: 111)	(2) 2000
PGQPS–**2013**	Queen's Portrait set of £5 coins, (4754 – 4757) gold proofs (Issued: 148) .	(4) 8000
PG31S–**2013**	Thirtieth Anniversary set of three £1 coins, (4590, 4334 and 4604) gold proofs (Issued: 17)	(3) 3000
PGC14–**2014**	Proof 'Queen Anne' £5, (4758), 'Bimetallic' 'Trinity House' £2 (4734), 'Bimetallic' 'World War I' £2 (4735), 'Bimetallic' £2 (4570) 'Royal Shield' £1 (4604), 'Northern Ireland' £1 (4722), 'Scotland' £1 (4723.), and 50 pence 'Commonwealth Games' (4630), gold proofs (Edition:)	(6)
PGC4P–**2015**	Fourth Portrait 'Bimetallic' £2 (4570) 'Royal Shield', £1 (4604), 50 pence to 1 pence (4620, 4636, 4652, 4672, 4691 and 4711), gold proofs, (Edition: 500	(8) 3800
PGC5P–**2015**	Fifth Portrait 'Bimetallic' £2 (4736) 'Royal Shield', £1 (4604), 50 pence to 1 pence (4632, 4636, 4652, 4672, 4691 and 4711), gold proofs, (Edition: 500)	(8) 3800

£

PGC15–**2015**	Proof Churchill £5, (4764), Waterloo £5, (4765) 'Bimetallic' 'Magna Carta' £2 (4737), 'Bimetallic' 'Royal Navy' £2 (4738), 50 pence 'Battle of Britain' (4632), gold (Edition: 100)	(5)	5500
PGC16–**2014**	World War 1. Set of six £5, Renumbered (4850 – 4855), gold proofs (Edition: 20)	(6)	9999
PGC17–**2015**	World War 1. Second Set of six £5, (4856 – 4861), gold proofs (Edition: 25)	(6)	9999

Platinum Coin Proof sets

PPBCS1–**2007**	Britannia Proofs £100, £50, £25, £10 (4454A, 4464A, 4474A and 4484A) (Issued: 250)..	(4)	2800
PPBCS2–**2008**	Britannia Proofs £100, £50, £25, £10 (4455A, 4465, 4476A, and 4485A) (Edition: 250)...	(4)	2800
PPEBCS–**2008**	'Emblems of Britain', 'UK' £1 (4590), 'Britannia' 50 pence (4610) and 20 pence to 1p (Issued: 250)	(7)	3500
PPRSAS–**2008**	'The Royal Shield of Arms', 'Royal Shield' £1 (4604) to 1p (4611, 4631, 4651, 4671, 4691, 4711) (Issued: 184)	(7)	3500

Pattern Proof sets

PPS1–**2003**	Silver proof set of £1 designs with plain edge and hallmark (4595A, 4596A, 4597A, 4598A) (Edition: 7,500)	(4)	75
PPS2–**2003**	Gold proof set of £1 designs with plain edge and hallmark (4595A, 4596A, 4597A, 4598A) (Edition: 3,000)...	(4)	2300
PPS3–**2004**	Silver proof set of £1 designs with plain edge and hallmark (4595B, 4596B, 4597B, 4598B) (Edition: 5,000)	(4)	75
PPS4–**2004**	Gold proof set of £1 designs with plain edge and hallmark (4595B, 4596B, 4597B, 4598B) (Edition: 2,250...	(4)	2300

LONDON 2012 OLYMPIC AND PARALYMPIC GAMES

OCNS1–**MD**	Set of 29 50 pence coins in individual card packs (4960 to 4988)	(29)	90
OCNS2	Gold Medal Winners set of 50 pence Cuni and £5 Olympic 2012 £5, (Athletics, 4960, Boxing, 4967, Canoeing, 4968, Cycling, 4961, Equestrian, 4969, Rowing, 4978, Sailing, 4979, Shooting, 4980, Taekwondo, 4982, Tennis, 4983, Triathlon, 4984 and £5, 4924) (Edition: 2,012)	(12)	45
OCNS3	Five pounds.(crowns). Set of the four Countdown issues and the Official Olympic and Paralympic £5 cuni coins. (4920 to 4925). (Edition: 2,012)	(6)	70
OCNS4	Five pounds. (crowns). Set of four Countdown issues (4920 – 4923)	(4)	45

Silver coin sets.

OSS1–**2009**.	The Mind of Britain. Set of six £5 silver proofs (4930, 4931, 4932, 4933, 4934 and 4935) (Edition: each coin 95,000)	(6)	300
OSS2–**2010**	The Body of Britain. Set of six £5 silver proofs (4936, 4937, 4938, 4939, 4940 and 4941) (Edition: each coin 95,000)	(6)	300
OSS3–**2010**	The Spirit of Britain. Set of six £5 silver proofs (4942, 4943, 4944, 4945, 4946 and 4947) (Edition: each coin 95,000)	(6)	300
OSS4–**MD**	Great British Icons. Set of 6 £5 silver proofs (4930,4931,4938,4944,4945, 4946) (Edition: 10,000 taken from individual coin limits of 95,000)	(6)	550

£

			£
OSS5–**MD**	The Mind, Body and Spirit of Britain. Set of 18 £5 silver proofs (4930 to 4947)	(18)	1650
OSS6–**2011**	Set of 29 50 pence silver brilliant uncirculated coins (4960 to 4988)	(29)	900
OSS7–**2011**	Gold Medal Winners set of 50 pence silver brilliant uncirculated coins and £5 Olympic 2012 silver proof, (Athletics, 4960, Boxing, 4967, Canoeing, 4968, Cycling, 4961, Equestrian, 4969, Rowing, 4978, Sailing, 4979, Shooting, 4980, Taekwondo, 4982, Tennis, 4983, Triathlon, 4984 and £5, 4924), (Edition: 999 but coins taken from individual issue limits)	(12)	550
OSS8–**2011**	Accuracy. Set of six 50 pence silver brilliant uncirculated coins depicting various sports (Badminton, 4964, Basketball, 4965, Fencing, 4970, Football, 4971, Hockey, 4975, and Tennis, 4983) (Edition: 2,012 but taken from individual issue limits)	(6)	280
OSS9–**2011**	Agility. Set of six 50 pence silver brilliant uncirculated coins depicting various sports (Boxing, 4967, Equestrian, 4969, Gymnastics, 4973, Judo, 4976, Sailing, 4979, and Taekwondo, 4982) (Edition: 2,012 but taken from individual issue limits)	(6)	280
OSS10–**2011**	Speed. Set of six 50 pence silver brilliant uncirculated coins depicting various sports (Athletics, 4960, Aquatics, 4962, Canoeing, 4968, Cycling, 4961, Rowing, 4978, Triathlon, 4984) (Edition: 2,012 but taken from individual issue limits)	(6)	280
OSS11–**MD**	Five pounds.(crowns). Set of the four Countdown issues and the Official Olympic and Paralympic £5 proof silver coins. (4920 to 4925). (Edition: 800 taken from individual issue limits)	(6)	500

Gold coin sets.

			£
OGS1–**2008**	**(Previously listed as PG2PCS).** 'Bimetallic' 'Centenary of Olympic Games of 1908' £2 (4585) and 'Bimetallic' 'United Kingdom Olympic Handover Ceremony' £2 (4951) gold proofs (Edition: 250)	(2)	1000
OGS2–**2010**	'Faster' 2-coin proof set, two £25, (4905 and 4906) (Edition: taken from individual coin Limits)	(2)	1200
OGS3–**2010**	'Faster' 3-coin proof set, £100, and two £25, (4915, 4905 and 4906) (Edition: 4,000)	(3)	3500
OGS4–**2011**	'Higher' 2-coin proof set, two £25, (4907 and 4908) (Edition: taken from individual coin limits)	(2)	1200
OGS5–**2011**	'Higher' 3-coin proof set, £100, and two £25, (4916, 4907 and 4908) (Edition: 4,000)	(3)	3500
OGS6–**2012**	'Stronger' 2-coin proof set, two £25, (4909 and 4910) (Edition: taken from individual coin limits)	(2)	1200
OGS7–**2012**	'Stronger' 3-coin proof set, £100, and two £25, (4917, 4909 and 4910) (Edition: 4,000)	(3)	3500
OGS8–**MD**	'Faster', 'Higher' and 'Stronger' set of three £100 (4915 – 4917) and six £25 (4905 – 4910) (Edition: 1,000 taken from individual coin limits)	(9)	10500
OGS9–**MD**	'Countdown to London' set of four £5 gold proof coins (4920 – 4923)	(4)	11500
OGS10–**2012**	Set of £5 proof London Olympic Games and Paralympic Games (4924 and 4925) (Edition: taken from individual coin limits)	(2)	5500